Conquering Consumerspace

Marketing Strategies for a Branded World

Michael R. Solomon

AMACOM
American Management Association

New York • Atlanta • Brussels • Buenos Aires • Chicago • London • Mexico City
San Francisco • Shanghai • Tokyo • Toronto • Washington, D.C.

Special discounts on bulk quantities of AMACOM books are available to corporations, professional associations, and other organizations. For details, contact Special Sales Department, AMACOM, a division of American Management Association, 1601 Broadway, New York, NY 10019.
Tel.: 212-903-8316. Fax: 212-903-8083.
Web site: www.amacombooks.org

This publication is designed to provide accurate and authoritative information in regard to the subject matter covered. It is sold with the understanding that the publisher is not engaged in rendering legal, accounting, or other professional service. If legal advice or other expert assistance is required, the services of a competent professional person should be sought.

Various names used by companies to distinguish their software and other products can be claimed as trademarks. AMACOM uses such names throughout this book for editorial purposes only, with no intention of trademark violation. All such software or product names are in initial capital letters or ALL CAPITAL letters. Individual companies should be contacted for complete information regarding trademarks and registration.

Library of Congress Cataloging-in-Publication Data

Solomon, Michael R.
    Conquering consumerspace : marketing strategies for a branded world / Michael R. Solomon.
       p.   cm.
    Includes bibliographical references and index.
    ISBN 0-8144-0741-2 (hardcover)
    1. Brand name products—Marketing.   2. Consumers' preferences.
    3. Customer relations.   I. Title.
    HD69.B7S65   2003
    658.8'27—dc21   2002155062

Printing number

10   9   8   7   6   5   4   3   2   1

To Gail
Beloved Empress of Consumerspace

Contents

Preface

Welcome to consumerspace. Once upon a time, marketers barraged "couch potato" customers with hard-sell tactics. Today, we use products to define ourselves and others. We no longer are swayed by corporate-generated hype, but we are passionate about consumer-generated buzz. That means successful companies now need to shift their focus away from marketing *to* people and toward marketing *with* them. In consumerspace, firms partner with customers to develop brand personalities and create interactive fantasies. The winners understand that we buy products not just because of what they do, but because of what they mean. Market share is out, share of mind is in.

In the old days of *marketerspace*, companies called the shots. They broadcast glitzy ads to massive market segments, assuming that the consumers they lumped into broad demographic categories such as race or gender all would respond like automatons, obediently snapping up their me-too, mass-produced products. Doing business was a zero-sum game, where players advanced by convincing homogeneous blocs of customers to choose sides (at least for now). The winners racked up the most points, measured as market share. The customer was a coveted game piece, a trophy to be acquired and occasionally polished.

That view of the consumer as couch potato is so twentieth century. In today's *consumerspace*, firms partner with customers to develop brand personalities and create interactive fantasies. The winners understand that we buy products because of what they mean, rather than what they do. In consumerspace, each of us charts our own identity by picking and choosing the brands that speak to us. We reward those that do with our loyalty but also with our reverence and yes, sometimes even our love. Market share is out, *share of mind* is in. In marketerspace, companies sell to us. In consumerspace, they sell with us.

What will *consumerspace* look like, and how can cutting-edge firms help build it—and control it? This book is about that branded reality. In the pages to come, we'll explore what that means, both for those who buy the dream and those who sell it.

Welcome to consumerspace.

Acknowledgments

I relied upon the inspired work and suggestions of numerous colleagues and students in the writing of this book. I would like to thank my doctoral students Natalie Wood and Caroline Muñoz for their dedication and for their helpful work on such topics as Web avatars and virtual communities. I referred to several personal Web sites suggested to me by Prof. Hope Schau. I built upon Prof. Russell Belk's development of the extended-self concept to make my argument about the intertwining of products with consumer identity. Prof. Susan Fournier's work on brand relationships also was very helpful in this context. Profs. Al Muniz and Tom O'Guinn first used the term *brand community* to describe online product-based bonding. Profs. John Sherry and Rob Kozinets generously shared their work on themed retail environments. Some of my research on ethnic authenticity was conducted with Profs. Ron Groves and Darach Turley. Prof. Gary Bamossy gave me valuable feedback about this book and life in general. Finally, my colleague, friend, and business partner Prof. Basil Englis was instrumental in much of my academic work cited in this book as well as in the commercial applications we fielded together on behalf of Mind/Share, Inc. These friends and many others play a prominent role in my consumerspace.

CHAPTER 1

Now Entering Consumerspace
Welcome to a Branded World

Welcome to consumerspace, where reality is branded. Where we avidly search for the products and services that will define who we are and who we want to be. Where we are what we buy—literally. This book is about that branded reality. In the pages to come, we'll explore what that means, both for those who buy the dream and for those who sell it.

This Book Brought to You By . . .

In the video game Cool Borders 3, characters ride past Butterfinger candy bar banners and wear Levi's jeans while attempting to beat opponents' times that are recorded on Swatch watches. A Sony PlayStation game called Psybadek outfits its main characters in Vans shoes and clothing. According to a Sony executive, ''We live in a world of brands. We don't live in a world of generics. . . . If a kid is bouncing a basketball in a video game, to us it makes sense that it should be a Spalding basketball.''[1]

It isn't news that products matter. But, the extent to which we rely today upon brands to define our identities and to make sense of the world around us is extraordinary. Skeptical? Consider the five people who are being paid $800 each by a British marketing firm to legally change their names for one year to Turok. He is the hero of a video game about a time-traveling American Indian who slays bionically enhanced dinosaurs. The company hopes to turn each of the chosen few into an ambassador for the game, since at the least, each warrior wannabe will have to patiently explain the new moniker to friends, loved ones, and curious strangers. According to a company spokesman, they will be ". . . walking, talking, living, breathing advertisements." This experiment in *identity marketing* follows an earlier promotion by a Web site called Internet Underground Music Archive (IUMA) that paid a Kansas couple $5,000 to name their baby boy Iuma.[2]

In "the old days," we used products strategically to manage the impressions we made on others. The quest for status is very much alive today, but brands do a lot more than help us keep up with the Joneses. Today, we use these material props to look good to ourselves, to validate our identities, to find meaning in our social environments. Today, we buy products because of what they mean, rather than what they do.

Our quest to define our very identities with the aid of brands that have deep meanings to us reflects a transition from *marketerspace* to *consumerspace*. In marketerspace, companies create mass-produced products targeted to the preferences of homogeneous market segments. In consumerspace, each of us charts our own identity by picking and choosing the brands that speak to us. In marketerspace, companies sell *to* us. In consumerspace, they sell *with* us.

In the chapters to come, we'll see how things work in consumerspace. Along the way, we'll highlight opportunities for marketers who appreciate how what they sell truly has become part of what we are. But first, a little history.

The Good Old Days of Marketerspace

In the beginning, there was marketerspace, a commercial system where producers dictated what we buy, when, and where. Henry

Ford's production-line approach to manufacturing revolutionized the business world by making mass-produced Model T cars available to virtually everyone, even to the workers who actually built the "Tin Lizzie." The workingman could now reap the fruits of his labor, but the selection was pretty bland. As Ford famously observed, you can have any color Model T you want—as long as it's black. Drivers back then didn't seem to mind. By 1921, the Model T Ford controlled 60 percent of the automobile market. But that was before people could choose from among a Ford, Maserati, or Hummer.

A heavy-handed approach works fine in a seller's market, but along came the Great Depression. As money got very tight, shoppers got very picky about parting with their scarce cash. Desperate to move their inventories, companies turned to the hard sell. This strategy continued on past World War II, when American factories that had dutifully increased their capacity to churn out supplies for the war effort once again turned their attention to producing consumer goods. The great industrial machine created in wartime had to be fed in peacetime as well.

By the 1950s, the competition for consumers' pocketbooks got too heated to depend upon the skills of super salesmen who could "sell ice to Eskimos." Once again the automotive industry led the way. This time it was General Motors that created a new paradigm by pushing the concept of *market segmentation*: Don't try to sell everyone a Chevrolet. Identify a specific market, create a product to appeal to that market (Chevy for the working man, Cadillac for his boss, and so on), and differentiate your product so people in that market will prefer it to the competition. The modern marketing era was born.

The Consumer as Couch Potato

The stars of marketing executives began to rise in corporations that came to depend upon clever promotional strategies to "sell the sizzle" instead of the steak. But this ascendancy was not without its critics, who were alarmed by what they viewed as the exploitation of the masses by Madison Avenue. The social critic Vance Packard wrote over forty years ago, "Large-scale efforts are being made, often with impressive success, to channel our unthinking habits, our purchasing decisions, and our thought processes by the use of insights gleaned from psychiatry and the social sciences."[3] The economist John Kenneth Galbraith also chimed in, indicting radio and television as tools of manipulation. Because virtually no literacy is required to use these media, they allow repetitive and compelling communications to reach almost everyone.

Trashing the marketing system became fair game for both ends of the political spectrum. On the one hand, some members of the Religious Right preached that marketers contribute to the moral breakdown of society by presenting titillating images of hedonistic pleasure. On the other hand, some leftists argued that these seductive promises of material pleasure buy off people who would otherwise be revolutionaries working to change the system.

According to this argument, the marketing system creates demand—demand that only its products can satisfy. A classic response to this criticism is that the basic need is already there; marketers simply recommend ways to satisfy it by channeling our needs into desires. They humbly suggest, for example, that we slake our thirst with Coca-Cola instead of goat's milk, water, or perhaps designer water.

While many critics are quick to accuse marketers of manufacturing desire for superfluous products, this conspiracy theory is a bit hard to buy. Remember the midi dress or the Edsel? Considering that the failure rate for new products ranges from 40 percent to 80 percent, it seems more likely that at the end of the day, marketers succeed when they try to sell us good products and fail when they try to unload lemons.[4]

Critics on the left and right had something in common with the businesspeople they were censuring. Both marketers and their accusers painted a picture of consumers as helpless automatons who had to be saved from themselves. If one pushed the right buttons by wrapping a product in a classy package or depicting it in use by a ravishing model, buyers would line up like lemmings to possess the Next Big Thing. It all became a matter of who did a better job of pushing those buttons. Keep us fat and happy on our Barcaloungers as we absorb the latest directives courtesy of Madison Avenue.

This view of a compliant customer just drooling to receive his marching orders from the boob tube was strongly influenced by a group of theorists known as the Frankfurt School, which dominated communications research for most of the twentieth century. These scholars charged that those in power use the mass media to brainwash the population. The receiver of propaganda is basically a "couch potato" who is duped or persuaded to act based on the information he or she is fed by the government.

This accusation certainly had some validity as mass media vehicles like cinema became more sophisticated and widely available. Joseph Goebbels clearly understood how to use the media to mobilize the Nazi war machine. So did the U.S. government when it responded to Axis aggression by creating a character like Rosie the Riveter to encourage women to take up the slack in domestic factories while their men went off to war. Indeed, our government funded some of the seminal academic research in communications during World War II. One objective: to devise strategies that would persuade civilians to eat more sweetbreads in order to leave the choicer parts of cattle for our soldiers fighting overseas. Out of these humble beginnings arose much of what we know about how to design messages that will result in, as Jimmy Buffett sang, changes in attitudes.

Broadcasting Is Dead. Long Live Narrowcasting

After World War II, the race to identify the needs of large consumer segments was on. Marketers figured out that if they could just identify what certain consumer blocs such as middle-class housewives or blue-collar factory workers wanted, lo and behold they could deliver products designed to meet their needs. Market share became the currency by which business success was measured.

This "radical" idea—identify a need and satisfy it—took a giant step toward creating a consumer-centric marketplace. But this model still hinges on a company's ability to convince a sizable group of like-minded people to buy into its solution to that need. The segmentation model eventually breaks down because it persists in viewing all consumers (at least those who belong to the same segment) as essentially the same. By this logic, it should be possible to develop a "positioning strategy" embracing product design, packaging, and communications elements that will strike a chord among all or most people who share some set of defining characteristics such as gender, age group, ethnic identification, or even psychological traits such as innovativeness or extroversion. If we do a good enough job crafting a message that will ring the right bells and whistles, our consumers will be happy as pigs in a trough—and so will our shareholders.

The mass segmentation approach worked quite well so long as it was possible to comfortably pigeonhole each consumer into a convenient category. In more recent times, that's become a problem. We're no longer as easy to categorize in broad terms (if we ever were). Going, going, gone are the monolithic audiences of consumers we used to be able to reach on a handful of network TV stations. Today the market is fragmenting rapidly, creating new niches that mutate even as we try to measure them. Broadcasting just doesn't work in this environment. Narrowcasting rules.

Goodbye White Bread. Hello Bagels, Tortillas, and Croissants

One of the obvious factors behind this slivering of the population is simple demographics. It's no longer about selling stuff to a cross-section of white-bread America. We're rapidly diversifying in many ways, both in terms of "ascribed characteristics" like race, and "achieved characteristics" like lifestyle. The Census Bureau projects that by the year 2050, non-Hispanic whites will make up only 50.1 percent of the population (compared to 74 percent in 1995). Gay and lesbian consumers are an increasingly vocal presence; they spend in the range of $250 billion to $350 billion a year, and over 70 percent of them make purchases online. Alternative lifestyles, alternative medicine, alternative music. Even those traditional white-bread consumers are experimenting with bagels, tortillas, and croissants.

Take a look at the magazine section of any decent bookstore, and this splintering is obvious. This is not your parents' *Life* magazine.

Between 1998 and 1999, the specialty magazine *WWF* (World Wrestling Federation) gained 913,000 readers and *4 Wheel & Off Road* gained 749,000, while mainstream *Reader's Digest* lost over three million readers and *People* lost over two million. The explosion of media alternatives means we are exposed to many different interpretations of "the good life." In our affluent consumer society, we have the luxury of changing our minds frequently.

And change them we do—which explains why companies need to invest substantially in tracking these shifting tastes. It's a bit like nailing Jell-O to a wall. Liz Claiborne spends $300,000 a year to buy the services of color- and trend-consulting firms that help the apparel company stay on top of what is happening in the ever-changing world of fashion. Efficiencies realized by communications technologies that allow marketers to mail a catalog to this house, but not the one next to it, are enhancing the ability of businesses to profitably develop niche products. For example, recognizing a captive audience when it sees one, Sony capitalized on America's burgeoning incarceration rate (triple that of 1980) and now sells over $1 million of specialized headphones designed just for prison inmates.

We are confounding those marketers who want to assign us to little boxes and keep us there for years. Instead we're becoming more chameleon-like, changing our stripes at whim and trying on new identities. We're not swearing loyalty to one cologne; we're buying a fragrance tool kit that is adaptable to different social situations. Some of us are even going online and pretending to be someone else (and in many cases even switching genders, at least while we're logged on).

In addition, because our product preferences often change so rapidly, it can be futile to try to reach consumers where they are now: By the time they get the message, they've moved on. We've found that it makes a lot more sense to target people in terms of where they think they're going to be down the road. Companies must practice *aspirational marketing* by focusing on consumers' ideal states. You must anticipate what consumers' emerging tastes will be in the next six months to five years and determine what emerging brands you think will be part of their product repertoires down the road. Consumers are a moving target. It helps to aim at their likely trajectories rather than trying to catch them in your sights now. They certainly aren't going to wait around for you to acquire the target and shoot.

Old-time venerable brands are changing as well, morphing into new versions to keep up (or die trying). For example, General Motors, which brought us the wisdom of market segmentation, now has the temerity to introduce, of all things, a Cadillac SUV—and then (perhaps the ultimate commercial oxymoron?) a Cadillac pickup truck. This GM division can no longer stand still and wait for its core segment of affluent older drivers to ante up for their new Caddy. For one thing, those folks have a nasty tendency to die off. The Escalade SUV has already been co-opted by youth culture; young artists like Jennifer Lopez, Outkast, Jay-Z, and Jermaine Dupri conspicuously refer to it in their songs. Not exactly the Brat Pack.

No, segmentation isn't dead. But today's segments are smaller, less homogenous, and much more subtle—Cadillac even sees the driver of its Escalade EXT pickup as quite a different person from its Escalade customer. The brand manager says that while these two Caddy owners may live in $2 million homes right next to each other, the pickup owner is probably five years younger, he might have inherited his father's construction business, he may or may not have attended college, and he is still connected to his high school buddies. In contrast, the SUV driver is more likely to sport an MBA from Harvard and to have forsaken his high school haunts for more worldly cronies.[5]

THE BOTTOM LINE

A segmentation strategy based upon identifying large, homogeneous blocs of consumers that share some basic characteristics such as age or income is not as effective today. Our lifestyles are splintering and morphing; people pick and choose from a mixture of brand possibilities as they construct their own unique identities. Mass media vehicles are no longer an effective way to reach many important target segments. In addition, these rapid

> changes make it more desirable to track consumers' aspirations rather than their current preferences in order to develop new brands and messages that will resonate with these evolving ideals.

Getting to Know You

The transition from broadcasting to narrowcasting means that marketers have to find new ways to connect with customers who increasingly are jaded and hard to reach by conventional means. That's what fueled the stampede in the late 1980s toward *relationship marketing*. The logic was simple: It's a lot less expensive to keep an existing customer than to win a new one. Building long-term bonds with consumers became the mantra. Branding is back. Loyalty is in.

Don't panic. This book is not about relationship marketing—nor about micromarketing, permission marketing, 1:1 marketing, liberation marketing, or naked marketing. Those are all terms used by some smart people to describe strategies for talking to a consumer base that has become too diverse to be reached by one tired old thirty-second TV spot. What this book *is* about is how these strategies impact on consumers themselves. The accelerated trend toward using consumption data to define both our neighbors and ourselves means that we are actively incorporating the information we receive via marketing communications of all stripes—whether delivered as personalized 1:1 messages, pop-up ads online, flashy billboards, edgy commercials, or glimpses of that hot blouse J-Lo is wearing in her latest music video.

That means we have to back off from the idea that marketers do things to consumers and instead think about the communications process as more of a two-way street. As the "permission marketing" concept reminds us, we don't have to just sit there and take it. We have a voice in deciding what messages we choose to see and when—and we exercise that option more and more. Just ask some of the more than a million people who are now using DVRs (digital video recorders) like

TiVo to watch TV shows whenever they wish—and who are skipping over the commercials.

The traditional view of the submissive consumer whose allegiance is swayed by the most compelling message is not entirely wrong. All things equal, we still are more likely to be persuaded by credible communicators who deliver a convincing message in an appropriate format. This viewpoint just doesn't tell the whole story—especially in today's dynamic world of interactivity, in which consumers have many more choices available to them and exert greater control over which messages they will choose to process.

THE BOTTOM LINE

> The traditional view of the consumer as a passive recipient is no longer accurate or very useful. Consumers often want to exert control over the amount and nature of marketing information being transmitted to them. They also will increasingly expect to be able to choose when they will receive sales pitches and other kinds of marketing communications—and they will be eager to absorb information *they* have requested.

Consumer.com

One obvious reason for this change is that we are steadily becoming a wired society. In a sense, many of us have become our own self-contained TV stations that send and receive reams of marketing information to one another 24/7. The number of total worldwide wireless data users is estimated to exceed 1.3 billion by 2004. Providers like AT&T Wireless, Verizon, and Sprint PCS are offering customized Web portals, accessible at home, in the mall, on the beach, or in the car, that include content such as weather, stocks, news, movie-theater listings, and sports scores. Clearly we're no longer a nation of passive consumers reclining in our Barcaloungers, just waiting to watch whatever some big network decides to show us. We're players now. Bring it on.

You Say Tomato . . .

This change in consumer behavior is mirrored by a bit of a revolution that is still shaking up the scientists who study these phenomena. The intellectual perspective known as *interpretivism* or *postmodernism* questions many of the field's long-standing assumptions about why we buy. A traditionalist tends to view a purchase as the last step in a neat and orderly sequence of persuasion attempts that results in a measurable change in a person's attitudes toward a product. The field's Young Turks argue that this highly structured, rational view of behavior ignores the complex social and cultural world in which we live. Being linear is so twentieth century.

Interpretivists stress the importance of symbolic, subjective experience, and the idea that meaning resides in the mind of the person, not the objective stimulus. We each construct our own meanings based on our unique and shared cultural experiences, so there are no right or wrong answers. In this view, the world in which we live is composed of a pastiche, or a mixture of images jumbled together from many different places. To understand that idea, just go to the food court at the local mall and watch shoppers gleefully assemble a smorgasbord of tacos, cheeseburgers, and sushi—perhaps washed down with Irish beer or French wine. The value placed on products because they help us to create order in our lives is replaced by an appreciation of the power of consumption to offer us diverse experiences.

One ramification of this outlook is that it helps us to think in terms of people today as *Homo commercialus*. We thrive on marketing. Rather than waiting obediently for those marketing messages, we proactively search for meaning in the products and ads surrounding us, interpret these according to our own idiosyncratic biases, and then absorb these meanings into our self-concepts. Instead of measuring the effectiveness of a brand in terms of simple market share, we need to evaluate it in terms of its ability to capture *share of mind*. This more dynamic process is consistent with the so-called *uses and gratifications perspective* of communications. According to this school of thought, we don't just passively process advertising to get information about the latest sale or the newest whiz-bang features. Instead, the commercial messages surrounding us are part and parcel of our daily lives. A study of young people in Great Britain, for example, found that they rely on advertising for many reasons, including entertainment (some report that the "adverts" are better than the programs), escapism, play (some report singing along with jingles, others make posters out of magazine ads), and self-affirmation (ads can reinforce their own values or provide role models).

It's important to note that this perspective is not arguing that media play a uniformly positive role in our lives, only that recipients are making use of the information in a number of ways. For example, marketing messages have the potential to undermine self-esteem as women internalize images of stick-thin models that establish unrealistic standards for their own appearance. A comment by one participant in the aforementioned British study illustrates this negative impact. She observes that when she's watching TV with her boyfriend, ". . . really, it makes you think 'oh no, what must I be like?' I mean you're sitting with your boyfriend and he's saying 'oh, look at her. What a body!'"[6]

THE BOTTOM LINE

> Advertising is about much more than communicating information about products and services. Consumers zealously absorb the imagery and messages from commercial stimuli and incorporate these into their lives in many ways. In consumerspace, advertising is part entertainment, part reality check.

I Consume, Therefore I Am

Recently a young man named John Freyer sold all his possessions on eBay to see if our "stuff" really defines who we are. Those who bought any of the artifacts he listed for sale registered them on a Web site called allmylifeforsale.com. Freyer then undertook a decidedly nonspiritual odyssey as he set out to "visit" all of his possessions in their new homes around the world. In this case, selling literally became an art form—the University of Iowa's Museum of Art bought his false teeth for $27 and plans to build an exhibit devoted to them.[7]

Freyer truly believes that what we own constitutes a large part of what we are. Many consumer researchers would agree with him. Although the traditional perspective on buyer behavior views each of us as a rational information processor, it's difficult to deny the irrational side of consumption after visiting yard sales where neighbors eagerly scoop up each other's "junque" or checking out that diamond-encrusted bra for sale in the Neiman-Marcus catalog.

That's why many of us who work in this field now acknowledge the need to move beyond buyer behavior (Why do we buy?) and onto consumer behavior (Why do we consume?). Those are two very different questions. Nowadays almost anything is fair game when it comes to the study of consumption, whether canned peas, a massage, democracy, or hip-hop music.[8] In a sense our field has caught up with Andy Warhol, who understood early on that Marilyn Monroe and a Campbell's soup can have a lot more in common than first meets the eye.

The Ties That Bind

Every year roughly 50,000 Harley owners converge on South Dakota to take part in a rally that affirms their "Harleyness." The publisher of *American Iron*, an industry magazine, observed, "You don't buy a Harley because it's a superior bike, you buy a Harley to be a part of a family."[9] Brands often mean something to us because they also mean something to others. Common ownership links us together in the way that religion, family, and community did in bygone times. Love me, love my Hog.

You don't have to be a biker to belong to a brand family; it's a very common way to commune with others in consumerspace. Each week at the Niketown store in Boston, as many as eighty runners show up for a weekly running club to meet, greet, run—and talk Nike. Joined by their enthusiasm for a product , these groups of people who meet either in the flesh or in online gatherings are what marketing experts call a *brand community*. Whether the chatter is about Nikes—or Harleys, Barbies, or Palm Pilots—this scene takes place thousands of times each day. In consumerspace, brands are the ties that bind.

THE BOTTOM LINE

Affirmation of group identities is a major motivation to consume. Consumers form bonds with others based upon common ownership, and their dedication to a brand may galvanize them to share the love in brand communities. Marketers like Harley-Davidson understand that customer loyalty can be cemented by providing resources that encourage their customers to express their enthusiasm with kindred spirits.

"He Who Dies with the Most Toys Wins . . ."

During World War II, members of "cargo cults" in the South Pacific literally worshiped items salvaged from crashed aircraft or washed ashore from ships. These people believed that the ships and planes passing nearby were piloted by their ancestors, and they tried to entice them to return home to their villages. They went so far as to construct fake planes from straw in hopes of luring the aircraft to their islands.

We don't go so far as to worship everyday products—or do we? At the least we certainly live in a highly materialistic society where people often gauge their own worth and that of others in terms of how much they own. The popular bumper sticker, "He Who Dies with the Most Toys Wins" is a comment on this philosophy. And, some growing religious movements literally do revere possessions—or at least the money it takes to buy them. In Africa, new places of worship like the Winners Church are at the forefront of a booming Pentecostal movement. This philosophy is based upon similar dogmas in the United States and elsewhere which preach that success comes to those who pray, a Prosperity Theology celebrating both the earthly and spiritual virtues of accumulating wealth.

It's easy to take our comfortable lifestyles for granted until we remember how recent this abundance is. Even a fairly downscale person living in America today lives better than most gentry did 200 years ago (at the least, they are likely to bathe more than once a month). This comfortable standard of living is a fairly new development. In 1950 two out of five American homes did not own a telephone, and in 1940 half of all households still did not have indoor plumbing. Today, though, many Americans now energetically seek "the good life," which abounds in material comforts. Forget about toilets—most middle-class kids can't imagine a world without their own personal cell phones, pagers, computers, and credit cards.

One way to think about marketing is as a system that provides a certain standard of living to consumers. To some extent, then, our lifestyles are influenced by the standard of living we have come to expect and desire. We measure our success quite tangibly, and perhaps this spiraling cycle of acquisition blinds us to other priorities. Many feel that marketers arbitrarily link products to desirable social attributes, fostering a materialistic society in which we are measured by what we own. One critic even argued that the problem is that we are not materialistic enough—that is, we do not sufficiently value goods for the utilitarian functions they deliver but instead focus on the irrational value of goods for what they symbolize. According to this view, for example, "Beer would be enough for us, without the additional promise that in drinking it we show ourselves to be manly, young at heart, or neighborly. A washing machine would be a useful machine to wash clothes, rather than an indication that we are forward-looking or an object of envy to our neighbors."[10]

Many, though certainly not all, social critics share these sentiments about the evils of consumption. Most notably, the scholar James

Twitchell celebrates consumption in his thoughtful examination of our affection for luxury products. He argues that this pursuit of status in fact has positive effects on us and on our society. Unbridled admiration for Fendi bags or Mercedes sedans is a great unifier that transcends our political, economic, or religious differences.[11] Let's go shopping!

Whether or not our desire for more, more, more is bad, bad, bad, clearly many of us relish our toys. Materialists are more likely to value possessions that bolster their status, in contrast to those who tend to prize products that connect them to other people or that provide them with pleasure in use. Products valued by materialists are more likely to be publicly consumed and more expensive. A study that compared specific items preferred by materialists versus others found that those who equate goods with self-worth were attached to products such as jewelry, china, or a vacation home. In contrast, low materialists cherished such things as a mother's wedding gown, picture albums, and a rocking chair from childhood.[12]

But the pursuit of products is about much more than status. Indeed, many of our most valued possessions may not even be visible to others, whether these take the form of a slinky teddy from Victoria's Secret or a collection of McDonald's Happy Meal boxes. A focus on the role of goods in "keeping up with the Joneses" is narrow at best. It blinds us to the many other reasons we are driven to consume. Susan Fournier at Harvard looked at the specific kinds of brand relationships people tend to have. She identified the connections a person might have with a product, including these:

- *Self-Concept Attachment*—The product helps to establish the user's identity.

- *Nostalgic Attachment*—The product serves as a link with a past self.

- *Interdependence*—The product is a part of the user's daily routine.

- *Love*—The product elicits emotional bonds of warmth, passion, or other strong emotion.[13]

Products are at the very heart of many (if not all) of our social functions, as we'll see throughout this book. They affirm our place in society, enable us to perform prescribed rituals that affirm this place, and even provide guideposts for our behavior in different settings. It's not just that we do things to products. They do things to us by evoking strong feelings, reminding us of prior experiences, and enhancing or deflating our feelings of self-worth. Some social scientists may derogate the study of consumption and consign it to the backwaters of science, but many others (as well as their more thoughtful peers in the "real world" of marketing) understand that it's more likely the opposite—the things we buy open a window into the underlying heart and soul of human social behavior. The old saw that "you are what you wear, eat, etc." may be truer than you thought. As one of my distinguished colleagues likes to say, even sleep can be viewed as the consumption of sheets!

THE BOTTOM LINE

The pursuit of status is very much alive, though because attaining luxury goods (or knockoffs that resemble them) is easier today, status symbols are more likely to take the form of singular experiences like luxury services and adventure travel. But as central a motivation as status is to consumption, it is by far not the only driver of purchases. Products often play key roles in our social lives by helping us to express love, independence, and many other feelings. In a very real sense, we are what we buy.

The Global Village: Exporting Nike Culture

The dominance of the marketplace in defining social identity is a global phenomenon. It's true that Americans are net exporters of popular culture—much to the dismay of many intellectuals who bemoan the creeping "McDonaldization" of local traditions (including the

Frenchman who famously derogated Euro Disney as a "cultural Chernobyl"). Indeed, renditions of the American "good life" influence the lifestyles of others around the globe, as many consumers have learned to equate commercial icons like Levi Strauss, McDonald's, Nike, and Harley-Davidson with modernity, sophistication, or rebellion.

In Japan, Starbucks became a household name by teaching young urbanites how to drink coffee in shops featuring comfortable sofas and American hip-hop music rather than taking tea in dimly lit parlors. Some Japanese pay the equivalent of one-half million dollars for shrunken versions of U.S. homes. The more avid fans of American popular culture have been known to stage cookouts around imported brick barbecues and trade in their Toyotas for expensive imports such as Chevy vans. Teenagers in Tokyo who wish to emulate California cool can occasionally be seen cruising the streets with surfboards strapped to the tops of their cars even though the ocean is nowhere to be seen. In China, new housing compounds bear names like Orange County and Manhattan Gardens, and a high-end Buick is esteemed as a luxury car.

But it's not all about America, by any means. Over sixty countries have a gross national product of less than $10 billion, while there are at least 135 transnational companies with revenues greater than that. The dominance of these marketing powerhouses is fueling a *globalized consumption ethic*. People the world over are increasingly surrounded by tempting images of luxury cars, glam rock stars on MTV, and gleaming appliances that will make their lives easier. They forsake local traditions for a common vision of prosperity.

This shift brings with it a hunger for well-known global brands that will bring people the world over a step closer to this ideal, whether this means coveting Levi's jeans from the United States, Nokia cell phones from Finland, Hermès scarves from France, or BMW cars from Germany. In transitional economies such as the former Soviet bloc countries, shopping is slowly evolving from a wearisome struggle to a leisure activity. Possessing coveted items becomes a mechanism to display one's status, often at great personal sacrifice. In Romania, for example, Kent cigarettes double as an underground currency even though the cost of smoking a pack a day of foreign cigarettes would cost the average citizen there his or her entire yearly salary. As one analyst observed, ''. . . as former subjects of the Soviet empire dream it, the American dream has very little to do with liberty and justice for all and a great deal to do with soap operas and the Sears Catalogue.''[14]

So, the United States is clearly a major entrant in the race to brand our selves. However, our global consumer culture is not necessarily driven by a desire to emulate America. Indeed, in one recent survey conducted by a marketing research firm in Beijing, nearly half of all children under twelve thought that McDonald's is a domestic Chinese brand. The reality is that there's a lot of quid pro quo among industrialized nations that covet each other's status symbols. We fall for this as much as anyone else; in the United States, we happily pay a premium for brands with foreign cachet, whether Chanel or Häagen Dazs (a made-up name for a product that's really produced in New Jersey). Japanese brands like Hello Kitty and Pokemon sell out all over the world.

THE BOTTOM LINE

Global brands are the new currency. The rise of multinational corporations that distribute recognizable, branded goods around the world is creating a globalized consumption ethic. Increasingly it makes little sense to segment consumers in terms of nationalities. A young professional in Paris has more in common with a similar person in Tokyo or Buenos Aires than she does with a working-class person in Nice. People scattered around the world are more likely to share common value structures based upon similar exposure to popular culture in the form of movies, music, and other media vehicles.

Whether in the form of Italian shoes, German autos, or American sneakers, brands are the fundamental building blocks of modern society. That's because these icons are bought for what they mean, not for what they do. Let's see why.

Products as Symbols

Brands carry meaning largely because they place us in social categories. Contrary to "rational" economic perspectives on purchase decisions that dominate the calculus of many firms, choosing Brand X over Brand Y is about more than a careful calculation of a cost-benefit ratio. It is a statement about who one is and who one is not. Group identities, whether of devotees of a musical genre, extreme athletes, or drug users, gel around forms of expressive symbolism. The self-definitions of group members are derived from the common symbol system to which the group is dedicated. Sociologists have described these systems with such labels as *taste public*, *symbolic community*, and *status culture*.

Understanding symbol systems and exploring their contents is more than academic, however. This discovery process goes to the heart of *lifestyle marketing strategies* that build a collection of brands with a common appeal to a certain type of person. Increasingly, companies recognize (at least intuitively) the value of building such a *lifestyle portfolio*. For example, Pepsi and Mountain Dew plan to create an apparel line that will be synergistic with their beverage marketing efforts. Leveraging a well-defined brand image to other categories is, of course, a popular strategy: In the year 2000, corporate licensing revenues were $982 million.[15] We'll take a closer look at the strategic ramifications of such portfolios later in the book.

THE BOTTOM LINE

The brands we buy place us in social categories. We use these cues to place others (and ourselves) with consumers who we believe will share similar lifestyles and values. Lifestyle marketing

> strategies recognize the potency of these bonds. They build a brand portfolio that enables members of a category to express their underlying identity in a variety of concrete ways, from food to apparel to music.

By Your Toys Shall They Know You

An individual's pattern of consumption often overlaps with the brand choices made by many others who happen to have similar social and economic characteristics. That overlap is at the heart of market segmentation strategies. Still, each person also provides a unique "twist" to the pattern that allows him or her to inject some individuality into a chosen lifestyle. For example, a "typical" college student (if there is such a thing) may dress much like his or her friends, hang out in the same places, and like the same foods, yet still indulge a passion for marathon running, stamp collecting, or community activism that makes him or her a unique person.

Our observations about what others do, eat, wear, drive, and so on satisfy more than our morbid curiosity about our neighbors. We use this information to categorize people very quickly: Good or bad? Friend or foe? Cool or uncool? In preindustrial society, these judgments were easier. The odds were we knew everyone we encountered, and if we didn't, we could quickly determine who they were by answering a few simple questions: Are they from my village or elsewhere? Are they a member of my religion? Are they gentry or serf? We didn't need to know much more.

Today, things are different. In postmodern society we still have a psychological need to categorize those we meet, but the cues are far more complicated. Most likely, we no longer live in the place we grew up. Religion is no longer a defining characteristic for many. Instead, we make our inferences based on a person's choice of leisure activities (e.g., squash versus bowling), food preferences (e.g., tofu and beans versus steak and potatoes), cars (Lexus versus Ford pickup), and so on. We're often surprisingly good at this. People who are shown pictures of someone's living room, for example, are able to make surprisingly accurate guesses about his or her personality.

And, in the same way that a consumer's use of products influences others' perceptions, the same products can help to determine his or her own self-concept and social identity. Cycling back to our brief discussion of postmodernism, each of us constructs a unique pastiche of imagery that is a mixture of shared elements and idiosyncratic ones. The continual evolution of this work-in-progress is at the heart of the consumption experience, and is the "life project" in which we each engage as modern consumers. It's not just a job, it's an adventure.

The Brand Personality

The following memo was written to help an advertising agency figure out how a certain client should be portrayed in advertising: "He is creative . . . unpredictable . . . an imp. . . . He not only walks and talks, but has the ability to sing, blush, wink, and work with little devices like pointers. . . . He can also play musical instruments. . . . His walking motion is characterized as a 'swagger.' . . . He is made of dough and has mass."[16]

The Pillsbury Dough Boy is one of many commercial characters that have taken on a life of its own. The genesis of this creative activity can be traced to 1886, when the Quaker Oats man first appeared on boxes of hot cereal. Quakers had a reputation in nineteenth-century America for being shrewd but fair, and peddlers sometimes impersonated them to capitalize on this stereotype. When the cereal company decided to "borrow" the same image to adorn its package, this signaled the recognition that potential buyers might associate qualities they inferred from the package to its contents. The *spokescharacter* was born.

Of course, branding in one form or another far predates the 1880s—the ancient Greeks and Romans figured out the value of distinguishing one product or service from another with a unique name or symbol. Branding serves many functions, including reducing the perceived risk of purchasing an unknown. We are predictable animals; we tend to prefer the familiar. That's why it's fairly easy to teach us to "look for the union label."

Today, brand names have become so valuable that it's fairly common to find them valued in accounting terms just like any other tangible asset. *Brand equity* refers to the value a brand brings to its producer over and above what the generic product would be worth sans the name. This kind of equity may be so integral to a company's output that it literally is all the firm produces. Some firms are completely outsourcing production to focus on nurturing the brand. Nike doesn't own any sneaker factories, and Sara Lee sold off many of its bakeries, meat-processing plants, and textile mills to become a "virtual" corporation. Sara Lee's CEO commented, "Slaughtering hogs and running knitting machines are businesses of yesterday."[17] Selling the meaning behind branded products is the business of today, and the economic foundation of consumerspace.

So, how do people think about brands? Advertisers are keenly interested in this question, and several major agencies conduct extensive consumer research to help them understand how consumers connect to a brand before they roll out campaigns. DDB Worldwide does a global study called "Brand Capital" of 14,000 consumers; Leo Burnett's "Brand Stock" project involves 28,000 interviews. WPP Group offers a system called "BrandZ," and Young & Rubicam has its "Brand Asset Valuator." DDB's worldwide brand planning director observes, "We're not marketing just to isolated individuals. We're marketing to society. How I feel about a brand is directly . . . affected by how others feel about that brand." The logic behind this bonding approach is that if a consumer feels a strong connection with a brand, she is less likely to succumb to peer pressure and switch brands.[18]

These connections often are highly personal. Many of us form stronger attachments to our clothes, cars, or homes than to our neighbors. Consumers appear to have little trouble assigning personality qualities to all sorts of inanimate products, from personal care products to more mundane, functional ones—even kitchen appliances. Whirlpool's research showed that people felt its products were more feminine than competing brands. When consumers were asked to describe the company's appliances as if they were real people, they typically imagined a modern, family-oriented woman living in the suburbs—attractive but not flashy. In contrast, the company's KitchenAid brand was envisioned as a modern professional woman who was glamorous, wealthy, and who enjoyed classical music and the theater.[19]

THE BOTTOM LINE

Brands help us to make sense of the world and to decide where we fit in it. We use evidence gleaned from observing others' choices of leisure activities, cars, clothing, music, food, and so on to determine our compatibility with them. Consumers view brands as having personalities and prefer those marketing offerings that are similiar to how they see themselves or to the type of person they want to become.

Is It Real or Is It . . .

How in the world can people look at a refrigerator and see a woman? This process can be understood in terms of *animism*. In many cultures, inanimate objects are given qualities that make them come alive. Sacred objects, animals, or places are believed to have magical properties or to harbor the spirits of ancestors. It's customary in some cultures to wear something that belonged to a foe defeated in battle in order to absorb his life energy (or sometimes even to eat a body part, but we won't go there). In our society, objects may be "worshiped" in the sense that they are believed to impart desirable qualities to the owner, or they may in a sense become so important to a person that they can be viewed as a "friend."

Animism can occur at different levels of intensity. In some cases, we simply associate a brand with a loved one, alive or deceased ("My grandmother always served Knott's Berry Farm jam"). Or, we may go a step further and believe the object is possessed by the soul of a being, as when kids (and maybe some adults as well) feel that by putting on their Air Nikes they magically absorb some of the athletic ability of Michael Jordan. Preposterous? A recent movie called *Like Mike* was based upon this very storyline.

As part of a project I conducted for Levi Strauss that examined people's deep attachments to Levi's blue jeans, I analyzed letters written to the company over more than a century. This archive was rich and revealing; many people, including coal miners and sailors, believed their lives had been "saved" by a resilient pair of denim jeans that stood between them and injury from jagged rocks, eruptions of steam, and other perils. In some cases their gratitude was so intense they could not bear to dispose of the pants even after twenty or thirty years. Some owners even mailed the jeans back to the company with the request to give them a "proper burial."

This kind of animism is not confined to blue jeans. In Japan, it's not unusual for people to conduct a highly ritualized burial ceremony for worn-out household appliances that have finally given up the ghost after years of exemplary service to the household. We may not stage a funeral for everything we own, but it's certainly not unusual for objects to be imbued with human characteristics. We often anthropomorphize the things we own. Many of us give names to our cars, and some of us take it personally when our computers "decide" to crash.

Embodying made-up figures with human characteristics to represent brands is, of course, a very common practice that's been in use at least since someone decided to create that Quaker Oats man. We seem to readily accept familiar spokescharacters such as Charlie the Tuna, the Keebler Elves, or Bibendum, the Michelin Man. In research that Grey Advertising did for Sprint Business Services, customers were asked to imagine long-distance carriers as animals. They envisioned AT&T as a lion, MCI as a snake, and Sprint as a puma. Who said the telecom industry isn't a jungle?

Signposts of Meaning
If these meanings run so deep, how can we get a handle on them? For assistance in understanding how consumers interpret the meanings of

symbols, some marketers turn to a field of study known as *semiotics*. This discipline is devoted to the study of meanings, and its method-ologies can be very useful to demystify the hold exerted upon us by marketer-created icons, whether the Marlboro Man, the Ford Mustang, or even Britney Spears. As one set of researchers put it, ". . . advertising serves as a kind of culture/consumption dictionary; its entries are products, and their definitions are cultural meanings."[20]

According to the semiotician Charles Sanders Peirce, signs are related to objects in one of three ways: They can resemble objects, be connected to them, or be conventionally tied to them:[21]

- An *icon* is a sign that resembles the product in some way. Bell Telephone uses an image of a bell to represent itself.

- An *index* is a sign that is connected to a product because they share some property. The pine tree on some of Procter & Gam-ble's Spic and Span cleanser products conveys the shared property of fresh scent.

- A *symbol* is a sign that is related to a product through either conventional or agreed-upon associations. The lion in Dreyfus Fund ads links the animal's attributes of fearlessness and strength to the company's investing philosophy.

From a semiotic perspective, every marketing message has three basic components: an object, a sign or symbol, and an interpretant. The *object* is the product that is the focus of the message (e.g., Marl-boro cigarettes). The *sign* is the sensory imagery that represents the intended meanings of the object (e.g., the Marlboro cowboy). The *interpretant* is the meaning derived (e.g., rugged, individualistic, American).

As shown in Figure 1.1, connecting symbols to their underlying meanings is a valuable exercise for advertisers to understand *how* their messages mean. The Marlboro Man was a brilliant embodiment of the American values of freedom, individuality, and masculine rug-gedness. When this cowboy rode into town courtesy of the Leo Burnett

Figure 1.1: A semiotic analysis of the Marlboro Man.

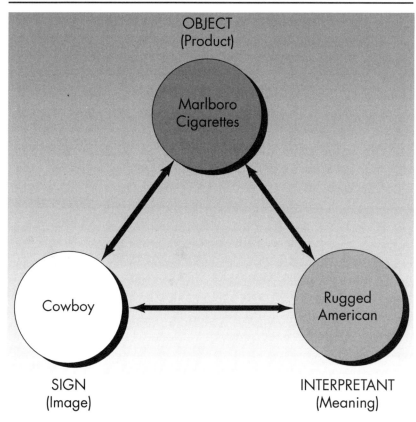

OBJECT
(Product)

Marlboro
Cigarettes

Cowboy

Rugged
American

SIGN
(Image)

INTERPRETANT
(Meaning)

SOURCE: Michael R. Solomon, *Consumer Behavior: Buying, Having, and Being,* 5th ed., ©
2002, p. 63. Reprinted by permission of Pearson Education, Inc., Upper Saddle River, N.J.

agency, he was able to almost single-handedly change the meaning
of this tobacco product from a woman's cigarette (complete with red-
tipped filter to hide lipstick marks) into one of the most successful
brand franchises in history.

THE BOTTOM LINE

Products are often endowed with human qualities. Even fabricated fantasy characters become real to us as we form relation-

> ships with the symbols created by marketers to signify the underlying meanings of their brands. Semiotic approaches to understanding meaning can help marketers to comprehend how consumers associate arbitrary qualities with concrete products.

Pssst. Wanna Buy a Bootleg Steveland Morris Hardaway CD?

All sorts of products, from dishwashers to deodorants, communicate meaning by virtue of the symbols with which marketers associate them. The same process is at work when we package people for mass consumption. From actors and musicians to superstar athletes and supermodels (and yes, even a few academic superstars), the famous and near famous jockey for market position in popular culture. Michael Jordan will most likely turn out to be one of the best-selling brands of all time. These personae are carefully cultivated and managed by troupes of handlers who connive to get them exposure on television shows such as *Oprah,* starring roles in movies, recording contracts, or product endorsements. "Colonel" Tom Parker figured this out almost fifty years ago when he saturated the market with Elvis belt buckles, black velvet portraits, and other mementoes of the King.

Like other products, celebrities often strategically name themselves to craft a "brand identity" using the same strategies employed by packaged goods companies to ensure that their products make an impression on consumers, including memorability (Evel Knievel), suitability (fashion designer Oscar Renta reverted to his old family name of de la Renta because it sounded more elegant), and distinctiveness (Steveland Morris Hardaway became Stevie Wonder).

Successful agents typically choose a branding strategy to maximize the impact of their "product" in the celebrity marketplace. Here are some common approaches described by Philip Kotler and his colleagues in their book *High Visibility:*[22]

   ■ In the *pure selling approach,* an agent presents a client's qualifications to potential "buyers" until he finds one who is willing to act as an intermediary. The agent might send a singer's tapes to talent scouts at record companies or photos of an aspiring model to beauty magazines. In this case, the celebrity is sold to distributors, just as the representative of a snack foods company tries to get grocery retailers to give her product adequate shelf space.

■ Using the *product improvement approach,* the agent works with the client to modify certain characteristics that will increase market value. This means changing the person's repertoire or image to conform to whatever is currently in demand. For example, Madonna's image changed over consecutive albums from East Village punk to lacy virgin to Marilyn Monroe clone to country cowgirl, and she continues to transform herself with each succeeding release.

■ An agent relies upon a *market fulfillment approach* by scanning the market to identify unmet needs. After identifying a need, the agent finds a person or a group that meets a set of minimum qualifications and develops a new "product." These "manufactured stars" are common, for example, in the music world. The Monkees, the New Kids on the Block, the Spice Girls, and more recently O-Town, 'N Sync, and the Back Street Boys were created from whole cloth by producers who carefully auditioned hundreds of photogenic young singers and musicians until they discovered just the right combination of teen idols.

From Hype to Hyperreality
In consumerspace, we've gone well beyond the simple linkage of images like the Marlboro Man to product attributes like masculinity. Sometimes it's just not possible to identify what a symbol stands for because its referent is as artificial as the symbol itself. In fact the reasons to buy a product may be built from whole cloth by enterprising marketers. Hallmark has helped to "invent" holidays like Grandparents' Day, many firms from McDonald's to Budweiser have turned a relatively obscure Mexican holiday called Cinco de Mayo into an American celebration (to the bewilderment of many Mexicans), and the deBeers diamond company was instrumental in teaching us to cement a nuptial agreement with an engagement ring.

Indeed, postmodernists argue that we should not even attempt to connect a symbol with its underlying reference because there is no such objective reality—there is no "there" there. Theorists (most notably Jean Baudrillard) claim that we now live in a condition of *hyperreality*, where the true relationship between the symbol and reality is no longer possible to discern.[23] The symbol becomes the reality, as when consumers line up to buy copies of a cookbook revealing Aunt Bee's favorite recipes. Maybe it's a bit of a wake-up call to remember that the actress who portrayed the fictional spinster on the old TV sitcom *The Andy Griffith Show* doesn't do much cooking these days—she's been dead for many years.

A more vivid example of hyperreality can be found in Switzerland, where a region of the country has been renamed "Heidiland" to commemorate the supposed "birthplace" of the imaginary girl. In the town of Maienfeld, new Heidi attractions are flourishing. A Heidi trail leads to a Heidi refreshment stand, and from there to an actor who poses as Heidi's grandfather. Initially officials refused to permit the posting of "Welcome to Heidiland" highway signs, because Swiss law allows only real place names. The volume of tourists making a pilgrimage to the "home" of this mythical character apparently changed their minds. Hyperreality is big business in consumerspace.

The Church of McDonald's

Brands matter deeply to us, and they're not just about status. Our reasons for cherishing products go much deeper than that. Some of the roles they play are similar to those of magic amulets or witches' potions in days of old. Antiaging cosmetics, exercise programs, and gambling casinos often imply that their offerings have "magical" properties that will ward off sickness, cellulite, old age, poverty, or just plain bad luck. People by the millions play their "lucky numbers" in the lottery or carry rabbits' feet and other charms to ward off "the evil eye." Many hang on to lucky clothing, display St. Christopher medals in their cars, or (much to the chagrin of their spouses) refuse to throw out other products they believe will bring them good fortune.

Sometimes consumers regard "extraordinary" activities such as extreme sports as magical. For example, white-water river rafters report that the rites and rituals they practice on their trips have transformed their lives in profound ways. Software developers even supply "wizards" that help guide the uninitiated through their programs! Indeed, the computer is regarded with awe by many consumers as a sort of "electronic magician," with the ability to solve our problems (or in other cases to cause data to magically disappear!).

Zeus Meets Nike

A *myth* is a story containing symbolic elements that expresses the shared emotions and ideals of a culture. In our society many seemingly mundane products take on mythic qualities. All it takes is five minutes of watching professional wrestling, where outlandish characters representing virtue and vice engage in "mortal combat," to understand how central these stories are in our daily lives. In a typical month the World Wrestling Foundation Web site attracts almost two million unique visitors, each of whom spends an average of nearly twelve minutes at the site, according to Jupiter Media Metrix. This is valuable time spent marketing T-shirts, video games, and other paraphernalia that let viewers pay monetary tribute to their favorite standard-bearers of good or evil.

We look to the commercial world to provide us with the "stories" that used to be supplied by priests to help us find our way. The crackling fire where we used to gather to hear tales of bravery and cunning has been replaced by the glowing TV tube or computer monitor. In some cases a brand's communications platform (most likely unconsciously) takes the form of a mythic structure. A famous Coke commercial featuring the football player Mean Joe Greene and an adoring little boy who helps him out in a pinch follows the same plot structure as the fairy tale of the lion and the mouse. For years McDonald's ads depicted the triumph of good over evil as Ronald McDonald continually came up with new ways to confound the Hamburglar.

Corporations often do their part by passing down myths to newcomers. Nike designates senior executives as "corporate storytellers" who explain the company's heritage to other employees, including the hourly workers at retail outlets. They tell legends about the founders of Nike, including the coach of the Oregon track team who poured rubber into his family's waffle iron to make better shoes for his team—the origin of the Nike waffle sole. The stories emphasize the dedication of runners and coaches involved with the company to reinforce the importance of teamwork. Rookies even visit the track where the coach worked to be sure they grasp the importance of the Nike legacy.[24] Acolytes who are admitted to the inner sanctum (purportedly including CEO Phil Knight) get Nike swoosh tattoos in sensitive places to cement their corporate bonds.

Brands also are deeply embedded in many of our *rituals*, which are sets of multiple, symbolic behaviors that occur in a fixed sequence and that tend to be repeated periodically. Bizarre tribal ceremonies, perhaps involving animal or human sacrifice, may come to mind when people think of these practices. In reality, though, many contemporary consumer activities are ritualistic. The regimen of brushing one's hair for 100 strokes every morning, hitting Starbucks for that obligatory midmorning buzz, or decompressing in a hot bath accompanied by Mozart and white wine all qualify as ritual behaviors.

Though they may not think in these terms, many businesses owe their existence to rituals—and to consumers' needs for the artifacts required to perform them. These include service providers like wedding photographers and undertakers, as well as manufacturers of a huge range of products including birthday candles, diplomas, specialized foods and beverages (e.g., wedding cakes, ceremonial wine, or even hot dogs at the ballpark), trophies and plaques, band uniforms, and greeting cards.

THE BOTTOM LINE

Products often take on magical qualities and are objects of worship in modern society. Many are incorporated into modern versions of rituals that affirm our place in society and help to bring order to our daily lives. Marketing messages based upon mythic themes resonate with consumers.

Love Me, Love My Brand

Guests who stay at a Holiday Inn in Lake Buena Vista, Florida, can choose from such corporate theme rooms as the Minute Maid suite and the Edy's Ice Cream suite. A Coca-Cola executive (there is a polar bear motif in the Coca-Cola suite) comments, "[Families] . . . feel like they can actually interact with our brands within a room."[25] Sleeping with your favorite brand? That's consumerspace in a nutshell.

Now Appearing at a Department Store Near You

Brands arguably are the preeminent symbols of contemporary consumer culture. They are part of our vocabulary—"Where's the beef?" "Is this a Kodak moment?" "Just do it." Sometimes they are our friends and sometimes they are the objects of our obsessions (think Imelda Marcos's shoe closet). As represented in advertising, product placement, merchandising, artistic depictions, and word of mouth, brands are inextricably woven into the fabric of our cultural universe.

The notion that brands are part and parcel of what we see, what we do, and perhaps who we are is not entirely new, of course. In the early days of television, advertisers paid production costs and developed shows like the Colgate Theatre and Texaco Star Theater. An entire genre, the soap opera, was so named because of the daytime TV sponsorship of Procter & Gamble.

The difference is that in those days the companies paid for the ticket and invited you into the show. Sponsors hovered respectfully outside the door until you chose to take a break from the program. Contrast that separation with the new evil adversary Susan Lucci's character Erica Kane faces on the modern soap *All My Children*. Kane runs a cosmetics company called Enchantment. Now in addition to her other trials and tribulations she has to put up with the wheelings and dealings of a rival firm—Revlon. In return for becoming a major plotline for three months, Revlon agreed to spend several million dollars in advertising on the show.

Kane's predicament is hardly unique. Many of the environments in which we find ourselves, whether housing developments, shopping malls, sports stadiums, or theme parks, are largely composed of images and characters spawned by marketing campaigns. Wherever we turn, we are bombarded by advertising messages, in places we expect like network commercials but also increasingly in places we don't. Beach 'n Billboard imprints brand logos in the sand for a fee, while a French firm called JC Decaux specializes in the "street-furniture business" and plasters ads on public toilets, bicycles, bus shelters, newsstands, and any other public places it can find. On a party planning Web site called evite.com, people who download a template to create an invitation to an event will find that it's sponsored by an advertiser. Amstel Light ads show up on happy-hour invitations, girls' night out invites include ads for Crest teeth-whiteners, and Pizza Hut promos appear on pizza-night notices.

The scramble to get advertising out there is so intense that now some marketers are considering the idea of piggybacking ads for other brands onto their own! Suntory Ltd. pioneered this approach by slapping an ad for a clothing company onto a low-malt beer product. Consumerspace abhors a vacuum.

Indeed, in consumerspace brands are not just the backdrop. They are the stars. Now we have *Lucky*, a magazine devoted entirely to shopping. No need to bother with the pretense of including those bothersome articles to fill in the gaps between ads. In France, people pay good francs to watch twenty-four-hour marathons of commercials shown in movie theaters. A TV show now being shopped by the producer of *Who Wants to Be a Millionaire* called *Live from Tomorrow* will work sponsors' products into variety/news segments. One of the executives involved with the project explained, "We wanted to create a show that would in a contextual way showcase products in a really fun and unique way so that you wouldn't need 30-second commercials."[26]

One result of these ubiquitous messages is that we are no longer sure (and perhaps we don't care) where the line separating this fabricated world from reality begins and ends. Sometimes, we gleefully join in the illusion. A story line in a recent *Wonder Woman* comic book features the usual out-of-this-world exploits of a vivacious superhero. But, it also includes the real-world marriage proposal of Todd McDevitt, the owner of a chain of comic book stores who persuaded DC Comics to let him woo his beloved in the issue. One shudders to think what he has in mind for the honeymoon.

THE BOTTOM LINE

In consumerspace, brands no longer serve as just the backdrop to our daily lives. They are often the stars. TV shows, books, music, and movies increasingly are built around products. In our hyperreal society, the boundary between the fabricated and the real is no longer clear. Consumers often enjoy the opportunity to buy into fantasy by selecting products used by fictional characters.

Can I Play? Participatory Marketing

All of this talk about brands pervading our lives smacks of the criticisms generated by members of the Frankfurt School almost a century ago. Have we come full circle to the point where we are mindless automatons who blithely do the bidding of the Evil Empire (aka Madison Avenue)? Do we live to buy rather than buy to live? That accusation still holds water in some cases, but such a dour picture may not be accurate in many others. This time around, we as consumers are hardly unsuspecting dupes in a conspiracy to control our hearts, minds, and pocketbooks. On the contrary, we are enthusiastic players who demand a seat at the table. The old ties that bind have been replaced by the brotherhood of shopping.

Many of us (particularly Generation Y, as we'll see in Chapter 3) absorb all of the hype with a wink and a nod. We know it's all a game, and we like it—as long as we get to choose the terms. Informed consent is the watchword. This attitude is epitomized in the "consent condom," a new product on sale in Great Britain. Perhaps the ultimate in "permission marketing," this device is intended to eliminate potential charges of date rape by storing a couple's fingerprints and the current date to indicate that both parties have agreed to the merger.

Some may claim that we are all victims of rape by the commercial establishment, but that kind of consumer militancy is seeping into many people's attitudes regarding the relationships (rather than one-night stands) they choose to establish with each other, as well as with the companies that sell to them. In many ways, both online and off, consumers are avidly playing the marketing game. Slowly and steadily the balance of power is shifting. Marketers aren't exactly powerless, but they need to be a lot more willing to share decision-making responsibility with those who (they hope) will buy their products and services. In the new era of participatory marketing:

- Customers log on to priceline.com and dictate what they will choose to pay for a hotel room or an airline ticket.

- Fans help to determine if a new movie will be a winner or a turkey before it's even released by sharing their predictions on Web sites like E! Online or aintitcoolnews.com. The Hollywood Stock Exchange (hsx.com) offers a simulated entertainment stock market where traders predict the four-week box office take for each film. Major studios and actors cannot afford to ignore this customer community when making their "real" development and marketing decisions.

- When the owner of Bare Escentuals sells her eyeliners, blush, and other products on QVC, she first contacts 1,000 cosmetics groupies by phone and online who serve as guinea pigs to evaluate potential new offerings. Customer suggestions have paid off numerous times, and this input is responsible for one of the company's most popular lipsticks as well as a self-tanning lotion.

THE BOTTOM LINE

In consumerspace, people are not unwitting dupes of the marketing machine. Even though our lives are defined by commercial messages as never before, we now want to be part of the action. Participatory marketing strategies accelerate consumers' involvement in the marketplace by encouraging customers to join in with producers to create and consume the products they buy.

A few years ago, the director of strategic planning at Saatchi & Saatchi New York predicted, ". . . any space you can take in visually, anything you hear in the future will be branded, I believe. It's not going to be the Washington Monument. It's going to be the Washington Post Monument."[27] In the chapters to come, we'll see that she was probably right.

Welcome to consumerspace.

CHAPTER 2

How Products Get Their Meaning in Consumerspace

The Internet search site Lycos was the first company to sponsor a team in the Collegiate Professional Basketball League. The league is hoping that eventually Team Lycos will play such opponents as Team Nike, Team America Online, etc. The league's founder says, "I don't think of us as a basketball league, but as an advertising vehicle built around basketball."[1]

One way to think about *consumerspace* is as an advertising vehicle built around reality. Our allegiances to sneakers, musicians, or even soft drinks help us define our place in modern society. These choices also help each of us to form ties with others who share similar preferences. This comment by a participant in a focus group captures the curious bonding that can result: "I was at a Super Bowl party, and I picked up an obscure drink. Somebody else across the room went 'yo!' because he had the same thing. People feel a connection when you're drinking the same thing."

Just where do these linkages come from? Clearly advertising is one source, but a great conceit of marketers is that it's the only one. In *consumerspace* people learn which brands are naughty and which are nice from all sorts of places—the products celebrities use, store

39

windows, that stunning blonde down the hall. And they don't just buy
a product. They buy sets of products that combine to express themselves. Ask your friends to guess what kind of watch that yuppie driving the BMW Boxster is wearing. Count how many say Rolex versus
Timex. A no-brainer.

In this chapter, we'll take a look at the big picture of *consumerspace*. We'll start by examining just why people need products to
express who they are because that helps to explain why we form such
strong bonds with inanimate objects. We'll move on to an overview
of how new products compete for our favor as they fight the good fight
to succeed in the marketplace. Finally, we'll conclude with a discussion of the *style funnel*: The filtering mechanism that separates the
wheat from the chaff. As we'll see, those who operate this machinery
are very powerful people. They are *cultural gatekeepers* who play a
key role in determining which brands get admitted to *consumerspace*
and which ones get left on the cutting room floor.

Actors on the Stage of Consumerspace

When the Bard wrote, "All the world's a stage . . ." he wasn't just
waxing poetic. A sociological school of thought known as *role theory*
takes the view that much of consumer behavior is just like a play. Each
of us learns our lines and goes about acquiring the props and costumes necessary to put on a good performance. And we're very busy
actors because we are involved in many plays at one time, whether
as an extra or a star. The self is essentially defined by the "play" we
find ourselves in at any point in time, and how well we feel we are
acting out the role demanded of us in that particular performance.

This dramatic perspective reminds us of the complex and important relationships each of us has with the props and costumes that help
to define our very being. Expressions like "You are what you wear"
or even "You are what you drive" are not so far-fetched when viewed
in this light. We don't just use products to express ourselves—we rely
on them to remind us who we are and to maintain our sense of self.

Objects can act as security blankets by reinforcing our identities, especially in unfamiliar situations. For example, students who deco-rate their dorm rooms with personal items are less likely to drop out of college. This coping process may protect the self from being diluted in a strange environment.[2] Similarly, victims of burglaries and natural disasters commonly report feelings of alienation, depression, or of being "violated." One consumer's comment after being robbed is typ-ical: "It's the next worse thing to being bereaved; it's like being raped."[3] Burglary victims exhibit a diminished sense of community, lowered feelings of privacy, and less pride in their houses' appear-ance than do their neighbors.

I've found in my own research that you can alter people's behav-ior and self-concept by manipulating the clothing they wear: In one study that simulated a job interview, for example, men who were dressed "professionally" on average actually asked for a starting sal-ary many thousands of dollars higher than those who were dressed casually (the two groups were assigned to each clothing condition randomly to rule out the possibility that more assertive people just hap-pen to be better dressers as well). Evidently, the coat-and-tie guys were better able to pull off the professional role and were more confident in their abilities as a result.

THE BOTTOM LINE

Consumers use product cues to guide their behaviors, especially when they find themselves in unfamiliar roles or situations. This regulatory function presents opportunities for new products (like portion-controlled snacks) that provide this guidance.

Marketers can use this regulatory mechanism to their advantage by finding ways to let their products help people control their behav-iors. In developing a new line of snack cakes, for example, Sara Lee found that consumers low in self-esteem preferred portion-controlled snack items because they felt they lacked self-control.[4] Many advertisers intuitively understand that if they want to sell products, they need to convince people that their performance will improve if they buy them. Linking a brand to success in a social situation, whether a round of golf, a family barbecue, or a night at a glamorous club surrounded by "jet-setters," is a common advertising strategy. Thus people, products, and settings combine to express a certain consumption style as shown in Figure 2.1.

Are You What You Buy?

If we were, in fact, shaped by our possessions, we would expect to find that people resemble what they own—sort of like the popular notion that over time dog owners start to look like their canine companions! Chapter 1 introduced the idea of a brand personality: Do people prefer products with brand personalities similar to their own?

Research tends to support this idea. One of the earliest studies to

Figure 2.1: Linking products to lifestyles.

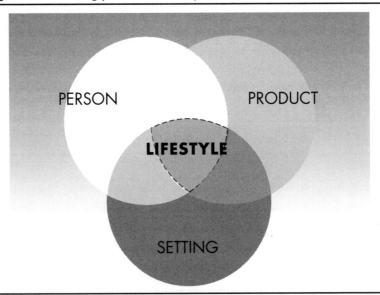

Source: Michael R. Solomon, *Consumer Behavior: Buying, Having, and Being,* 5th ed., © 2002, p. 175. Reprinted by permission of Pearson Education, Inc., Upper Saddle River, N.J.

examine this linkage found that car owners' ratings of themselves tended to match their perceptions of their cars: Pontiac drivers saw themselves as more active and flashy than did Volkswagen drivers. This convergence has also been reported between consumers and their most-preferred brands of beer, soap, toothpaste, and cigarettes relative to their least-preferred brands, as well as between consumers' self-images and their descriptions of their favorite stores.

The Extended Self

After being jilted by his girlfriend, a Tennessee man tried to marry his car. His plan was thwarted, however, after he listed his fiancée's birthplace as Detroit, her father as Henry Ford, and her blood type as 10 W40.[5] Under Tennessee law, only a man and a woman can legally wed. So much for that exciting honeymoon at the car wash.

Matrimony aside, it's not that uncommon to find people who are quite attached to a two-ton piece of metal—just witness the vaguely erotic weekend car-washing rituals in any suburban neighborhood as weekend warriors lovingly soap up their chariots and rub them down. We tend to define ourselves in terms of the products that are near and dear to us—whether one is a "meat and potatoes man," a "Ford kind of guy," or a Cabernet connoisseur. As a result, our self-concepts are influenced not just by our appraisals of our good looks, intelligence, or other internal qualities. The quality of our product inventories also reflects upon what we think of ourselves. Russell Belk has labeled those external objects that we consider a part of us the *extended self*.[6]

Thus, many brands take on additional meanings because they come to be associated by consumers with certain roles or lifestyles. Often it's the consumers themselves who make these connections rather than their being the result of some scheme cooked up by a marketer. For example, executives at Subaru discovered to their great surprise that lesbians are four times as likely as the average consumer to own one of their cars. They made this discovery accidentally, never having intended to go after this group. If you can't beat 'em, join 'em: Today the company deliberately targets this segment by running ads in gay media depicting happy same-sex couples driving its cars.[7]

In some cultures, people literally incorporate objects into the self—they lick new possessions, take the names of conquered enemies (or in some cases eat them), or bury the dead with their possessions. We don't usually go that far, but some people do cherish possessions as if they were a part of themselves. Many material objects, ranging from personal possessions and pets to national monuments or landmarks, help to form a consumer's identity. Just about everyone can point to something that has a lot of the self wrapped up in it, whether the item is a beloved photograph, a trophy, an old shirt, a car, or a cat. Indeed, it is often possible to construct a pretty accurate "biography" of someone just by cataloging the items on display in his or her bedroom or office. If you don't believe it, just try it.

I Am Not, Therefore I Am

Do real men eat quiche? A humor book published in 1982 chronicled the supposed demise of masculinity by identifying things that "real men" shouldn't do. While most enlightened men today worry more about the cholesterol threat posed by a quiche than by its challenge to their machismo, this book was right about one thing. The products we use do not only define us. They also help us to decide who we are not. This means that some brands are actively used to orient us away from certain identities we believe will be perceived negatively, whether Slutty Woman, Nerd, Yuppie Scum, etc. Anyone who doesn't believe this premise obviously has never tried to buy "respectable" clothing for a teenager.

The extended self thus includes the brands from which we try to distance ourselves. Our research supports the notion that many consumers harbor strong feelings about *avoidance brands*. Indeed, we've found that the brand personalities assigned to negatively valued products tend to be even more vivid and widely shared than the traits ascribed to brands we like. Given the scathing reactions one often gets from consumers when they are asked to describe people who use brands they themselves despise, it's surprising how little the avoidance idea is used in marketing research. One obvious application is in comparative advertising. A marketer who wants to subtly demean the competition might do so by embedding rival brands in contexts where negatively valued people display products that research has shown to be avoidance items for a particular market segment.

THE BOTTOM LINE

> The extended self is composed of products we value and those we despise. By identifying sets of both positively and negatively valued brands for a particular consumer profile, a marketer can use this information to position his or her brand by linking it to the positive ones and/or linking rival brands to the negative ones.

Product Constellations: The Forest or the Trees?

Unless you're deeply into experimental theater, you wouldn't put on a play with no props. In the same way, when we act out a social role, we tend to use many props, costumes, and stage settings. This underscores the strategic importance of looking at how brands fit together on a symbolic level, even if they have nothing to do with each other on a functional one. Many products and services seem to "go together," usually because they tend to be selected by the same types of people. In many cases, products just don't make sense if unaccompanied by companion products (e.g., fast food and paper plates, or a suit and a tie) or are incongruous in the presence of others (e.g., a Chippendale chair in a high-tech office or Lucky Strike cigarettes with a solid gold lighter).

Product complementarity occurs when the symbolic meanings of functionally dissimilar products are related to each other in consumers' minds. We use these sets of products, which I have termed *consumption constellations*, to define, communicate, and perform social roles. For example, many of us would describe the prototypical American "yuppie" almost solely in terms of such possessions as a Rolex watch, BMW automobile, Gucci briefcase, a squash racket, fresh pesto, white wine, and Brie cheese. And, it's worth noting that the cachet of these products has faded dramatically since the heyday of the yuppie; now many carry the stigma of avoidance products due to their strong association with this narcissistic, high-maintenance lifestyle.

An important part of lifestyle marketing is to identify the set of products and services that seem to be linked in consumers' minds to a specific social role. And research evidence suggests that even a relatively unattractive product becomes more appealing when it shows up in the company of other, better-liked products. Marketers who pursue *cobranding strategies* intuitively understand this: That's why L. L. Bean and Subaru are teaming up for a cobranding deal. According to the vice president of marketing at the car company, "L. L. Bean is a natural partner for Subaru, as both companies provide outdoor enthusiasts with products that enhance their lives."[8] No word yet whether L. L. Bean also intends to rope those Subaru-driving lesbians into its franchise.

Identifying product constellations is key to navigating consumerspace, yet brand managers tend to be myopic about this strategy. As we saw in Chapter 1, someone managing, say, an automotive brand worries a lot about market share—not share of mind. That is to say the chief concern is, "How many drivers are purchasing my brand versus other cars and how can I alter this equation in my favor?"

This manager probably doesn't think a lot about the other (nonautomotive) products that also tend to be associated with ownership of one car versus others. Basically, the focus of the lion's share of marketing research is on *brand substitutability*, not brand complementarity. We obsess about whether consumers prefer Brand A to Brand B within a product category, overlooking the extent to which Brand A is associated with Brand X in a different product category.

As shown in Figure 2.2, a constellation perspective stresses the important—and frequently overlooked—role of context in consumerspace. The same product can take on vastly different meanings depending upon the other products with which it is paired, just as the same prop can be used in many different plays. This contextual importance is illustrated by data from the PRIZM system developed by Clari-

Figure 2.2: A product constellation.

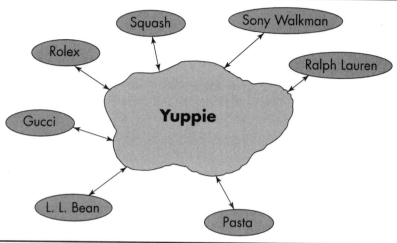

© Michael R. Solomon, 2001.

tas, Inc. This sophisticated clustering system classifies every U.S. zip code into one of sixty-two categories, ranging from the most affluent "Blue-Blood Estates" to the least well-off "Public Assistance."[9]

Each PRIZM cluster is essentially a map of a product constellation; it shows what people in that cluster consume at a much greater rate than average and also what they avoid. Although consumers in two very different clusters may purchase some products at an equivalent rate, these similarities end when other purchases are taken into account. For example, people in "Urban Gold Coast," "Money and Brains," and "Blue-Blood Estates" communities are more likely than average to buy high-quality binoculars. But then again so are consumers in the "Grain Belt," "New Homesteaders," and "Agri-Business" clusters. The difference is that the former groups use the binoculars to watch birds and other wildlife, while the latter use them to help line up the animals in their gun sights. Furthermore, whereas the bird-watchers do a lot of foreign travel, listen to classical music, and host cocktail parties, the bird hunters travel by bus, like country music, and belong to veterans' clubs.

THE BOTTOM LINE ━━━━━

A product constellation perspective highlights the crucial strategic importance of linking disparate products in terms of lifestyle rather than function. The same product takes on very different meanings depending upon the context in which it is consumed and the other products used along with it. The typical focus on brand substitutability within a product category overlooks the importance of brand complementarity across product categories.

Learning the Script

How do people suddenly decide that certain props are required to play a role? It's partly a matter of learning to want that special something—attaching free-floating desire to something concrete like a pair of Diesel jeans or a Bang & Olufsen stereo system. Suddenly, it seems, the newest new thing pops up on the radar screen, and in a flash the inhabitants of consumerspace are scrambling to obtain it.

Cool Radar

Of course, that's not really the way it works. More likely, a few cutting-edge connoisseurs tune in to the latest hip brand and then eventually it becomes a "must have" for the rest of us. Social scientists use the term *diffusion of innovations* to describe the process whereby a new product, service, or idea spreads through a population. The rate at which a product diffuses varies. For example, within ten years after its introduction only 20 percent of the population owned a TV, but cable TV was used by 40 percent of U.S. households after a decade.

Roughly one-sixth of the population (so-called *innovators and early adopters*) is very quick to adopt new products. At the other end of the spectrum, one-sixth of the people, known as *laggards*, will try something new only under duress—they are the Archie Bunkers of consumerspace. The other two-thirds, so-called *late adopters*, are somewhere in the middle, and these consumers represent the mainstream public. They are interested in new things, but they do not want them to be too new.

Even though innovators make up only about 2.5 percent of the population, marketers eagerly seek them out. And for good reason: These are the brave souls who are always on the lookout for novel developments and who will be the first to try a new offering. Consumers who are tuned in to the latest trends (and especially those who help to set them) are an incredibly valuable source of marketing intelligence; they are spies in the land of cool. We'll look more closely at young trendsetters in Chapter 3. For now, though, it shouldn't be surprising to learn that innovators tend to have more favorable attitudes toward taking risks, boast relatively high educational and income levels, and are socially active.

How can we predict which products will diffuse and which will die, what styles will be in fashion and what styles will be here today (if that long) and gone tomorrow? That question is the holy grail of marketing. One of the first and most influential explanations was proposed way back in 1904 by sociologist Georg Simmel. His *trickle-down theory* states that there are two conflicting forces that drive fashion change. First, subordinate groups try to adopt the status symbols of the groups above them as they attempt to climb up the ladder of social mobility. Dominant styles thus originate with the upper classes and trickle down to those below. At this point the second force kicks in: Those people in the superordinate group are constantly looking below them on the ladder to ensure that they are not imitated. They respond to the attempts of lower classes to "impersonate" them by adopting still newer styles. These two processes create a self-perpetuating cycle of change—the machine that drives fashion.[10]

Simmel's elegant explanation holds less water in the twenty-first century, where class differences aren't nearly so distinct, where mass communication makes it possible for virtually everyone to learn about new styles at the same time, and where the inspiration for many designs comes "from the streets." If anything, it's more accurate in today's Hip-Hop Nation to talk about *a trickle-up theory*—by the time the rich folks figure it out, it's probably passé.

A more contemporary approach adopts a medical model: fashion as epidemic. In his book *The Tipping Point*, Malcolm Gladwell eloquently describes the process that turns a sleeper into a phenomenon in short order. A brand like Hush Puppies, for example, might just slog around—sometimes for years and years. It's initially bought by a small number of people, but change happens in a hurry when the process reaches the moment of critical mass. This moment of truth is Gladwell's *tipping point.* For example, he observes that Sharp introduced the first low-priced fax in 1984 and sold about 80,000 in that year. There was a slow climb in the number of users for the next three years. Then, suddenly in 1987 enough people had faxes that it made sense for everyone to have one—Sharp sold a million units that year. Cell phones followed a similar trajectory.[11]

More generally, this way of looking at diffusion is helpful in understanding how ideas circulate in consumerspace, as articulated in an emerging perspective called *meme* (mēēm) *theory.* A meme is an idea or product that enters the consciousness of people over time—examples include tunes, catch phrases ("Is that your final answer?"), or styles like the Hush Puppy. In this view memes spread among consumers in a geometric progression, just as a virus starts off small and steadily infects increasing numbers of people until it becomes an epidemic. Memes "leap" from brain to brain in a process of imitation.

The memes that survive tend to be distinctive and memorable, and the hardiest ones often combine aspects of prior memes. For example, the *Star Wars* movies evoked memes relating to Arthurian legend, religion, heroic youth, and 1930s adventure serials. Indeed, George Lucas studied comparative religion and mythology as he prepared his first draft of the *Star Wars* saga, "The Story of Mace Windu."[12] The new science of memetics, which tries to explain how beliefs gain acceptance and predict their progress, was spurred by Richard Dawkins, who in the 1970s proposed culture as a Darwinian struggle among "memes" or mind viruses. The meme idea is catching on. A

Web site called memepool.com is a pool for ideas that attracts 7,000 users a day who post random thoughts others may adopt.[13]

The Meme Messengers

Finding themselves with less money to spend on advertising, companies like Palm are trying to boost sales of handheld devices by wooing people they call *influencers*. These folks run Web sites that review handheld products or they manage fan clubs devoted to personal digital assistants (these people should probably get out more . . .). Palm has figured out that many consumers turn first to these influencers' recommendations before making a purchase. So it makes sense to get these guys in your court. Palm even recruited employees whose sole job is to stay in touch with influencers. The chosen few now receive special Palm T-shirts and marketing kits and get access to restricted Internet discussion groups.

Palm's efforts are a potent reminder of the power of some individuals to make or break a market. Marketers spend lavishly to inform us about their brands, to cajole us into liking them. Ironically, advertising is relatively ineffective at getting us to try new stuff. Still, a much more influential source is the personal recommendation: *Word of mouth* (WOM) is product information transmitted by individuals to individuals. Because we get the word from people we know, WOM tends to be more reliable and trustworthy than recommendations we get through more formal marketing channels. And unlike advertising, WOM often is backed up by social pressure to conform to these recommendations.

The power of WOM was demonstrated by the meteoric rise of an obscure, 200-year-old breath mint called Altoids. Sure, the retro-style ads we see everywhere now are clever, but the Altoids craze really predates these tongue-in-cheek messages. In fact, the manufacturer did virtually no advertising for most of the brand's history. The mint's revival started when it began to attract a devoted following among smokers and coffee drinkers who hung out in the blossoming Seattle club scene during the 1980s. Until 1993, when manufacturer Callard & Bowser was bought by Kraft, only those "in the know" used the mints. The brand's marketing manager persuaded Kraft to put a bit of cash into promoting the cult hit. Suddenly, the tipping point kicks in and we're in the midst of a breath mint fad. According to Dunhill's director of marketing, "mints have become the latest gentlemanly accessory."[14]

THE BOTTOM LINE

The diffusion of a new product through a population resembles the spread of an epidemic, starting out with key innovators and then making its way to the mainstream. Identifying "influencers" within a product category is an invaluable early warning system that helps companies stay ahead of the new product development curve.

The Style Funnel: Building Up and Breaking Down

It seems so simple on the face of it: Marketers decide what they want us to know about their brands, they create clever advertising messages to tell us about them, and we go to stores or log on to Web sites to choose from among competing alternatives—a pair of Seven jeans today, a 7-Up tomorrow. The company that comes up with the catchiest slogan or the most eye-catching package wins. Democracy rules at the mega mall.

Cultural Selection: Survival of the Coolest

In this view, our biggest problem is to wade in among the myriad options and find the ones we like. Indeed, if anything, it seems we have too many choices: Just buying a tie or a tube of lipstick can require lengthy deliberation and create a faintly dizzy feeling. Consumers may at times feel overwhelmed by the sheer number of choices in the marketplace. A person trying to decide on something as routine as a necktie has many hundreds of alternatives to choose from (more on this issue in Chapter 10). Despite this seeming abundance, however, the options available to consumers at any point in time actually represent only a small fraction of the total set of possibilities out there. The selection of certain alternatives over others—whether automobiles, dresses, computers, recording artists, political candidates, religions, or even scientific methodologies—is the culmination of a complex filtration process resembling a funnel, as depicted in Figure 2.3. Many possibilities initially compete for adoption, and these are steadily winnowed out as they make their way down the path from conception to consumption in a process of *cultural selection*.

Despite the abundance of choices available to us—thousands of CDs, hundreds of blouses, coffee tables too numerous to count—these options represent only a small fraction of the teeming jungle of products that is consumerspace. Most of the choices never make it to the retail level. They were filtered out along the way by experts whose thumbs-up or -down can make or break a product.

Sociologists have looked at this narrowing down process in great detail, though not typically as it pertains to branded merchandise. They study how "cultural products" such as paintings or music get produced and selected. These same processes that help to explain the production of culture also happen to serve us well in understanding the odyssey of a brand from conception to consumption. In both cases it's useful to think of a *culture production system* at work. Populated by many players (who don't often realize they are part of the system to begin with), this system works organically to decide which dresses we will see on the rack at Bloomingdale's or which songs will make it into the Top 40 this week.

This perspective assumes that the organizations in a culture influence the nature of the symbols produced. For example, one study of the country music industry showed that the songs produced in Nashville tend to be more diverse when there are more industry competitors and more homogenized when power is concentrated with a few big labels.[15]

A culture production system has three major subsystems: (1) a *creative subsystem* responsible for generating new symbols and/or prod-

Figure 2.3: The culture production process.

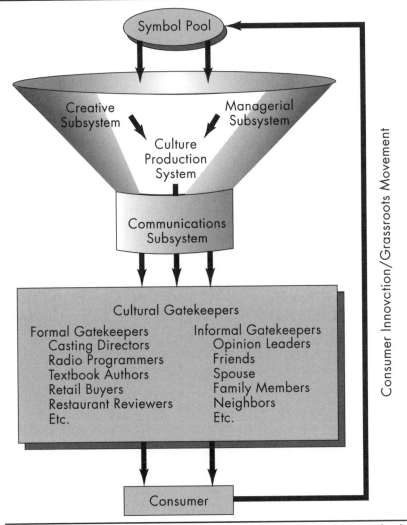

SOURCE: Michael R. Solomon, *Consumer Behavior: Buying, Having, and Being*, 5th ed., © 2002, p. 491. Reprinted by permission of Pearson Education, Inc., Upper Saddle River, N.J.

ucts; (2) a *managerial subsystem* responsible for selecting, making tangible, mass-producing, and managing the distribution of new symbols and/or products; and (3) a *communications subsystem* responsible for giving meaning to the new product and providing it with a symbolic set of attributes that are communicated to consumers. An example of the three components of a culture production system for a record would be (1) a singer (e.g., rapper Puff Daddy, a creative subsystem); (2) a company (e.g., Bad Boy Records, which manufactures and distributes Puff Daddy's CDs, a managerial subsystem); and (3) the advertising and publicity agencies hired to promote Puff Daddy's output (a communications subsystem).

The sociologist Howard Becker conducted a classic study of how this process works. He probed the enigmatic world of *haute couture* in a quest to understand the fashion industry. After attending some runway shows, Becker observed that many of the buyers seemed to follow a formula: At a typical Paris show over one hundred designs are shown to about two hundred buyers, yet insiders can easily pick out the thirty or so that will be seriously considered. Becker's recounting of this event is telling: "When the buyers were asked why they chose one dress in preference to another—between which my inexperienced eye could see no appreciable difference—the typical, honest, yet largely uninformative answer was that the dress was 'stunning.'"[16] These experts can't necessarily articulate their reasoning, but the high level of convergence among them (despite the fact that they are competing against one another to bring back unique selections that will differentiate their stores) implies that their "intuition" is more than just a subjective reaction to a "stunning" garment.

Cultural Gatekeepers: Guarding the Doors of Consumerspace

To borrow from an old cliché: Those who can't do, teach. Those who can't teach, criticize. Some of the most important arbiters of culture—the players who determine what's hot and what's not—don't design the products, make them, package them, or sell them. Many judges or "tastemakers" influence the products that are eventually offered to consumers. These *cultural gatekeepers* are responsible for filtering the overflow of information and materials intended for consumers. Gate-keepers include movie, restaurant, and car reviewers, interior design-ers, disc jockeys, retail buyers, and book/magazine editors.

Music to Our Ears

To understand the importance of this cultural filtering process, think about the music industry. For years we've had an abundance of music to choose from. Browsing in a record store can eat up a day, but life today is even more complicated now that we can download free stuff to our heart's content (to the chagrin of the record labels of course) from sites like Morpheus and KaZaA.

There's a catch to this cornucopia of tunes: Each year more than 30,000 music titles are released into a very cluttered space—there literally are not enough hours in a lifetime to listen to all of them. That's why even in the age of free music, producers and reviewers will con-tinue to make a living. Their role as filtering agents grows in impor-tance as the number of choices on the market mushrooms. Increasingly we will rely on them to sift through the noise and recommend which of the ten million albums we can expect to be produced over the next fifty years merit our attention.

Some analysts feel that this is the bedrock of the new business model for this industry: It will be easier to buy selected material than get free music that you have to spend time evaluating. The president of a company that compiles soundtracks sold in stores like the Gap and Victoria's Secret exemplifies this gatekeeping function. He sees himself as streamlining the music-buying process. Thumbing labori-ously through the new-release rack in a record store may be fine for teenagers, he said, "but for people who are beyond that part of their life and they have jobs and maybe have families, the reality is they don't have two hours to go hang out at Tower Records." So, he said, when a trusted brand name (like the Gap!) offers them its take on good music, they accept.[17] We'll talk more about this editing function in Chapter 10.

Decoding the Formula

Like the classic comment by a Supreme Court justice that he couldn't define pornography but he knew it when he saw it, cultural specialists (like Becker's retail buyers) just seem to "know" what they like. Very often there is substantial agreement among these experts. That's because many forms of popular culture, such as literature, decorating styles, or apparel, tend to follow a *cultural formula*.

Fiction is a great example. Detective stories, Western novellas, or science fiction series typically contain predictable symbols that clue us in to what to expect. That's why cowboy movies always had the good guys in the white hats and the bad guys in the black ones. Romance novels are an even more extreme case. Computer programs even allow users to "write" their own romances by systematically varying certain set elements of the story. TV sitcoms almost always have a father figure (whether Ward Cleaver, Jerry Seinfeld, or an animated Homer Simpson), a mother figure (June Cleaver, Jerry's Elaine, or Marge Simpson), and "children" (whether the Beaver, Seinfeld's Kramer and George, or that irascible Bart Simpson).

Reliance on these formulas also leads to a recycling of images, as members of the creative subsystem reach back through time for inspiration. Thus, young people watch retro shows like *Gilligan's Island* and remakes of *The Brady Bunch*, designers modify styles from Victorian England or colonial Africa, hip-hop DJs sample sound bits from old songs and combine them in new ways, and the Gap runs ads featuring now-dead celebrities including Humphrey Bogart, Gene Kelly, and Pablo Picasso showing off their khakis. With easy access to VCRs, CD burners, digital cameras, and imaging software, virtually anyone can "remix" the past.

CASE STUDY

A study I conducted illustrates the potency of these formulas. In a simulated preproduction task, I asked twenty-five professional property masters to "dress a set" for a coffee commercial. I systematically varied the context to see how lifestyle cues might influence their choices. Each person was given a basic storyboard and he or she was told only that the actor would be a male or female and what kind of music would be playing in the background (classical or country).

Based upon this vague information, respondents had to choose an exterior house shot, an ensemble of living room furniture, and a specific coffee mug that would be featured in a close-up shot. The outcome? Although all choices were made individually, I found an extremely high level of consensus. For example, nineteen out of the twenty-five set dressers chose the same contemporary living room style for a male who liked classical music. As the gender and musical taste of the person was varied, we observed consistent shifts in the decor associated with this "slice of life." Our property masters, whose choices help to educate millions of viewers about lifestyles they have not directly experienced, seemed to be following the same cultural formula.

With all of the thousands of choices at their fingertips, why do we see so much conformity in these choices? Put simply, individual gatekeepers live in the same mass culture as the rest of us. Often they base their predictions or analyses on the same limited set of observations as others in the industry, creating a self-fulfilling prophecy. Political pundits may echo what others are saying. In industries ranging from apparel to automotive, design executives buy color-forecasting information that tells them which hues will be popular in a year, three years, and five years. Should we be surprised when suddenly all the designers are introducing their new lines in that same ghastly shade of purple?

These cultural specialists share many of our stereotypes (e.g., a classical music lover must be sophisticated and prefer contemporary decor) and are affected by cultural trends, shifts in values, and so on. Although symbolic alternatives vie for acceptance, they often adhere to the same dominant style, whether New Wave or nouvelle cuisine. Movies influence fashions: Remember the hat craze inspired by *Urban Cowboy*? Car design is influenced by other technological developments. That's why those funny-looking tailfins were so popular in the 1950s: The space race, instigated by the *Sputnik* launch, brought rocket ships and "cities of the future" to the forefront for young Americans. If you couldn't fly to the moon, at least you could go cruising for a Moon Pop in your snazzy new Cadillac.

THE BOTTOM LINE

Cultural gatekeepers such as reviewers and editors play a pivotal role in deciding which new products will succeed or fail. Marketers need to be sure they understand who pulls the strings within a particular channel and ensure that they are doing their best to convince these players (in addition to end consumers) of their offering's value. Part of this persuasive process involves identifying the stereotypes or cultural formulas that influence gatekeepers' assumptions about what products will succeed and who will be most likely to adopt them.

So, a paradox of consumerspace is that the abundance of choice is in some ways illusory. In reality, many of the selections we make are predetermined, largely influenced by the judgments of cultural gatekeepers who steadily winnow down the options before we ever see them. These editors do their best to estimate what we will like or loathe, and there's often a self-fulfilling prophecy as they too are influenced by trends in popular culture and assumptions about what the mass market will accept. And, even when the stylistic "winners" do make it to market, some of us will decide if they will pass muster among the masses well in advance of the rest of us. These consumer innovators play a key role in spreading the "disease" of new fashions. These "carriers" are likely to be our sons and daughters, as we'll see in Chapter 3.

CHAPTER 3

O Pioneers!
Scanning Global Youth Culture

In some cultures, an adolescent boy is sent off into the jungle to do combat with lions or tigers or bears (oh my!). Upon his (hopefully) triumphant return with carcass trophy in hand, he is awarded the status of manhood and all the perks that come with it. In our society, that man-child returns home with his driver's license. Let the games begin.

Teen Angels

We accept without hesitation that there will be a period when boys make the transition to men and girls flower into womanhood. Adolescence is a time fraught with both magic and insecurity as kids find their way and figure out just who they are and who they are supposed to be. Typically we send them away for four years to let them answer these questions while exploring the wonders of fraternity initiations and spring break excursions.

Puberty has been with us for a long time, but the concept of being a teenager actually is a fairly new idea. Most cultures throughout history did not build in this transition period. Young people were expected to shoulder the responsibilities of their parents early on (remember that Shakespeare's Juliet was all of thirteen when she tried to hook up with Romeo). The teen years are a cultural construction we have created to form a safe harbor for adolescents, a buffer zone to cushion the rude awakening of maturity.

Our thinking on this subject started to change in the last century as a youth culture started to coalesce. The magazine *Seventeen*, born in 1944, was built on the revelation that young women didn't want to look just like a junior version of Mom. Frankie Lymon and the Teenagers became the first pop group to identify themselves with this new subculture. The stage was set for teens to rule the world.

And rule it they do. So-called Generation Y kids (children born between 1977 and 1995) number seventy million and make up 21 percent of the population. The percentage of Generation Yers in the total population is expected to increase at twice the rate of the population until 2010, and by 2020 this percentage will have reached 32 percent. Generation Y is an ethnically diverse generation. While minorities make up 24 percent of baby boomers, they form 34 percent of Generation Y.

Unlike their cynical Gen X predecessors, Gen Yers tend to be more upbeat about their lives and their prospects. According to a survey by *U.S. News and World Report,* alcohol consumption among high school seniors dropped from 72 percent in 1980 to 52 percent in 1998. Drug usage, pregnancy, and homicide rates among teens also are declining. There is a bit of a renaissance of family and religious values, and sociologists are predicting a surge in younger marriages and bigger families as these kids come into their own in a few years. Although some grownups who have seen one too many tongue piercings would argue we are on the brink of the apocalypse, these trends imply that we are actually raising a generation that looks like more like Eisenhower Republicans who have swapped their cloth coats for Abercrombie & Fitch lo-rise jeans. Kids (as always) are hard to figure out, but marketers who try can be amply rewarded. The future of consumerspace lies in the hands of its young pioneers.

Consumers-in-Training

Once known for discouraging kids from hanging out in its aisles, 7-Eleven is targeting teens in a big way. The chain is adding eighty new products and limited-time exclusives on teen favorites such as Gatorade and Mountain Dew (a Mountain Dew Code Red Slurpee is in the works). It already struck gold with such youth faves as Pokemon cards, scooters, and prepaid cellular phones.

The chain figured out that, whether they're buying skateboards or junk food, teens are an economic force to be reckoned with. Collectively, American teens spent $172 billion in 2001—that's a lot of Slurpees. According to Teenage Research Unlimited, the average teen spends $84 per week, of which $57 is money he or she actually earns.[1] Learning from their parents, many young residents of consumerspace have figured out they don't even need to have cash on hand: 42 percent of teens aged 18 and 19 already have a credit card in their own name. Another 11 percent say they have access to a parent's credit card. Debit cards like Splash Plastic and Smartcreds further encourage teen spending. A market research firm specializing in this segment has gone so far as to label teens *Skippies*—school kids with income and purchasing power.

A lot of this money goes toward "feel-good" products like cosmetics, posters, and fast food, with the occasional nose ring thrown in as well. That's not the whole story, however. Marketers need to understand that teens may also be participating in more far-reaching purchase decisions, especially as fewer live in traditional families with parents who have ample time to do the grocery shopping. One survey of sixteen- to seventeen-year-old girls found that over a three-month period a significant proportion of them purchased staple items such as cereal, frozen meals, cheese, yogurt, and salad dressing. Marketers are beginning to respond to these changes. The number of pages devoted to food advertising in *Seventeen* magazine increased by 31 percent in one year.

Gen Y kids appear to be materialistic, but they're hardly an easy sell. They are very savvy about marketing strategies and are quite aware that advertisers are doing whatever they can to get them into their franchise. Pandering messages are a major turnoff. Advertisers need to tread carefully in cynical waters. Marketers of entrenched brands like Nike, Pepsi, and Levi Strauss are tearing their hair out over

Gen Y consumers. Image-building campaigns (e.g., Michael Jordan endorsing Nike) are not as effective as they once were—kids have figured out that someone's paying these guys to endorse this stuff.

Still, because kids are so interested in many different products and have the resources to obtain them, the teen market remains an attractive target. Toyota, for example, created a special marketing unit called Genesis Group just to reach young adults. Genesis launched its first campaign to support Toyota's new crop of youth-oriented models like the Echo.

Marketers view teens as "consumers-in-training" because brand loyalty often develops during adolescence. A teenager who is committed to a brand may continue to purchase it for many years to come. Such loyalty creates a barrier-to-entry for brands that were not chosen during these pivotal years. For this reason advertisers sometimes try to "lock in" adolescent consumers so that in the future they will buy their brands more or less automatically. As one teen magazine ad director observed, "We . . . always say it's easier to start a habit than stop it."[2]

THE BOTTOM LINE

Teens are alluring targets for "feel-good products," but marketers in mainstream categories also may find it advantageous to cultivate brand loyalty at an early age. In addition to discretionary items, many teens participate in grocery shopping and household maintenance. They form bonds with products that will serve as barriers-to-entry for rivals who seek their business later in life.

Reaching Kids Where They Live (and Learn)

The raw materials for a branded reality emanate from many sources. Marketing propaganda bombards young people virtually everywhere they turn—including school. Indeed, one of the most controversial interfaces between marketers and consumers occurs when companies wrap advertising in the guise of "educational materials." In some schools third graders practice math by counting Tootsie Rolls. Others use reading software sporting the logos of Kmart, Coke, Pepsi, and Cap'n Crunch cereal. Many firms including Nike, Hershey, Crayola, Nintendo, and Foot Locker provide free book covers that happen to be swathed in ads. Almost 40 percent of secondary schools in the United States start the day with a video feed from Channel One, which exposes students to commercials in the classroom in exchange for educational programming. Education is turning into "aducation."

Youth Is Wasted on the Young

To paraphrase Dickens, adolescence truly is both the best of times and the worst of times. Many exciting changes happen as individuals leave the role of child and prepare to assume the role of adult. These changes create a lot of uncertainty about the self, awakening the contradictory needs to belong to a secure group while at the same time discovering one's unique identity. Choices of activities, friends, and clothes often are crucial to social acceptance. Teens actively search for cues from their peers and from advertising for the "right" way to look and behave. That's why advertising geared to teens typically is action-oriented and depicts a group of cool teens using the product.

Adolescents have a number of psychological needs, including experimentation, belonging, independence, responsibility, and approval from others. Product usage is a significant medium to express these needs. While it may be news to us, today's kids largely accept the fact that they are what they buy. Brands like Nike or retailers like Hot Topic are enthusiastically adopted by teens to express their developing identities. According to a study by Teenage Research Unlimited (TRU), teens describe their generation as motivated primarily by entertainment and social activity. When asked to choose a statement that characterizes their peer group, the number-one answer chosen by 50 percent of respondents was "we're about fun."[3] Not bad work if you can get it.

It turns out having fun can be hard work. As the vice president of TRU explained, "Today's teens enjoy an enormous amount of freedom, both personally and financially. However, they also know that their world is changing quickly and that greater responsibility is just around the corner. Consequently, many young people admit they feel pressure to squeeze as much fun into their teen years as possible." This need to multitask may explain why teens' second-place choice in TRU's survey was the statement "high-tech is such a (huge) part of our lives." Many teens use technology like cell phones and pagers to help them organize social calendars that make their parents' schedules look downright tranquil.[4]

According to research by the Saatchi & Saatchi advertising agency, there are four themes of conflict common to all teens:

1. *Autonomy Versus Belonging:* Teens need to acquire independence so they try to break away from their families. On the other hand, they need to attach themselves to a support structure, such as peers, to avoid feeling alone.

2. *Rebellion Versus Conformity:* Teens need to rebel against social standards of appearance and behavior, yet they still need to fit in and be accepted by others. Cult products that cultivate a rebellious image are prized for this reason. Hot Topic caters to this need by selling such "in your face" items as nipple rings, tongue barbells, and purple hair dye.

3. *Idealism Versus Pragmatism:* Teens tend to view adults as hypocrites, whereas they see themselves as being sincere. They have to struggle to reconcile their view of how the world should be with the realities they perceive around them.

4. *Narcissism Versus Intimacy:* Teens are often obsessed with their own appearance and needs. On the other hand, they also feel the desire to connect with others on a meaningful level.

Global Youth Culture: It's a Small World After All

Walk down a street in Amsterdam, Buenos Aires, or Hong Kong and it's easy to have a feeling of déjà vu. The kids look surprisingly familiar: Nike shoes, Levi's jeans, Chicago Bulls T-shirts wherever you look. Indeed, the National Basketball Association is fast becoming the first truly global sports league. About $500 million of licensed merchandise is sold *outside* of the United States in a typical year. U.S. firms like Nike and Levi Strauss find it easy to go global because of the special appeal American products have around the world. They benefit from their strong association with innovation, rebellion, and a casual lifestyle fueled by youth idols from Elvis Presley to Kurt Cobain.

Multinational marketers know that their best chances to succeed in foreign markets lie in identifying consumer segments that share a common worldview. Other than affluent business travelers, the best candidates are young people whose tastes in music and fashion are strongly influenced by MTV and other media that broadcast many of the same images to multiple countries. Viewers of MTV Europe in Rome or Zurich can check out the same "buzz clips" as their counterparts in London or Luxembourg.

We are witnessing the rise of a *global youth culture*, fueled by the Internet and communications networks like MTV, that transcends national borders. Even rave parties are going global. Companies with names like BringItOn! Travel (motto: "On the beach 'til 7 P.M. In the clubs 'til 9 A.M.) and Hiptrips.com specialize in "Adventure Travel Party Scene" packages that unite ravers from many countries in the common pursuit of ecstasy.

It seems that kids are the same everywhere. The *New World Teen Study* surveyed over 27,000 teenagers in forty-four countries and identified six values segments that characterize young people from Cairo to Caracas. The results of this massive segmentation exercise have been used by companies like Coca-Cola and Royal Phillips Electronics to develop ads that appeal to youth around the world. Figure 3.1 summarizes some of the findings from this massive study.

THE BOTTOM LINE

Young consumers are not a monolithic market segment any more than their older Gen X counterparts were. Some subgroups hold highly traditional values and are achievement-oriented. Only a minority conform to the extreme sports and body-piercing stereotype. Marketing strategies targeted to youth must recognize this diversity and develop a portfolio of brand personalities that align with the unique profiles of different subsegments.

Marketing: The New Esperanto

Hip-hop dancing is all the rage among China's youth, who refer to the style as *jiew*, or street dancing. The emulation of a musical genre that originated on the other side of the world underscores the popularity of American culture in China, despite the two nations' rocky political ties and the misgivings many Chinese feel toward U.S. military power.

If plugged-in kids around the world belong to the same club, its secret password is musical. MTV provides the codebook that lets young pioneers speak to one another. Our research that compared MTV videos in the United States and Europe found many similarities in content (though the American releases tended to contain more overt references to drugs and weapons). These videos are about much more than entertainment. They provide a window into different music-oriented youth subcultures, each with its own "code" that includes acceptable clothing styles, cars, body ideals, and so on.

As kids open these windows, they crack the code by absorbing reams of information about how to consume. When we showed videos from a range of musical genres (e.g., rock, alternative, hip-hop) to kids with the sound turned off, they still were able to tell us with great accuracy what messages the videos were transmitting. These clips literally serve as "training videos" in that they teach kids how to belong to a certain subculture. That helps to explain the co-optation of the music video grammar by companies hoping to embed their brands into the lesson. The deliberate usage of "MTV-style" editing by companies like Nike makes it more likely that kids will absorb the message

(Text continues on page 73)

Figure 3.1: Highlights of the New World Teen Study.

Segment	Key Countries	Marketing Approach	Driving Principles	Overview
Thrills & Chills	Germany, England, Lithuania, Greece, Netherlands, South Africa, United States, Belgium, Canada, Turkey, France, Poland, Japan, Italy, Denmark, Argentina, and Norway	Fun, friends, irreverence, and sensation	Stereotype of the devil-may-care, trying-to-become-independent hedonist. For the most part, they come from affluent or middle-class parents, live mainly in developed countries, and have allowance money to spend.	Respond to sensory stimulation. Tend to get bored easily so stale advertising messages will escape their notice. They want action ads with bells and whistles, humor, novelty, color, and sound. Edgier than their peers. Constantly seek out the new. First ones to hear of the newest technology or the hippest Web site. Experimenting is second nature. Wear all sorts of body rings and wear their hair in different shades.
Resigned	Denmark, Sweden, Korea, Japan, Norway, Germany, Belgium, Netherlands, Argentina, Canada, Turkey, England, Spain, France, and Taiwan	Friends, fun, family, and low expectations	Resemble the thrills-and-chills teens, often decorating their bodies with rings and dye. However, they are alienated from society and very pessimistic about their chances for economic success. The punk rockers of the world, who sometimes take drugs and drink to excess. Respond to heavy metal and grunge music that emphasizes the negative and angry side of society.	Do not have as much discretionary income to spend as teens in other segments. Infrequent consumers save for some fast food, low-ticket clothes items, tobacco, and alcohol. They are drawn to irony and to ads that make fun of the pompousness of society.

(continues)

Figure 3.1: (Continued).

Segment	Key Countries	Marketing Approach	Driving Principles	Overview
World Savers	Hungary, Philippines, Venezuela, Brazil, Spain, Colombia, Belgium, Argentina, Russia, Singapore, France, Poland, Ukraine, Italy, South Africa, Mexico, and England	Environment, humanism, fun, and friends	A long list of do-good global and local causes that spark their interest. The intelligentsia in most countries who do well in school. Class and club leaders who join many organizations. They attend the same parties as the thrills-and-chills kids, but they are more into romance, relationships, and strong friendships. Eagerly attend concerts, operas, and plays. They exhibit joie de vivre and enjoy dancing or drinking at bars and cafés with friends. They love the outdoors as well, including camping, hiking, and other sports activities.	Attracted by honest and sincere messages that tell the truth. Offended by any ad that puts people down or makes fun of another group. Piggyback a promotion with a worthwhile cause.
Quiet Achievers	Thailand, China, Hong Kong, Ukraine, Korea, Lithuania, Russia, and Peru	Success, anonymity, anti-individualism, and social optimism	Value anonymity and prefer to rest in the shadows. Least rebellious of all the groups, they avoid the limelight, and do not ever want to stand out in the crowd. These are bookish and straight kids who study long hours, are fiercely ambitious, and highly goal-directed. Their top priority is to make good grades in school and use higher education to further their career advancement. Most of the quiet achievers live in Asia, especially Thailand and China. But they also exist in the United States, where they are sometimes regarded as being techies or nerds.	Love to purchase stuff. Part of the reward for working diligently is being able to buy products. Their parents will defer to their children's needs when it comes to computers and other technological products that will aid in homework. This group is also keen on music; they are inner-directed and adept at creating their own good times. Prefer ads that address the benefits of a product. They are embarrassed by ads that display rampant sexuality. And they do not respond to the sarcastic or the irreverent.

| Bootstrappers | Nigeria, Mexico, United States, India, Chile, Puerto Rico, Peru, Venezuela, Colombia, and South Africa | Achievement, individualism, optimism, determination, and power | Most dreamy and childlike of the six segments. They live sheltered and ordered lives that seem bereft of many forms of typical teen fun and wild adult-emulating teen behavior. Spend a lot of time at home, doing homework and helping around the house. Eager for power; they are the politicians in every high school who covet the class offices. They view the use of authority as a means for securing rewards, and they are constantly seeking out recognition. Geographically many of these teens come from emerging nations such as Nigeria and India. In the United States, bootstrappers represent one in every four teens. Moreover, they represent 40% of young African Americans. A major error of U.S. marketers is to misread the size and purchasing power of this ambitious African American segment. | Young yuppies in training. They want premium brands and luxury goods. Bootstrappers are also on the lookout for goods and services that will help them get ahead. They want to dress for success, have access to technology and software, and stay plugged in to the world of media and culture to give them a competitive edge. They are attracted by messages that portray aspirations and possibilities for products and their users. |

(continues)

Figure 3.1: (Continued).

Segment	Key Countries	Marketing Approach	Driving Principles	Overview
Upholders	Vietnam, Indonesia, Taiwan, China, Italy, Peru, Venezuela, Puerto Rico, India, Philippines, and Singapore	Family, custom, tradition, and respect for individuals	Traditions act as a rigid guideline, and these teens would be hard-pressed to rebel or confront authority. They are content to rest comfortably in the mainstream of life, remaining unnoticed. The girls seek mostly to get married and have families. The boys perceive that they are fated to have jobs similar to their fathers'. Predominate in Asian countries such as Indonesia and Vietnam that value old traditions and extended family relationships. Teens in these countries are helpful around the home and protective of their siblings. Moreover, many upholders are in Catholic countries where the Church and tradition guide schooling, attitudes, and values.	Advertisers and marketers have had success selling to upholders using youthful, almost childlike, communication and fun messages. These are teens who still watch cartoons and are avid media consumers. They are highly involved in both watching and playing sports, particularly basketball and soccer. More than any other group, they plan to live in their country of birth throughout adulthood. Essentially, upholders are homebodies. They are deeply rooted in family and community and like to make purchase decisions that are safe and conform to their parents' values. Brands that take a leadership stance will attract upholders for their risk-free quality, value, and reliability.

SOURCE: Adapted from "The Six Value Segments of Global Youth," *Brandweek*, 22 May 2000, 41, No. 21, p. 38, based upon data initially presented in *The $100 Billion Allowance: How to Get Your Share of the Global Teen Market* by Elissa Moses (New York: John Wiley & Sons, 2000).

because the commercial is more like a real music video than a conventional ad. Similar strategies are employed by advertising organizations such as College Television Network (now owned by MTV Networks) that beam hip messages directly to college dorm rooms and cafeterias.

Youth Tribes

Music is one of several types of "social glue" that hold kids together. They form allegiances based upon taste cultures as a way to bolster still-tentative self-concepts and to clearly mark group boundaries. The need for acceptance remains as acute as for previous generations. In a survey of 2,000 teens conducted by Teenage Research Unlimited, only 11 percent of respondents view themselves as "popular."

In the old days, we called them cliques—groups of kids who had similar interests and who often made membership desirable because they mostly focused on keeping others out of the inner circle. Today, organized youth gangs are more powerful; they dominate many urban high schools, and their reach is steadily expanding beyond their origins in New York, Chicago, and Los Angeles. Young people around the country proclaim their allegiance to a gang, often by the display of its colors (red for Bloods, blue for Crips). This boundary marking is so pervasive that recently Michelin came under fire in California for its new "Scorcher" tires that feature yellow, red, or blue treads. A San Francisco supervisor says, "These colored tires may appeal to gangs who will use red and blue skid marks to mark their turf and insult rival gangs."[5]

Now some analysts find it useful to think in terms of even larger cliques or *youth tribes* that unite kids by means of shared interests or values rather than geographic proximity or a shared interest in criminal activity. Although these tribes are often unstable and short-lived, at least for a time members identify with others through shared emotions, moral beliefs, styles of life, and, of course, the products they jointly consume as part of their tribal affiliation.

In France, a tribe of in-line roller skaters holds gatherings of as many as 15,000 young people who congregate to affirm their shared interest. There are specialized Web sites for members of the skating tribe to meet for chatting and to exchange information about the latest skate models and looks. Within this tribe there are subdivisions such as fitness skaters versus stunt skaters, but all members share a connection to the overarching activity.

The challenge of *tribal marketing* is to link one's product to the needs of a group as a whole. In-line skating, for example, provides manufacturers with an opportunity to strengthen the tribal bond by selling ritual artifacts (as described in Chapter 1) such as shoes, key chains, belts and hats, backpacks, and T-shirts to members. Although many brands of skates are available, including K2, Razors, Oxygen, Tecnica, and Nike, the original Rollerblade product retains cult status within the tribe. Companies like Tatoo, the pager arm of France Telecom, build upon tribal bonds by sponsoring skating events as well as hosting a Web site dedicated to the activity. Some companies like Pawn, Senate, and USD have targeted just a section of the tribe known as stunt skaters that have their own special dress codes and rituals.

In the United States, a similar tribe is built around skateboarding. California-based shoe manufacturer Vans is most closely identified with this movement, and the company aggressively seeks opportunities to cement this linkage. Instead of relying on mass-media advertising, Vans sponsors activities, produces documentary films, and even builds skateboard parks to celebrate the outlaw nature of the sport—and in the process promote its specialized shoes.

The *New World Teen Study* described earlier reminds us that while most adolescents are actively seeking an identity, the way they go about this is not necessarily the same. Many group identities gel around some form of symbolism, whether music (followers of neo–Grateful Dead groups like Phish), clothing (think "Valley Girls"), or sports. For example, the Bad Blue Boys (BBB) is a tribe of young male Australian soccer fans from the western suburbs of Sydney who (to put it kindly) exhibit aggressive and homophobic tendencies. Their nationalistic identity is supported and driven by their obsession with soccer.

Closer to home, an American sneaker company called And 1 appeals to members of a basketball tribe that sets admission standards based on the ability to blow by a defender on the court. The company carefully cultivates a trash-talking, street image (distributing shirts with slogans like "I'm sorry. I thought you could play"), and it recruits street players to match its renegade brand image. This group, known as the Entertainers Tour, puts on shows of hoops and music at playgrounds and appears in And 1's TV advertising. Footage from the events was blended with some unreleased rap music to produce a videotape that was handed out at playgrounds, parks, and clubs by street teams to spread the word about this upstart company.

Made in Japan

The tribal phenomenon is most pronounced in Japan, where teenagers invent, adopt, and discard fads with lightning speed. Teen rebellion is a new phenomenon in Japan, a country known for rigid conformity and constant pressure to achieve. Now more and more teenagers seem to be making up for lost time. The dropout rate among students in junior and senior high school increased by 20 percent in a two-year period. More than 50 percent of girls have had intercourse by their senior year of high school.[6]

Teenage girls in Japan exhibit what science fiction writer William Gibson calls "techno-cultural suppleness"—a willingness to grab something new and use it for their own ends—matched by no other group on earth. According to one estimate, cell phones sit in the purses and pockets of about 95 percent of all Japanese teenage girls. Unlike American phones, these devices are connected constantly to the Internet and plug these girls into a massive network. Index, a Tokyo software start-up company, offers a Net-phone service called God of Love. For about $1.40 per month, users can tap the birth date of a potential mate into their phones and receive a computerized prediction of the relationship's future.

Japanese youth are very style-conscious, and at any time there are prominent tribes, each with very well defined looks and rules. A popular tribe for Japanese girls a few years ago was called the "Gals," easily recognized by their bleached yellow hair, salon-tanned skin, chalk-white lipstick, and seven-inch platform heels. Other groups included the Sports Clique (low-heeled Air Mocs and Gap clothing) and the Back-Harajuku Group (baggy sweatshirts, colorful jeans, sneakers, and long scarves).

To try to win the loyalty of young consumers in Japan, a group of big companies including Toyota, Matsushita, and Asahi Breweries formed a marketing alliance. They are introducing a range of products, from beer to refrigerators, all with the same brand name of Will (yes, Will). About thirty Will products are now on sale in Japan. Asahi Breweries' Will Smooth Beer nearly tripled its sales targets in the three months after launch. Matsushita's Will laptop was a disappointment, but its retro refrigerator offering did so well the company added a mini Will fridge and vacuum cleaner. The jury is still out on this ambitious project; critics are not sure the plan "Will" work because some of the companies are handicapped by traditional images that don't play well with their young targets.

Whether it does or not, this effort highlights the potential payoffs of using a constellation approach (as described in Chapter 2) to create a "lifestyle package" targeted to a specific lifestyle segment or tribe. Indeed, in the United States some major corporations are figuring out the value of teaming with very dissimilar players to develop youth-based products. For example, Nike and Polaroid have formed a partnership that lets teens personalize their sneakers by inserting pictures they take with the I-Zone camera directly into the shoes. Toyota is teaming with fashionable surf wear maker Roxy to create a surf-friendly version of its Echo sedan for the young female market, complete with water-resistant, neoprene-covered seats, a Yakima roof rack, and wet-gear storage bins. If this lifestyle strategy works, Toyota plans to roll out a male-oriented sport wagon or pickup linked to the trendy Quiksilver name.[7]

THE BOTTOM LINE

Marketers can connect with Gen Y consumers by teaming up with other companies to offer a lifestyle package of products specially designed to cater to young lifestyles. The constellation branding approach will work especially well with this age cohort, which is accustomed to thinking about products in terms of groupings linked to a youth tribe.

Connecting in Consumerspace

Some futurists believe that we'll soon reach a point where each of us is wired and online all of the time. We'll be issued a username and password at birth, and a computer device will be implanted in our bodies to keep us connected to the Web. That hasn't quite happened yet (though a primitive form of this technology already is being used to track wayward pets). But consider the service now offered by a Swiss company called Skim: Each user is issued a six-digit number that he or she wears on jackets and backpacks sold by the company. When you see someone on the street or in a club you'd like to get to know better, you go to skim.com, type in the person's number, and send him or her a message. Talk about wearing your heart on your sleeve. . . .

If our future is a wired one, the young pioneers of consumerspace are definitely at the vanguard. Adolescence is a time to reach out to others—but tentatively. A thriving Internet subculture has developed among many teens to serve this purpose. The Net is the preferred method of communication for many young people because its anonymity makes it easier to talk to people of the opposite sex or of different ethnic and racial groups.

Virtual Tribes

For teens, consumerspace is very much a virtual place. According to Teenage Research Unlimited, more than 80 percent of teenagers have Internet access, whether at home, school, work, a friend's home, or the library. In ancient times (i.e., before the Internet), kids would be parked in front of the TV all day watching *Gilligan's Island* reruns.

Today, they're much more likely to be banging away at a computer keyboard, instant messaging to buddies around the world. Young people are among the most enthusiastic Web surfers. For many, this activity has replaced the old-fashioned fun of watching the tube or hanging out at the mall.

This virtual space will continue to grow because the younger members of Generation Y are more tech savvy than any kids in history. A July 1999 survey by ISP Global Internet found two-thirds of children under the age of eleven first used a computer before they were five years old, while less than a quarter of those over eleven did so.[8] Jupiter Media Metrix estimates that there will be 26.9 million active Web surfers under the age of twelve by 2005.[9]

According to one market research firm, 62 percent of teenagers log on from home for at least four hours a week. They spend most of their online time doing research, sending and reading e-mail, playing games, or checking out things to buy. Teens are expected to spend $1.2 billion online at hip sites like Alloy.com and Bolt.com. To counteract parents' concerns about security issues, some start-ups such as icanbuy, Rocketcash, and Doughnet are creating "digital wallets" that let Mom and Dad set up an account and limit the sites at which money can be spent.

A study of almost 4,000 young respondents conducted by Harris Interactive found that e-commerce spending among online teens and young adults currently constitutes 13 percent of their total spending—a figure that is more than four times the rate of e-commerce spending among all adults. What are teens buying? Of teens who make purchases online, 57 percent have bought CDs/cassettes, 38 percent have bought concert or sports tickets, 34 percent bought books and magazines, 32 percent ordered clothing, and 9 percent ordered cell phones or pagers. As these sites get more sophisticated, they need to keep in mind that kids value their surfing time as a social experience in addition to its shopping value. Dot-com companies need to work on building in some fun and adventure to lure kids away from the mall. As one thirteen-year-old shopper put it, "The Net kinds of takes away the whole experience—the hunt, the get, and the buy. Web shopping is just too perfect! You type in 'gray cords' and there they are. It's not fun. The fun is in the hunt."[10]

Fantasies in Consumerspace

That comment is a reminder that kids are doing more than shopping online. They also are avid participants in virtual gaming sites as well as online communities forged around themes or characters (more on this in Chapter 6). On any given night, up to 50,000 people can be found roaming around a fantasyland in cyberspace called EverQuest. This is a "massively multiplayer game" that combines the stunning graphics of advanced gaming with the social scene of a chat room. And teens commune with each other about shared fantasies by establishing virtual communities devoted to fantasy characters. For example, *anime* sites like those devoted to Sailor Moon attract teens from around the world. Here are a few to check out:

- http://www.anime.de/
- http://www.fao.lv/sm-info/
- http://members.tripod.com/~saturnchild/sailormoon.html

The Web also provides a forum for experimentation that appeals to teens grappling with identity issues. Researchers report that teens value privacy when surfing the Web because they view it as a way to express their individuality—that's why it's common for them to have multiple e-mail accounts, each with a different "personality." Indeed, many teens are using the Web to experiment with different identities. More than half have more than one screen name or e-mail address. Nearly a quarter of this multimonikered group keep at least one name secret so they can go online without being recognized by friends. And, 24 percent of teens who use e-mail, instant messaging (IM), or chat rooms pretend to be someone else.

Instant Messaging, Instant Gratification

To promote its Kit Kat candy bar to youth in the United Kingdom, Nestlé sent text messages to the cell phones of 6,000 consumers aged 18 to 25. These alerted them when ads for the candy would air and in-vited them to take a quiz about the ad that would in turn enter them into a drawing to win a month's supply of Kit Kats (about 94 percent of British youth have cell phones with wireless messaging capabil-ity).[11] This technique, known as short-messaging system marketing (SMS), is becoming a popular way to reach customers in the United Kingdom and throughout Europe.

New technologies provide exciting ways to communicate with kids in consumerspace, who are entering consumerspace via their phones as well as their computers. Young consumers view a cell phone as a necessity, not a luxury. It's their primary means of staying connected with others. But a cell phone is not just a means of communi-cation. It is an accessory, a fashion statement, an instant messenger, a toy, a social prop. It is a symbol of independence second only to the car, many teenagers say, and an extension of their personality.

Phone manufacturers are scrambling to provide what kids want. The companies have their sights set on young people for good reason: Since only 38 percent of American teenagers have cell phones, the market has plenty of room for growth. Some firms are retooling exist-ing phone models, adding features like an FM radio or even access to AOL Instant Messenger. Others, like Wildseed, are designing fash-ionable phones for teenagers from the ground up. Its models have "smart skins"—replaceable taco shell–shaped faceplates with com-puter chips that allow teenagers to change functions as well as the phone's appearance. There are graffiti-splattered faceplates for skate-boarders, for example, that come with edgy urban ringer tones and gritty icons. Similarly, market leader Nokia has a line of what it calls "expression" phones, which have spawned secondary products like customized faceplates, add-on lights, and downloadable ringer tones.

The cell phone is a key access point that enables kids around the world to tune in to marketing messages. This medium's potential trajectory is huge as wireless penetration steadily increases. Consider a novel marketing campaign to promote a musical group that doesn't really exist, conducted in spring of 2002 by EMI Group PLC in Singa-pore. The music company gave fans of Gorillaz, a popular rock group consisting of four cartoon characters, the opportunity to exchange text messages over their mobile phones with the band member of their choice. Each member has a distinctive look and personality, and after a favorite character was selected, its cartoon face was sent to the recipient's mobile phone. Kids who shared the mobile numbers of their friends won stickers, posters, and a free CD-ROM.

These phone numbers are, of course, a potential gold mine for EMI, as they'll allow the company to communicate with music fans at will. EMI chose Gorillaz because its fan base is young, hip, and devoted. As the company's managing director observed, "For a very cool band like Gorillaz, the last thing you want to do is go mainstream." That explains why the text messages used in the promotion were distinctly anticorporate: A typical one read, "Greedy record company wants me 2 tell U 2 buy Gorillaz album. Record people suck. Buy or don't buy, up to you."[12]

EMI's foray into cell phone marketing makes sense because its young market is at the leading edge of *M-commerce*, promotional messages transmitted over mobile phones and other mobile devices such as personal digital assistants (PDAs). Right now, M-commerce is far more prevalent in Europe and Asia—the Philippine Long Distance Telephone Company estimates one million text messages are sent every day in that country alone.[13] The United States has the second-largest installed base of cell phone users (130 million; China has 148 million), but only 46 percent of the U.S. population had cell phones in 2001, compared with 82.5 percent in the United Kingdom and 75.3 percent for all of Europe according to the Yankee Group. They estimate mobile phone penetration by 2006 to be 66.9 percent in the United States, 91.6 percent in the United Kingdom, and 76.1 percent in Japan.[14]

THE BOTTOM LINE

Young consumers are more technology-savvy than any previous generation. They network electronically as a way to affirm their connections with other kids and with the companies they value.

American kids increasingly will learn about relevant products via such formats as mobile messaging, already a potent communications medium in Europe and Asia.

Slowly but surely, M-commerce is making its way to the United States. Even the MTV Music Video Awards now include a wireless advertising campaign to promote the event. Millions of consumers who use such networks as AT&T Wireless and Sprint will get messages urging them to tune in. Accelerating usage will open the door for M-commerce advertising campaigns like those now being conducted in other countries. One study predicts that despite the slow start, about 90 million Americans will be participating in M-commerce by 2007, generating more than $50 billion in revenues.[15] Wireless connections to consumerspace will be a prerequisite to being cool, to which our attention now turns.

In Pursuit of Cool

Attaining the status of *cool* is the holy grail when marketing to youth. It's an elusive concept that has defined cultural icons from James Dean to Puff Daddy. It seems so easy: Create a cool product and kids will flock to your brand in droves. But there's a nasty paradox afoot: If you have to work at being cool, by definition you're not. Kids have supersensitive BS detectors that go off at the slightest sign someone is just trying too hard.

Coolness can be thought of as a set of shared meanings (language, values, self-presentation, etc.) within a peer group that signal affiliation with a desirable lifestyle or clique. The desire to be cool seems to be fairly universal, though obviously the path to coolness varies across people and time. As we've seen, certain types of dress, musical tastes, etc., are used as props to support an uncertain self and provide validation. The emulation of admired groups, what youth scholar Marcel Danesi calls *signifying osmosis*, makes it more likely that a sycophant will be admitted into the exclusive club. By adopting group-endorsed behaviors and lifestyles, kids signify an affiliation that anchors individual identity to a larger community.[16]

Some colleagues and I asked young people in the United States and the Netherlands to write essays about what is "cool" and "uncool." We found that being cool has several meanings, though there are a lot of similarities between the two cultures when kids use this term. Some of the common dimensions include having charisma, being in control, and being a bit aloof. And many of the respondents agreed that being cool is a moving target: The harder you try to be cool, the more uncool you are. Some of their actual responses are listed here:

- "Cool means being relaxed, to nonchalantly be the boss of every situation, and to radiate that." (Dutch female)

- "Cool is the perception from others that you've got 'something' which is macho, trendy, hip, etc." (Dutch male)

- "Cool has something stand-offish, and at the same time, attractive." (Dutch male)

- "Being different, but not too different. Doing your own thing, and standing out, without looking desperate while you're doing it." (American male)

- "When you are sitting on a terrace in summer, you see those machos walk by, you know, with their mobile [phones] and their sunglasses. I always think, 'Oh please, come back to earth!' These guys only want to impress. That is just so uncool." (Dutch female)

- "When a person thinks he is cool, he is absolutely uncool." (Dutch female)

- "To be cool we have to make sure we measure up to it. We have to create an identity for ourselves that mirrors what we see

in magazines, on TV, and with what we hear on our stereos."
(American male)

Chewing the Phat: Cool Hunters and the Teen Safari

Attaining coolness is a matter of survival in the jungle of social acceptance. Kids have a lot to gain by staying on top of what's cool and a
lot to lose by getting lost in this jungle. They stay tuned to what's
"phat" and what's not by watching MTV and carefully observing the
trendsetters who seem to have it figured out (much as their parents
faithfully tuned in to *American Bandstand* or *Soul Train*). Some even
surf to virtual nightclubs to spy on the partyers whom the bouncer let
in at such sites as thewomb.com and digitalclubnetwork.com.

It's hard enough for kids to navigate this jungle. Think about the
marketer who has the bad fortune to be over thirty! That's why many
firms are aggressively ramping up their efforts to connect with kids on
their own terms and collect marketing intelligence on the streets and
in cyberspace. Staying on top of emerging ways to be cool is big, big
business:

■ Mountain Dew executives try to connect with cool kids one person at a time by handing out beverage samples at surfing, skateboard, and snowboard tournaments. A top marketing executive
explains, "There's a Pavlovian connection between the brand and the
exhilarating experience." By this logic, "Doing the Dew" isn't a rush
just because of the caffeine and sugar. It comes to be associated with
the hip places where the soft drink is consumed.[17]

■ Just before Arista Records released a new CD from Babyface,
the company flashed 10,000 e-mails to kids on fan lists. The e-mail
gave them a chance to buy the album before it hit stores, and recipients were encouraged to join the "Arista Army" and also to send the
message to others. The strategy worked: 62 percent of the e-mails
were passed along to others and the "Army" quickly grew from 600
Gen Yers to a brigade of more than 20,000.[18]

Still other youth-oriented companies tap into cool icons, particularly celebrities with an urban, street-smart image like tennis star Venus Williams or rapper Ja Rule. The *Wall Street Journal* reported in August 2001 that Reebok's sales of basketball and tennis shoes increased by more than 50 percent by tapping youth-oriented celebrities to tout its products.

Tracking a Moving Target

Research firms are coming up with innovative ways to tap the desires of teens, many of whom don't respond well to traditional survey techniques. Sometimes respondents are given a video camera and are asked to record a "typical" day at school—along with play-by-play commentary to help interpret what's going on. Greenfield Consulting Group uses what it calls the "teen-as-creative-director" technique. The firm gives teens camcorders and asks them to complete a two-part creative assignment that will be judged by their peers. A typical task is to create a video collage of the "coolest/hippest/whateverest" things they can find and write a song/poem/story that describes what "cool/hip" is all about. After the teens complete their assignments, they present their work to each other at a focus group facility, judge the work collectively, and award prizes of $250 each to the creators of the best video and song/poem/story.

One company sends researchers to spend the night with respondents so they can observe them up close and personal. During the evening they talk about important stuff like their skin-care routines but then in the morning the interviewer watches to see what teens actually do in the bathroom while primping before school. When the Leo Burnett advertising agency was revamping Heinz ketchup's image to make it cool, the account research team took teens to dinner to see how they actually used the condiment. These meals opened their eyes; new ads focus on teens' need for control by showing ketchup smothering fries "until they can't breathe" and touting new uses for ketchup on pizza, grilled cheese, and potato chips.[19]

Cool Hunters: Now Lukewarm?

The quest for cool has also spawned a cottage industry of *cool hunters* who scour the streets to report on emerging trends. Some of these amateur anthropologists rely upon a network of "correspondents" who periodically report back from the field. They are a bit like cool Tupperware Ladies (or is that an oxymoron?) who rely upon personal contacts and intuition to spot opportunities. Correspondents typically supply headquarters with videotaped interviews of cutting-edge kids spouting off on topics from spirituality to blue jeans, then these random bits of data are used to craft a cultural scouting report that is sold to clients like Nike and Coca-Cola.

This methodology was itself a fashion statement for several years within the marketing research community, a fad that had sex appeal if not staying power. The bloom is largely off the rose now because in hindsight the track records are disappointing. Relatively few new product successes have emerged from cool hunters. There are several possible reasons for this lackluster performance:

- By definition the real trendsetters don't like to be tracked or emulated and may be reluctant to share their insights with the masses.

- A quarterly report on emerging fads was not compiled quickly enough to really keep up with a fickle market.

- The insights largely were journalistic rather than scientific, relying upon the skill of the cool hunter to assimilate idiosyncratic feedback from multiple sources.

The principle behind cool hunting is still solid: Locate market leaders and create a conduit to share their opinions with product developers. However, more systematic, ongoing, and rigorous approaches are needed. Most likely these will be in the form of online research applications that allow a large network of respondents to provide visual feedback in real time. These interfaces can either be created specifically to track young people's product preferences, or, alternatively, analysts can mine existing Web sites where kids vent about products to track the ebb and flow of the ocean of style.

Teen CyberCommunities

Bolt knows what teens want—and why shouldn't it? About 95 percent of the site's content is written by teens themselves. The youth Web site is striving to maintain its lead as the place to reach Net-surfing teens between fifteen and eighteen years of age. With over 700,000 registered users, the majority clocking in at least once a week, Bolt has proved to offer the kind of personalized portal attractive to teens and those making the transition to collegiate surfer.

Bolt's real attraction is the teen-created content. Concrete Media, Bolt's parent company, while responsible for editorial decisions and page design, has a hands-off policy that allows the teen community to police what appears on the site. Teens are free to comment on opinion polls and news events, and even to submit entries unacceptable to their school newspaper editors. Subjects range from the latest music video to wrestling to concern over AIDS.

Trying to connect with kids is not exactly a new idea. After all, many local department stores have sponsored teen panels for years. What has changed is the ability to reach out to young consumers in electronic formats. Pizza Hut, for example, conducts roundtable discussions though e-mail with teens to make sure it is satisfying their tastes. Just to be sure, Pizza Hut sometimes invites some of them back to its own boardroom to have lunch with company executives.

More recently, an 800-pound gorilla named Procter & Gamble developed its own teen community Web sites, tremor.com and toe jam.com, to help identify young opinion leaders. The Tremor site is for market research and for recruiting teens and pre-teens for word of mouth campaigns. Tremor last year ran a pilot program with AOL Time Warner's WB network where teen panelists reviewed a script for *Dawson's Creek* before the show aired. Toejam (unpleasant connotations aside, this is an acronym for "teens openly expressing just about me") lets members preview new products and critique ads before they are widely distributed.[20]

THE BOTTOM LINE

Cool kids are the innovators of the youth market. Track their ever-changing preferences quickly and reliably, and stay ahead of the new product development curve. Use a collection of techniques including ethnographic work ("live with the natives"), online surveys, and simple observation of street culture to triangulate the direction of these trends.

CHAPTER 4

Here's Where You Can Stick Your Ad
Customers Talk Back

A few years ago, Lifesavers threw down the gauntlet. The company threatened to eliminate the pineapple flavor unless consumers went to its Web site and voted to keep it. More than 400,000 people rallied to the cause. Perhaps this was not the most momentous election in our history, but this kind of mass response hints at our willingness to get involved when the fate of our favorite goodies is at stake.

Consumers are control freaks. We enjoy the feeling of power that comes from having input into what we do, see, and buy—even if it just means getting to vote on a candy flavor. Many studies find a relationship between a feeling of control and good health. This craving for mastery makes us hungry for feedback that helps us stay on top of our performance, whether physical or financial.

We snap up products that let us know how we're doing. For example, a company called Body Media introduced a line of sensors attached to clothing that monitor a user's vital signs and upload this information to a Web site (bodymedia.com). The "sensewear" includes chest straps, armbands, and smart rings that monitor heart rate, respiration, and caloric burn rate. Data are mapped onto a personalized Web page. Users can compare their readings to population norms in order to be alerted if a vital sign is abnormal. Similarly, Micromass Communications is developing a site for the American Heart Association that generates pages for visitors based on individual psychological profiles. First-time visitors will respond to an online questionnaire about their health habits. Then, the site will show users who are at risk of heart disease specifically how to change their lifestyles and reduce cholesterol.

We want to be involved. We want to know if we're having an impact, and we hunger for the validation that comes from making the "correct" selections. Consumer research supports the benefits of letting people regulate the type and amount of product-related information they will receive, particularly in online environments. Even mundane products can build interest by creating avenues for consumers to learn more on their own. Dovespa.com, a Web site hosted by Unilever, gives skin-care tips and information on new Dove products. SlimFast.com lets users keep track of their weight loss.

Enhancing this feedback loop and building reciprocal bonds between brands and consumers is key to cultivating precious loyalty in a very competitive product landscape. This chapter will review some of the thinking behind this process and discuss some specific ways marketers can share control with their customers by letting them talk back.

THE BOTTOM LINE

Consumers want to be involved in the creation and delivery of what they buy. Promotions that encourage customer feedback heighten involvement with the producer and result in a potent barrier-to-entry to rival firms who must muscle in on an ongoing relationship.

From a One-Night Stand to a Relationship

Ever fantasize about going on the road with your favorite group? The Radiators are a popular New Orleans Cajun rock band that have joined a growing list of performers dabbling in the travel business. They offer tour packages to their followers so they can travel the circuit with them. The Radiators have figured out that maintaining personal contact with their hard-core groupies is the best way to keep them coming back for more.

Love, American Style

Like the Radiators, savvy marketers understand that it makes a lot of sense to build a lasting bond with customers. The bottom line is it's a lot cheaper to sell to the same person over and over than to win a new customer. A one-night stand might be fun, but a long-term relationship makes a lot more business sense. This insight has become so common-place in the commercial world that the term *relationship marketing* is practically a cliché.

Consumers often are willing partners in this courtship. They want to bond with companies as long as they're getting something out of the deal—and they don't want to wake up alone in the morning. People derive many benefits from products, over and above their functional uses. Susan Fournier at Harvard looked extensively at the types of relationships people form with products. She has identified different ways that everyday objects worm their way into our hearts and play important roles in our lives. The relationship metaphor comes in quite handy here as Fournier's research identifies numerous permutations of consumer-brand bonding. These include:

- *Best Friendships:* The brand is a true bud that is an integral part of the person's life.

- *Kinships:* An inherited preference for a brand that was used by a parent or other family member.

- *Childhood Friendships:* Nostalgic feelings are evoked during use.

- *Courtships:* Likely to commit to the brand but not there yet.

- *Flings:* Short-term engagement with high emotional rewards but no commitment.

- *Secret Affairs:* Highly emotional, private relationship considered risky if exposed to others.

- *Master/Slave:* A controlling relationship where the owner surrenders control to the product.[1]

THE BOTTOM LINE

People form different kinds of relationships with products, just as they do with other people. It's important to understand the dynamics of the relationship (e.g., short-term versus long-term, shared power versus dominant/submissive) consumers have with your product in order to know how to talk to them about it.

CRM: Getting Up Close and Personal

To enhance relationship building, many marketing experts now advocate *customer relationship management* (CRM) programs that allow companies to talk to individual customers and adjust elements of their marketing programs in response to each customer's reactions to elements of the marketing mix. Because it is always easier and less expensive to keep an existing customer than to get a new customer, CRM-oriented firms focus on increasing their *share of customer*, not share of market.

Don Peppers, a leading writer and consultant in this area, defines CRM as ". . . managing customer relationships. If I'm managing customer relationships, it means I'm treating different customers differently, across all enterprises. . . . The relationship develops a context over time, it drives a change in behavior . . . [this] means that I have to change my behavior as an enterprise based on a customer."[2] A CRM strategy allows a company to identify its best customers, stay on top of their needs, and increase their satisfaction.

CRM is about communicating with customers, but in its best incarnation it is also about customers being able to communicate with a company one on one. CRM systems include everything from Web sites that let you check on the status of a bill or package to call centers that solicit your business. When you log on to the Federal Express Web site to track a lost package, that's a CRM system. When you get a phone message from the dentist reminding you about that filling appointment tomorrow, that's a CRM system. And, when you get a call from the car dealer asking how you like your new vehicle, that's also CRM.

To appreciate the value of a CRM strategy, consider the experience of financial services firms Salomon Smith Barney and Fidelity Investments. In general, an investment banker needs to manage accounts as well as open new ones—often thirty to fifty per month. Just opening the account can take forty-five minutes, not a satisfying process for the banker or the customer. But with an automated CRM system, the banker can open an account, issue a welcome letter, and produce an arbitration agreement in ten minutes. She can create a unique marketing campaign for each client based on that person's life cycle—including such variables as when a person opened an account, his annual income, family situation, desired retirement age, and so on. The marketer can generate a happy anniversary letter to clients (to commemorate when they joined the firm, not when they got married) and include an invitation to update their investment objectives.

Many firms have found that this level of individualized attention results in a much higher rate of customer retention and satisfaction, so CRM creates a win-win situation for everyone. That success helps to explain why CRM is hot: Industry sources estimate that by 2005, companies will be spending $14 billion to purchase sophisticated software that will let them build these electronic bridges.

Even the Internal Revenue Service is buying a CRM software system worth more than $10 million. The system will allow taxpayers to obtain tax records and other information around the clock. An agency spokesman commented that this purchase is part of the IRS's ongoing effort to become more customer-friendly. By 2004, the agency hopes the system will be fully operational, which will allow many disgruntled taxpayers to receive quick (and hopefully accurate) answers automatically rather than sitting on the phone for hours.

Perhaps the most important aspect of CRM is that it presents a new way of looking at how to effectively compete in the marketplace. This begins with looking at customers as partners. CRM proponents suggest that the traditional relationship between customers and marketers is an adversarial one in which marketers try to sell their products to customers and customers seek to avoid buying. The customer relationship perspective sees customers as partners, with each partner learning from the other every time they interact. Successful firms compete by establishing relationships with individual customers on a one-to-one basis through dialogue and feedback. What does this customer really want?

To make life even a bit more interesting, a few companies are experimenting with interactive technologies that monitor consumers' Web-surfing patterns and intervene with a live customer service representative after the shopper has started to navigate through the site. For example, TechnoScout.com, a site that sells a wide range of consumer electronics and household goods, estimates that these "proactive chat" sessions now generate half of its sales. The company's sales representative can actually open Web pages directly on the customer's browser, rather than simply describing where to go, and can up-sell a customer to complementary or more upscale products if appropriate.[3]

Finding out precisely what an individual wants (even if he or she doesn't know it yet) often requires very sophisticated analyses of marketing intelligence. *Database marketing* involves tracking consumers' buying habits very closely and crafting products and messages tailored precisely to people's wants and needs based on this information. Sophisticated companies like American Express, General Motors, and Kraft General Foods are combining and constantly updating information from public records and marketing research surveys—with data volunteered by consumers themselves when they return warranty cards, enter sweepstakes, or purchase from catalogs—to build a complex database that fine-tunes their knowledge of what people are buying and how often. Vons has a customer loyalty program called Target Vons that boasts more than three million members. The program collects purchase data on participating shoppers in the chain's 335 stores. A central database sorts these transactions by store, department, category, brand, and UPC. Vons sends monthly mailings with tailored coupons to specific cardholders depending on their purchase history.

One Size Doesn't Fit All

To a denizen of the online world, a *skin* is a graphical interface that acts as both the face and the control panel of a computer program. Rather than settling for the boring skins that come with most programs, many people prefer to make and trade their own unique ones. According to the product manager for RealPlayer, "This kind of customization is a huge factor in driving product use. . . . We're getting into a world where one size doesn't fit all, and one of the great benefits of technology is having the experience tailored to you."[4]

In addition to the more than fifteen million skins that have been created for RealPlayer, many other games, including The Sims and the multiplayer Unreal Tournament, have Web sites devoted to user-created skins. Players swap skins of the Incredible Hulk or Rambo or even playable skins of themselves. Some companies market technologies that allow a player to impose his own photographic likeness on a game character. Movie companies and record labels now routinely commission artists to create promotional skins for films like *Blow* and *Frequency* and for music artists like U2, Britney Spears, and 'N Sync.

In a world of "me-too" products and services, *personalization* is key to setting oneself apart from the competition. This strategy accomplishes the two objectives described previously in this chapter: 1) It gives the user greater control over his or her environment, and 2) It lets the provider cement a relationship with that user.

One way to personalize is to customize the end product. Customization is hot: It's estimated that 20 percent of businesses will offer customized products or services by 2010, compared with only 5 percent today. New businesses like shoe company Customatix.com and Venturoma.Com, which lets the shopper create her own blend of massage oils, skin creams, or body washes, are thriving by letting end consumers design their own products. A recent survey found that 75 percent of American adults want more customized products and—more important—70 percent are willing to pay extra for them. This desire is even more acute among young people; 85 percent of eighteen- to twenty-four-year-olds want more customized products, particularly in such domains as clothing, shoes, electronics, and travel services.[5] We'll explore more aspects of customization in Chapter 5.

Personalization comes in many forms, but not all of them work well. Tailoring a product to the very specific needs of a customer is a way to personalize the offering, but so is that obnoxious waiter who informs you that his name is Wally and he'll be your server today. The downside is that a sincere effort to cater to customers' specific needs can be more demanding, time-consuming, and expensive. But, in many service environments this strategy pays many dividends, particularly as a form of competitive advantage. When is personalization worth the trouble? Most likely when some degree of risk is involved in the transaction—whether financial, physical, or social.

CASE STUDY

My colleague Carol Surprenant and I did one of the first studies on personalization. We created a simulation of an interaction between a bank platform officer and a customer who wanted to open a checking account. In each case the employee described the available options, but we varied how the information was presented in two ways. First, we injected what we called *cosmetic personalization* into the dialogue by building in a fair amount of small talk that gives the illusion that the customer is being treated as an individual rather than being on the receiving end of a canned script. Second, we provided differing amounts of what we called *customized personalization* by using the customer's responses to shape the dialogue so that the information presented truly was guided by his unique needs.

The results are not that surprising: Although programmed personalization positively affected evaluations of employee sociability and warm feelings about the bank, it had a negative effect on ratings of competence, trust, and satisfaction with the encounter. In contrast, customized personalization exerted a positive impact across the board. Not all personalization strategies are created equal; it's not enough just to talk the talk!

Personalization can be accomplished both offline and online. Retailers are experimenting with ways to let shoppers configure their selections. Numerous "make your own pottery" stores are springing up that let people design and make their own ceramics. Many music stores offer samplers that allow shoppers to check out the latest tunes before buying; in some cases listeners can burn CDs with their own mix and even design the clip art to personalize the cover label. The Ritz-Carlton hotel chain trains associates to enter detailed information into its database, so that if a guest orders decaf coffee from room service, she will also receive decaf on the next visit. Wyndham even tries to match guests with their preferred room decor.

Many of the exciting developments in personalization are occurring in the online space. Here are a few recent examples:

■ General Mills' Web site called MyCereal.com allows cereal lovers to design their own cereal. For about one dollar per serving, designers can choose from ninety ingredients.

■ Business portal FT.com has two million registered users, 60 percent of whom visit the site regularly. The site sends out hundreds of thousands of unprompted e-mails every day, giving individuals the headline news from the sectors that interest them.

■ Sony decided that personalizing its SonyStyle.com Web site was the best way to guide its customers through the maze of over 2,000 products on offer. The site is based on six personality types embodied by real live users. Using catchy personas like free agent, homelander, transcender, and virtual professional, Web customers are invited to pair themselves up with these guides to navigate through the Sony inventory.

■ General Motors is creating an internal personalized portal called mySocrates.com to offer Internet-accessed, self-service applications, as well as local news, sports, and weather to any GM employee. The carmaker feels this approach is an effective way to keep employees informed while giving them access to their own data. More than 70,000 of its employees have signed up for the service.[6]

THE BOTTOM LINE

Consumers are looking for ways to develop personal relationships with favorite brands. They want to feel special, not be just another name on a mailing list. Personalization strategies can accomplish this, but marketers must be careful to avoid cosmetic personalization and instead provide customized personalization—responses that let the consumer know his or her feedback is actually influencing the relationship.

Who Controls the Remote? Interactive Programming

In consumerspace we need interactive platforms that let consumers actually talk back to companies. The rapid development of new technologies is doing more and more to allow everyday people to control the flow of information in our society (that's why totalitarian regimes make it so hard for their citizens to own computers). One of the earliest breakthroughs in this communications revolution was the humble handheld remote control device. As VCRs began to be commonplace in homes, consumers suddenly had more input into what they wanted to watch—and when. No longer were they at the mercy of the TV networks to decide when to see their favorite shows, nor were they forced to choose between two shows airing in the same time slot.

Since that time, of course, our ability to control our media environment has mushroomed. Many people have access to video-on-demand or pay-per-view TV. Home-shopping networks encourage us to call in and discuss our passion for cubic zirconium jewelry live on the air. Answering machines and caller ID devices allow us to decide if we will accept a phone call during dinner and to know who is calling before picking up the phone. A bit of Web surfing allows us to identify kindred spirits around the globe, to request information about products, and even to provide suggestions to product designers and market researchers.

Cable companies, satellite TV, and even Microsoft are pouring billions into interactive TV. This medium is gaining critical mass in Europe, particularly in the United Kingdom. More than sixteen million European households subscribe to interactive TV, compared with about five million in the United States. American firms have been more attentive to technology than content, while our European counterparts are doing the opposite. As one U.S. executive observed, "Here we were focused on building a better mousetrap. In Europe they were figuring out what the mouse wanted to eat."[7]

The British can use a TV to place bets on races, change camera angles on sporting events, use "player-cams" that follow specific athletes during soccer games, and even interact with game shows. A cult hit called "Banzai" lets viewers vote by remote control to predict who will win such events as Magical Midget Climbs (two contestants try to climb a basketball player) and the Old Lady Wheelchair Chicken Challenge where two elderly contestants drive toward each other. A viewer's accuracy is tallied at the end of the show. Truly TV at its finest.

Levels of Interactive Response

A key to understanding the dynamics of interactive marketing communications is to consider exactly what is meant by a response.[8] The early perspective on communications primarily regarded feedback in terms of behavior—did the recipient run out and buy the laundry detergent after being exposed to an ad for it?

Make an ad, close a sale—that's not a bad outcome for a marketer. However, in addition to a transaction, other responses are possible as well, including building awareness of the brand, informing us about product features, reminding us to buy a new package when we've run out, and—perhaps most important—building a long-term relationship. Therefore, a transaction is one type of response, but forward-thinking marketers realize that customers can interact with them in other ways that may be more profitable than a single sale in the long run. For this reason it is helpful to distinguish between two basic types of feedback.

■ *First-Order Response:* Direct marketing vehicles such as catalogs and television infomercials are interactive—if successful, they result in an order, which is most definitely a response! So let's think of a product offer that directly yields a transaction as a first-order response. In addition to providing revenue, sales data are a valuable source of feedback that allow marketers to gauge the effectiveness of their communications efforts.

■ *Second-Order Response:* A marketing communication does not have to immediately result in a purchase to be an important component of interactive marketing. Messages can prompt useful responses from customers, even though these recipients do not necessarily place an order immediately after being exposed to the communication. Let's think of customer feedback in response to a marketing message that is not in the form of a transaction as a second-order response. Just as a first date may take the form of a "get to know you lunch in a neutral location," the first contact with the customer (or even the second or third) may not result in a purchase. Still, the marketer may have aroused the customer's interest, and the courtship begins.

When we recognize the value of second-order responses, many opportunities to conduct research and shape product offerings to the needs of specific segments become obvious. Coca-Cola demonstrated the power of this approach when it used RespondTV to let viewers click on an icon of its beloved Polar Bear Twins and have a free toy bear sent to them in the mail. Selling a can of Coke then and there clearly was not the objective.

THE BOTTOM LINE

Eliciting a response to a marketing message is key, but this reaction does not necessarily need to involve a transaction. In many cases the objective should be to arouse a second-order response to generate interest and motivate the consumer to begin a dialogue with the company that ideally will result in a deeper, long-term relationship. The goal is share of customer, not just market share.

New formats such as interactive television commercials can play a useful role in eliciting second-order responses. During the 2002 Winter Olympics, for example, viewers of NBC's broadcast coverage saw traditional commercials for AT&T. But households participating in a special program developed by a California-based company called Wink also saw a red "i" logo in the corner of their screens during those commercials. These viewers could press a button on their remote controls and then be led through a series of questions that appeared in a small window overlaid on the regular television commercial. These queries asked participants some basic but valuable questions such as "How interested are you in this?" "Are you an AT&T customer?" and "How much do you spend each month on long distance?" The more cynical among us might groan at this latest intrusion into our lives by companies selling long-distance service, but the potential for collecting real-time marketing data is enormous. Wink estimates it will have its interactive software installed in about one-tenth of America's television households in the near future.

Other advertisers are ramping up consumer involvement by letting viewers actually participate in the outcome of a commercial. Tommy Hilfiger's campaign for Tommy jeans featured finalists from an online talent search for unsigned musicians. In addition to voting, consumers were able to download music from the finalists; the winner collected a prize of $810,000 and a recording demo deal. Viewers who logged on to focus247.com were able to "direct" TV commercials for the Ford Probe by picking the cast and plot lines that would be used to create actual spots. Similarly, during its whatever.com campaign, Nike sent consumers to the Web to pick the endings of three cliff-hanger TV spots. A recent public service ad in the United Kingdom traces the story of Paul, a teenager from a troubled family. Things go from bad to worse for the boy, and viewers can click to make different choices for him. They can decide whether he should report his bullying stepfather to the police, or whether to prostitute himself ("To have sex for money press Green now"). Producers hope the ad will arouse viewers' empathy for the plight of the homeless.

User-Generated Content

Second-order responses can be more than letting the audience vote on a set of predetermined outcomes. Another way to let viewers re-spond is to let them generate their own marketing communications. The slow but steady penetration of high-speed Internet services (about one in five American users now subscribes to broadband) is encourag-ing more and more of us to get involved by posting our own content. Indeed, a study by the Pew Research Center found that broadband users spend almost four hours more online a week than do people who dial up. These users are twice as likely to contribute their own material—about 60 percent have produced Web sites of their own, participated in online discussion forums, and shared photographs or other files over the Internet.

The growing interest in interactive programming is encouraging to outfits like pseudo.com, Bolt.com, AtomFilms, and Swatch Group that are streaming original programming originating from the audi-ence. During the 2000 political conventions, ads on pseudo.com allowed viewers to reconfigure Bush's and Gore's facial features. Bolt.com gave cameras to teens to shoot their own commercial spots. New Line Cinema formed a partnership with garageband.com to give unknown bands a chance to be included in Adam Sandler's movie *Little Nicky.*

Another new source of marketing information is being mined by some companies that have figured out that what people say on their own Web sites can provide very valuable—and virtually free—insights into how everyday people are making sense of the products around them. In some cases users are working with existing material and creating new spins on it. For example, a Japanese fan of singer Bjork maintains a site devoted to remixing her songs (www.arktikos .com). Companies like Intelliseek are developing sophisticated algorithms that can analyze the textual content of Web sites and let companies know whether consumers are saying positive or negative things about them.

There also are multitudes of personal Web pages created by people who feel a need to express themselves online—and their brand allegiances often make up a prominent part of these shrines to the self. Hope Schau at Temple University has studied literally hundreds of these pages intensively. The pages take many shapes and are comparable to offline formats such as creative writing, essays, collages, and photo albums. She found that many of the personal Web sites utilize external links, which provide added and precise details about featured products, services, issues, and ideas.

Schau's analysis showed that most personal Web page authors don't hesitate to reveal their identities to visitors. Indeed, 71 percent of the pages she studied included a personal e-mail address, while half of the sites refer explicitly to the city and state in which the owner resides. And, 44 percent of the authors posted their picture as well. Many of the sites invoke celebrities with whom the author identifies in some way. Athletes are the most likely to be referenced, followed by musicians, movie stars, and TV personalities.

More important, these authors commonly flesh out their pages with links to companies like Amazon, Home Grocer, and CDNow, which are referred to by 30 percent of the personal site owners. Other businesses frequently included are home services (e.g., gardening, mortgage brokers, real estate agents and agencies, etc.) and health and beauty services (e.g., hair stylists, weight loss experts, herbalists, etc.). Nearly 10 percent of the sample referenced food (e.g., Godiva Chocolate) and beverage products (e.g., Pepsi One, Diedrich's Coffee). Finally, owners are likely to express their affiliations with education, government, and cultural institutions. Nineteen percent of the sample refers to an educational institution, usually one that the owner attends, attended, or aspires to attend. Finally, about one-fourth of the personal Web sites also link to a nonprofit organization such as Greenpeace or the World Wildlife Fund.

The newest form of online expression is the *Weblog*. These online personal journals have slowly built a following among Internet users who like to dash off a few random thoughts, post them on a Web site, and read similar musings by others. Some media analysts are praising *blogs* for their potential to undermine the hegemony of global media giants. Although these sites are similar to Web page services offered by Geocities and other free services, they employ a different technology that lets people upload a few sentences without going through the process of updating a Web site built with conventional home page software. This means bloggers can fire off thoughts on a whim, click a button, and quickly have them appear on a site. Weblogs frequently look like online diaries, with brief musings about the day's events, and perhaps a link or two of interest. A new blogger puts in his or her two cents every forty seconds, so this burgeoning *Blogosphere* (the name given to the universe of active Weblogs) is starting to look like a force to be reckoned with in consumerspace. Already, one media giant is smelling blood: Recognizing that many thousands of Brazilians are getting into blogging, Globo.com is licensing blogger software and is posting blogs from Brazilian *telenovela* (soap opera) stars like Boris, an 800-year-old vampire who wears armor and a horned helmet.

Turning the Tables: The Consumer as Producer

CRM is potentially a path-breaking way to look at marketing exchanges, but it still has a marketer-centric perspective insofar as it requires the manufacturer or retailer to initiate the relationship and keep up with it. One of the hallmarks of consumerspace is the advent of the consumer as producer. Here the tables are turned, as those who purchase also become those who take the initiative and spontaneously generate transactions. These involved consumers aren't exactly waiting for companies to come a-calling. They are forming their own consumption-based relationships with others who share their passions for merchandise ranging from *Star Trek* memorabilia to rare antiques.

Fandom and Hero Worship

Live long and prosper: The power of fandom is illustrated by twenty months of extensive fieldwork done by Robert Kozinets of Northwestern University. He literally did a doctoral dissertation on *Star Trek* fans, profiling in rich detail the incredibly strong bonds these consumers form with the show and with each other. While many of us are fond of the series and its many spin-offs (in one Harris Poll, 53 percent of Americans considered themselves fans), a hard-core group continues to boldly go where no fans have gone before.

Fan clubs, Web sites, and conventions abound, so Kozinets had little trouble finding sites to study. *Star Trek* fans are notorious for their devotion to the cause. The negative stereotype of the dweeb wearing fake Spock ears even surfaced on a classic *Saturday Night Live* skit, where ex-star William Shatner asks two hapless attendees at a Trekkie convention if they have ever kissed a girl. This stigma seems to only fuel the fire and unites fans as a dedicated subculture. An excerpt from a fan's e-mail as reported by Kozinets illustrates this devotion:

> I have to admit to keeping pretty quiet about my devotion to the show for many years simply because people do tend to view a *Trek* fan as weird or crazy. . . . [after attending her first convention she says]. . . . Since then I have proudly worn my Bajoran earring and not cared about the looks I get from others. . . . I have also met . . . other *Trek* fans and some of these people have become very close friends. We have a lot in common and have had some of the same experiences as concerns our love of *Trek*. . . .[9]

The fans derive satisfaction from their membership in this subculture on many levels, up to and including the spiritual. Kozinets found that many Trekkies, for example, are tuning in to creator Gene Roddenberry's utopian vision of a world without racism, nationalism, or poverty. Indeed, an analysis by another scholar showed that the quest for paradise was a theme employed in at least thirteen out of the original seventy-nine episodes filmed.

Others are attracted by the show's religious connotations: One fan explained in an e-mail "There is a kind of higher existence in the world of *Star Trek* that many of us wish to attain."[10] Kozinets notes a certain irony in all of this; despite the show's tendency toward anti-commercialism and generally negative treatment of merchants and money (remember the greedy Ferengi in a later spin-off), *Star Trek* is a merchandising empire that continues to beam up millions of dollars in revenues. Needless to say, it's not alone in this regard. Numerous other subcultures are out there, thriving on their collective worship of mythical and not-so-mythical worlds and characters ranging from *Star Wars* to the Grateful Dead to Hello Kitty.

Collectors

Collecting refers to the systematic acquisition of a particular object or set of objects. This widespread activity can be distinguished from *hoarding*, which is merely unsystematic gathering. Collecting typically involves both rational and emotional components. Their objects may obsess collectors, but they also carefully organize and exhibit their precious belongings. Consumers often are ferociously attached to their collections. This passion is exemplified by the comment made in one study by a woman who collects teddy bears: "If my house ever burns down, I won't cry over my furniture, I'll cry over the bears."[11]

Some consumer researchers feel that collectors are motivated to acquire their "prizes" in order to gratify a high level of materialism in a socially acceptable manner. By systematically amassing a collection, the collector "worships" material objects without feeling guilty or petty. Another perspective is that collecting is actually an aesthetic experience; for many collectors the pleasure emanates from being involved in creating the collection, rather than from passively admiring the items one has scavenged or bought. Whatever the motivation, hard-core collectors often devote a great deal of time and energy to maintaining and expanding their collections, so for many this activity becomes a central component of their identities.

Name an item, and the odds are that a group of collectors is lusting after it. The contents of collections range from movie posters, rare books, and autographs to *Star Wars* dolls, Elvis memorabilia, old computers, and even junk mail. The 1,200 members of the McDonald's collectors' club trade "prizes" such as sandwich wrappers and Happy Meal trinkets—rare ones like the 1987 Potato Head Kids Toys sell for $25.

The Topps Company, which makes bubblegum, candy, and trading cards, is taking the art of baseball card collecting to a new level by directing fans to its etopps.com Web site. There, a weekly round of six "I.P.O.'s," or initial player offerings, each costing less than $10, can be purchased by investors who can track the value of their portfolios based on prices in a secondary market run by eBay. Topps holds the actual cards in a climate-controlled warehouse in Delaware. Owners also receive a "performance bonus" when a baseball player performs above a statistical threshold set by Topps. We're talking real money here: The 2001 card of New York Mets infielder Edgardo Alfonzo, originally offered for $6.50, at one point traded for $276.

Other consumers collect experiences rather than products. Consider the man who has visited over 10,000 McDonald's restaurants. He keeps a list of unusual menu items and decor, and he defends his hobby this way: "I'm not an oddball or weirdo. I'm a collector of the McDonald's dining experience. So many issues from the last half of this century can be understood, at least partially, from a seat inside a McDonald's. What could be more quintessentially American?"[12] Supersize that?

Auctions and Swap Meets
Interesting consumer processes occur during *lateral cycling*, where already-purchased objects are sold to others or exchanged for still

other things. Many purchases are made secondhand, rather than new. Flea markets, garage sales, classified advertisements, bartering for services, hand-me-downs, and the black market all represent important alternative marketing systems that operate alongside the formal marketplace. In the last few decades, the number of used-merchandise retail establishments has grown at about ten times the rate of other stores.

Economic estimates of this underground economy range from 3 percent to 30 percent of the gross national product of the United States and up to 70 percent of the gross domestic product (GDP) of other countries. Trade publications such as *Yesteryear, Swap Meet Merchandising, Collectors Journal*, the *Vendor Newsletter,* and the *Antique Trader* offer reams of practical advice to consumers who want to bypass formal retailers and swap merchandise. In the United States alone, there are more than 3,500 flea markets—including at least a dozen huge operations such as the sixty-acre Orange County Marketplace—that operate nationwide to produce upwards of $10 billion in gross sales.[13]

And, of course, the Internet now makes this informal process even easier, especially thanks to the tremendous success of eBay. This mother of all auction sites started as a trading post for Beanie Babies and other collectibles. Now two-thirds of the site's sales are for practical goods. The site expects to sell $2 billion worth of used cars and $1 billion worth of computers a year. Coming next are event tickets, food, industrial equipment, and real estate.

Network Marketing: Virtual Tupperware Parties

The concept that drives *multilevel* or *network marketing* is simple: Enlist consumers to do the selling for you. Allow them to become distributors who in turn go out and recruit still other people. Give them a piece of the business by awarding them a fraction of the profits garnered by the people they recruit—and the people *they* recruit, and so on.

There are many variations on the theme, including the venerable Tupperware Party, as well as knockoffs that use the same approach to sell other products including adult novelties and lingerie. In these settings a company representative makes a sales presentation to a group of people who have gathered in the home of a friend or acquaintance. This strategy capitalizes on group pressures to boost sales since pressures to conform may be particularly intense and may escalate as more and more group members begin to "cave in" during a process social psychologists call the *bandwagon effect*. The latest incarnation is the upscale Botox Parties being held by enterprising dermatologists. Amidst a setting of champagne and hors d'oeuvres, wrinkled people find the courage to receive injections that will smooth them out—at least for three to six months until the facial paralysis wears off.

Network marketing is often associated with illegal pyramid or so-called *Ponzi schemes*. This type of scam was named after Italian immigrant Carlo Ponzi, who managed to find a way to rip off investors in the early 1920s by using money from new investors to pay the returns promised to earlier investors. Following a brief but pronounced spending spree, Ponzi's investors rioted at his offices and after riding high for only ten months Ponzi went to jail for four years. Despite his short-lived notoriety, his legacy lives on.

Multilevel marketing (MLM) is based on a similar pyramid structure, but unlike Ponzi's version, these businesses are not necessarily illegal. The appeal lies in the potential to shortcut the traditional retail distribution mechanism with all of its attendant support costs of marketing, sales, inventory, and distribution. MLM companies sell products to distributors at a deep discount compared with competitors. They fund the commissions and bonuses that drive the system by charging new distributors a nominal amount (usually less than $500) as a franchise fee for joining.

Ultimately, though, many MLM schemes self-destruct because they cannot recruit enough distributors to keep them going: If one person recruits six distributors, each of whom recruits six others, the total number of people in the program is forty-three by the third level. It's 9,331 by the fifth and jumps to more than ten million by the ninth! As one industry expert explained, the difference between legit and bogus schemes is that an illegal pyramid focuses on recruitment of new members to make money while a legitimate MLM program focuses on selling products.

Despite the potential downside, MLM programs do empower everyday consumers who want to experiment with the merchant role. For example, Shaklee relies on about 500,000 individual distributors to sell its food supplements, water filters, and personal-care and cleaning products. Many of these companies have found sales momentum builds quickest among tightly knit groups. The Amway Corporation, one of the bigger success stories with over $5 billion in sales in sixty countries, has historically had success in small, blue-collar towns. Salt Lake City–based Nu Skin Enterprises Inc. enrolls Mormons. Shaklee excels at recruiting salespeople from groups most companies would consider unrecruitable, including the Amish, Mennonites, and Hasidic Jews. The company has done so partly by accommodating the special needs of such highly insular communities. Shaklee awards "bonus buggies" instead of cars to its high-performing Amish and Mennonite salespeople. For its Hasidic distributors, company representatives hold separate meetings before the Sabbath and find synagogues for husbands to pray in on convention trips.[14]

THE BOTTOM LINE

> Whether acting as weekend merchants at a flea market or submitting ideas for commercials to corporate Web sites, consumers are constantly finding new ways to transform themselves into producers in the marketing process. Companies can profit by enlisting the aid of eager customers who value the opportunity to get involved.

Consumed Consumers

Finally, many individual consumers take on merchant status by literally selling parts of themselves. People who are used or exploited, willingly or not, for commercial gain in the marketplace can be thought of as *consumed consumers*.[15] The situations in which consumers are bought and sold as commodities range from traveling road shows that feature dwarfs and midgets to trafficking in body parts and babies. Some examples of consumed consumers:

■ *Dating and Mating*: Expenditures on prostitution in the United States alone are estimated at $20 billion annually. These revenues are equivalent to the amount of money Americans spend on shoes in a year. But you don't have to be a "pro" to be a player in the interpersonal marketplace. Yenta, a software program being developed at MIT, is designed to help individuals find others with common interests. Users communicate with each other anonymously until they decide to hook up and exchange identities. Then there are the hundreds of online dating services with names like singles-dating-online.com and 2hearts.com. Of course, if you're even too shy to meet prospective mates this way you can always try the Lovegety, a $21 device being marketed in Japan. It works this way: Boy sees girl. Boy is too shy to talk to girl. Instead he flicks on his male Lovegety and sends out an infrared signal. If the girl's Lovegety is within five meters of his, it starts to chirp with delight.

■ *Organ, Blood, and Hair Donors*: In the United States, over eleven million people per year sell their blood (not including voluntary donations). A lively market also exists for organs, and some women sell their hair to be made into wigs. Bidding for a human kidney on eBay went to over $5.7 million before the company ended the auction (it's illegal to sell human organs online—at least so far). The seller wrote, "You can choose either kidney . . . Of course only one for sale, as I need the other one to live. Serious bids only."[16]

■ *Babies for Sale*: Several thousand surrogate mothers have been paid to be medically impregnated and carry babies to term for infertile couples. Commercial sperm banks have become big business, and the market is international in scope, as many countries rely on imports to meet demand. The head of one of the largest companies boasts, "We think we can be the McDonald's of sperm." This company markets three grades of sperm, including an "extra" grade, which contains twice as many sperm as the average grade.[17]

This chapter has chronicled some of the many ways consumers are more than a final, passive link in the marketing chain. In consumerspace, many people play walk-on parts, and they're happy to do so. They are amateur merchants, artistes, and—as we'll see in Chapter 5—new product developers bursting with ideas to help companies make money. Let's see how.

CHAPTER 5

From Pawns to Partners
Turning Customers into Codesigners

More than 650,000 customers beta-tested Microsoft Windows 2000 before it went to market. The value of this R&D investment to Microsoft: more than $500 million. You do the math—not a bad deal for Microsoft.

Fail Early and Often

Why don't more companies do the equivalent of software beta-testing, where they share preliminary, bug-laden concepts with customers to get their feedback before it's too late? Ironically, many companies go to great lengths to hide their ideas until they are absolutely, positively perfect—at least according to their own designers.

Painful as it may be, it often makes sense to reveal what you are up to in the early stages, warts and all. In many contexts, consumers want to be engaged in the design process. As we saw in Chapter 4, they want to be part of an ongoing conversation with companies to ensure that they can choose from goods and services that fit their needs, not just the latest gizmos some whiz kid thought would be cool to sell.

Consumer products firms in particular need to think more like high-tech companies that incorporate the *lead user method*. This approach encourages sophisticated users to participate in a process of joint development with manufacturers. Studies of industrial product innovations show that the greater the benefit a user expects to obtain from a new product, the greater will be her investment in obtaining a solution. People want to be heard. They hate surprises like that really loud Father's Day tie—especially when the "gift" they receive doesn't match what they wanted.

It's not unusual these days to visit restaurants with open kitchens where diners can watch the chefs at work. Patrons sometimes even help out themselves by bussing their own tables or making their own salads. Indeed, many service businesses understand the value of enlisting their customers as *quasi-employees*. That's why the strategy usually referred to as *disintermediation* (in English, removing the middle man) has become all the rage in many service-intensive industries.

Sometimes these "helpers" aren't even aware of their contributions to a smooth operation, but they make them nonetheless. When a rental car agency gets people to obediently board a shuttle bus and then walk to the lot to claim their cars, it is making life easier for its employees. When a CPA firm sends a thick tax information form to a client to fill out in advance of a meeting, it's saving a lot of time for the accountant. When diners serve themselves in a buffet and even clean their tables when they're done, they're taking on the duties of wait staff—and paying for the privilege.

So, why not enlist the help of the people who will use the products you make? Involve them in the design process; get them to work as codesigners to be sure you are producing what they want to buy. When producers and consumers sign off on the process early on, everybody wins. There are a lot of ways to do this, from simply watching how people use what they buy all the way to getting them to design the product themselves.

THE BOTTOM LINE

Consumers often welcome the opportunity to participate in the delivery of services or products they purchase, especially when this allows them to exert more control over what they get. Enlist-

> ing customers as quasi-employees increases their satisfaction
> with their outcomes and can reduce costs for the service provider.

Build an Employee Suggestion Box

Feedback comes from a lot of places. First, try looking in your own backyard and ask your employees what they think. Here are some companies that get it:

- The 3M company allows its employees to spend 15 percent of their work time on their own projects.

- After U.K. retailer Asda started a suggestion program called "Tell Archie" (named after its former CEO), 1,000 suggestions a month began pouring in. One example: Why not install photo booths for disabled patrons? Employees receive goodies like pens and ties when they submit ideas, and then they collect points that can be redeemed for cash or gifts if any of their brainstorms are actually used.

- Nortel Networks, a producer of networking equipment, cut its development time for many products in half by involving its purchasing personnel at the concept stage before specs were written up.

- IDEO, the hot design firm that brought you such wonders as the Palm V, encourages its designers to fail early. The company creates a playroom atmosphere where employees hold "show-and-tells" about new design ideas.

IDEO understands that it's better to fall on your face early in the game. Companies generally underestimate the costs of failing later. Indeed, software development studies show that late-stage problems are more than one hundred times more costly than early-stage flaws. That may explain why the automotive industry is working hard to develop simulations that identify problems early on. Toyota made a major push in the 1990s to accelerate its development cycle. Its objective: to shorten the time from approval of a body style to the first retail sales of the style in order to keep up with the rapidly changing tastes of customers. Toyota involved more manufacturing engineers in the product and managed to slash development time by over 30 percent. Chrysler adopted a cross-functional design process back in the 1980s and cut development cycles by over 40 percent after pairing its design engineers with personnel from purchasing, manufacturing, finance, and some of its key supply partners.

THE BOTTOM LINE

Many companies fail to recognize that a great source of free feedback is literally in their own backyards—their own employees. Like customers, employees who participate in design and marketing decisions feel more invested in the results.

Learning by Observing: Do You Mind if I Watch?

Involving employees is a great first step—but keeping a close eye on customers is even better. Go to an auto show to look at concept cars, and you can bet someone is looking back at you. Volkswagen used feedback from shows as it refined its new Microbus concept. Attendees told the company the design was too austere (that's what happens when hippies grow into yuppies), so they added softer, larger seats in different fabrics. Go to the Web site at vw.com/microbus and tell VW what you think of the idea now. They're listening.

Sometimes just observing people as they go about their business each day can yield great insights. Many companies, such as Rubbermaid, Gillette, Black & Decker, and 3M, are more likely to watch consumers than to question them directly. Their investigators observe consumers as they choose products in stores, and they may even visit consumers' homes to watch how the products are actually used.

The Japanese have even coined a term to describe this process.

They call it "going to the *gemba*," the true source of information where the product actually delivers value to the customer. This experience can be a real eye-opener for managers who are used to thinking about their products in terms of internal processes rather than in terms of how they actually are used (or abused) by real people.

Warner-Lambert discovered just how important observation can be in research it did for its Fresh Burst Listerine mouthwash. A research firm paid thirty-seven families who agreed to allow cameras in their bathrooms (and this was before the popularity of "reality TV"). Users of both Fresh Burst and its rival Scope said they used mouthwash to make their breath smell good. But, Scope users swished the liquid around and then spit it out, while Listerine users kept the product in their mouths for a long time. One user kept the stuff in until he got in the car. He finally spat it out in a sewer a block away! These findings meant Listerine still hadn't shaken its medicine-like image. In some cases you can even identify needs that customers themselves may not recognize.[1] For example, the makers of Cheerios cereal discovered a new use for the product simply by watching carefully. They found that, contrary to their assumptions, breakfast wasn't always the primary occasion for eating the breakfast of champions. Parents of small children wanted to be able to carry bags of healthy O's to be doled out as snacks during the entire day. But, observation isn't just child's play: Quicken's "Follow Me Home" program sends developers to first-time buyers' homes to observe how they use the program. Their findings opened up a whole new market as they figured out that many small-business owners were using the package to run their firms as well as to keep track of their personal finances.

THE BOTTOM LINE

The best way to understand products and services from the user's perspective is to identify the situations where they are actually used and go to those places to observe people in action. The Japanese call this methodology "going to the *gemba*." These

> observations often are more reliable and informative than asking people how they would use a product or bringing them into a contrived setting like a laboratory to watch them.

Have It Your Way

People hunger for unique products that help them express their individuality in an impersonal world. We have what psychologists call a *need for uniqueness*. Everyone likes to feel that in some way, however small, they are special. That's why a perfume is marketed as: "Cachet. As individual as you are." This need creates enormous opportunities for companies that can convince us that what we buy is tailored just to us and that no one else in the world has anything quite like it.

As noted in Chapter 3, a desire for uniqueness is particularly robust among teens. The *L-Report*, a research service that watches the youth market, recently identified a trend it called "amateurism," a backlash against prefab. Punk designers such as Imitation of Christ create unpolished DIY looks. Frayed hems, exposed seams, and bleach stains are making a comeback. Final Home's cardboard couch exemplifies the use of pedestrian material in furniture. Cover Girl even markets a line of nail polishes called "Broken Mirror" that look cracked on purpose. One of the biggest insults my students utter is when they describe a brand or style as "corporate."

The Customization Revolution

The need to be special in an anonymous world has spawned a bit of a revolution in manufacturing. *Mass customization* occurs when individually tailored products are produced at nearly the cost of standardized procedures. Today, customers are configuring their own products, including computers (Dell), bicycles (Cannondale), CDs (CDNow), vitamins (Acumin), designer jeans (Levi's), and newspapers (the *Wall Street Journal Personal Journal*).

By giving everyone just what they want, the theory goes, we can build loyalty and drastically reduce the mountains of merchandise that sit unsold in stores. Levi Strauss pioneered the mass customization concept with its Personal Pair jeans for women who struggled with finding a pair off-the-rack that would fit them just so. The company's research told them that women typically try on as many as fifteen to twenty pairs before buying!

Other apparel companies also are experimenting with mass customization offerings. They are especially motivated to enhance the quality of fit if they sell a lot of merchandise online, since about one in three garments bought on the Web is returned. Lands' End introduced a service called Lands' End Custom that enables its customers to buy $54 chinos made just for them. Users of the feature are asked to type in a handful of measurements such as jacket size, weight and height for men, and height, weight, and bra size for women. They also answer questions about their body type, such as the proportions of their hips and thighs. A software system determines a customer's weight distribution from this information and the trouser measurements conforming to it, and then sends size specifications over the Internet to a factory in Mexico. The factory is equipped with computerized machines that cut the fabric for each order. Customers receive the pants directly from the factory, two to three weeks later.

Companies are finding a receptive market for products that reflect the individual in each of us. Indeed, consider the success of Reflect.com. A venture partially funded by Procter & Gamble, this operation delivers customized cosmetics within seven days. Women who order online can choose from more than 300,000 customized product permutations, even down to a personalized package.

THE BOTTOM LINE

Give consumers the latitude to configure their own unique products if possible. In addition to enhancing their satisfaction, this flexibility can serve as a valuable source of feedback to ongoing product design efforts. Monitoring which options are chosen most frequently provides behavioral data that can be shared with new product development specialists to guide future specifications.

On the other hand, perhaps that's too much of a good thing! As we'll see later in the book, consumers can sometimes be overwhelmed if they have to make too many choices. The multitude of choices offered by mass customization can lead to mass confusion, as when for example a furniture store offers sofas in 500 styles, 3,000 fabrics, and 350 leathers. We'll talk more about the crucial factor of simplification in Chapter 10.

Customization Comes in Different Flavors

How does mass customization work? *Modularization* is one way to achieve it. Components are broken down into modules, and then each is mass-produced at low cost and assembled in different configurations. Using this approach, Motorola's pager division was able to offer its customers twenty-nine million possible configurations while reducing the number of parts used and cutting manufacturing time in half.

Restaurant industry insiders refer to a similar process called *industrial cuisine* (not the most appetizing description one could think of). In the 1980s, Taco Bell was one of the pioneers of this technique. The fast-food firm reengineered its processing systems and centralized production in large commissary facilities. This enables the company to deliver fully prepared components to local stores, where bags of lettuce, tomatoes, beans, etc. are combined to form tacos, burritos, and chalupas.

Modularization is only one way to achieve mass customization, however. James Gilmore and Joe Pine, the "gurus" of this approach, describe four different ways to customize and provide helpful examples:[2]

1. *Collaborative Customization:* Conduct a dialogue with the consumer to articulate her needs and make customized products for her. This approach works best for people who get frustrated when forced to select from numerous options. Gilmore and Pine note that Paris Miki, a Japanese eyewear retailer, spent five years developing the Mikissimes Design System. This process takes a digital picture of a person's face, analyzes her features, and elicits statements from her about the look she wants. The customer receives a recommended lens size and shape in the form of a digital image superimposed on her photo.

2. *Adaptive Customization:* Offer one standard product that users can alter themselves. This is most appropriate when the consumer needs the product to perform in different ways on different occasions. For example, lighting systems made by Lutron Electronics Company connect different lights in a room. The user can program varying effects for parties, romantic moments, or reading.

3. *Cosmetic Customization:* A standard product is presented differently to different customers. Each uses it the same way, differing only in how they want it presented. Hertz's #1 Club Gold Program gives its preferred members a standard rental car. But, instead of waiting in a long line, the customer can look for his name in lights, go directly to his car, and find his name displayed on a personal agreement conveniently hanging from the mirror.

4. *Transparent Customization:* Provide the customer with unique goods without letting him know these have been customized for him. This approach is recommended when needs are predictable and when the customer does not want to have to restate his needs repeatedly. ChemStation of Dayton, Ohio, sells industrial soap that is used in car washes and for cleaning factory floors. The company custom-formulates a soap mixture that goes into a tank on the customer's premises. ChemStation monitors usage patterns remotely, so it can deliver a refill before the customer has to ask.

Getting Their Hands Dirty: The Customer as Codesigner

Mass customization is a great innovation, no doubt. But, the user still is only choosing from among a set of prespecified options rather than participating in defining what those options are. Can we go even further in enlisting consumers' input into design and merchandising decisions?

User-centered design tries to do just that. The idea is to incorporate your current knowledge of users in the early stages of design, confront users repeatedly with early prototypes, and redesign as often as necessary. For example, when Netscape introduced Navigator 2.0 to the market in January 1996, its designers immediately began developing the next version for release in August of that year. Within six weeks after the launch of 2.0, Netscape put up a Beta 0 version of its new prototype on an internal project Web site. Less than two weeks later, designers posted an updated version. A prototype was released to the public in early March and every few weeks thereafter until launch. Netscape's feedback from its users was critical, especially since it was locked in a neck-and-neck race with Microsoft for dominance of the browser market.

The Voice of the Consumer

How can firms do a better job of involving customers in the design process? In a *total quality management* (TQM) organization, the widely used *quality function deployment* (QFD) methodology includes a stage where the *voice of the consumer* (VOC) is formally injected into the process (process engineers like acronyms). This is where data collected at the *gemba* are supposed to be integrated with other components such as technical feasibility to inform decisions about new product development. In reality though, this voice typically is muted at best.

The VOC perspective is being implemented in a few cases, though primarily for business-to-business products rather than for consumer goods. Eric von Hippel (who originated the lead user concept) and his colleagues develop what they call "tool kits" to assist industrial clients. These tools use techniques like computer simulation and rapid prototyping to speed the product development process. For example, Bush Boake Allen (BBA), a global supplier of specialty flavors to companies like Nestlé, built a tool kit that enables its customers to develop their own flavors, which BBA then manufactures. On the consumer side, in work we are doing for DuPont the VOC is included at very early stages of identifying new technology platforms. This feedback guides the company in its development of innovative fibers engineered to deliver properties like "freshness" that end users of hosiery, shirts, and so on tell us they want. These insights at times contradicted assumptions the engineers had made about what qualities people looked for in garments and home textile products. This process resulted in fundamental changes in DuPont's product development initiatives.

Surprisingly, though, most firms don't really put the pedal to the metal in terms of actually gathering information about just what customers do want. And little research has been done to better understand the potential of codesign. Texas Instruments found this process can pay off: The company posted design specs for a new calculator at its Web site and invited feedback from high school teachers. TI then made significant changes to the prototype based upon the feedback it received from its users in the trenches.[3]

To paraphrase a popular TV show, this user feedback is indeed the weakest link in the marketing chain. Classic models of consumer behavior don't even address the possibility that consumers interact with competing providers prior to making a purchase, other than evaluating claims made in static advertising messages. These perspectives describe the process of product choice by assuming that people merely react to information they gather about alternatives before buying—a marketerspace rather than a consumerspace outlook if ever there was one.

As R&D continues to improve the ability to deliver rapid prototyping, the time required to produce customized products will shrink. This implies that a firm's capability to provide fast turnaround will become

a more important attribute when customers choose among competitors. If it takes CDNow three days to deliver a customized music compilation to your door and Amazon.com does the same in a week, you
know where you're going to be placing your order.

THE BOTTOM LINE

> Many companies only pay lip service to the value of integrating
> the voice of the consumer early on in the product development
> process. Most models of attitude change don't even address the
> possibility that the recipient of a marketing message might inter-
> act with the source. You should involve consumers as codesigners
> throughout the development cycle.

Design For, With, or By

So, how to do it? One way to think about this process is in terms of
the level of engagement by customers. They can be involved at several
stages in the development process, including *specification, conceptual development, detailed design, prototyping,* and *final product.*
This interaction can range from a simple "reality check" where customers react to ideas all the way to active participation in the brain-
storming process.[4]

A useful typology looks like this:[5]

- *Design For:* A product development approach where products
  are designed on behalf of the customers. This is the current standard, where (if you're lucky) a company will get input from
  specific customer groups in the form of interviews or focus
  groups.

- *Design With:* This approach includes information about customer preferences, needs, and requirements as well. In addition, though, customers are shown a set of possible solutions or
  product concepts and are asked to react to them.

■ *Design By:* Now we're getting somewhere. This denotes a product development approach in which customers are actively involved and partake in the design of their own product.

Various industries use different methods to bring customers closer to the design process. These can briefly be summarized as follows:[6]

■ *User-Oriented Product Development:* This describes a human factors/ergonomics engineering approach to product design. It typically is applied to products with man-machine development interface problems. In an iterative process, machine prototypes are developed and tested with users until the problems are solved.

■ *Concept Testing:* Makers of consumer packaged goods, durables, and industrial products may get customer feedback when they are coming up with initial product concepts. Typically, people are asked to react to sketches, models, mock-ups, or prototypes of the product-to-be.

■ *Beta-Testing:* As we've already seen, software firms like Microsoft typically beta-test programs to be sure the product does what it is designed to do in the customer environment.

■ *Consumer Idealized Design:* In a few isolated cases, makers of consumer durables involve consumers in the early phases of product design. The *idealized design process* is conducted as a group exercise similar to a focus group, where participants are selected because they represent the target market. The basic idea behind the approach is to get the customers to forget existing products and ignore the feasibility of new designs—the sky's the limit. Basically, the group brainstorms and eventually decides on a new design along with the reasons they think what they've come up with improves on what's out there.

■ *Lead User Method:* In industrial contexts, some firms realize that their key customers know an awful lot about what they need and that it's in the interest of the buyer to work with the provider on developing solutions to their needs. Indeed, in some high-tech industries it's estimated that between 30 and 70 percent of new product ideas actually originated with customers rather than with R&D people. As noted earlier, a *lead user* is a person whose needs are similar to the rest of the marketplace—with the exception that she will face these needs months or even years before the bulk of the marketplace encounters them.

■ *Participatory Ergonomics:* This approach is used in industrial settings to design work spaces. The basic idea is that the people who will actually be using the space are put into small groups that design their own working environment.

Virtual Codesign: Getting Online Feedback

Bringing consumers into the product development process can be time-consuming and expensive if it's done right. Fortunately, the Internet allows firms to get inexpensive feedback almost instantaneously— even though only a few companies are taking advantage of this medium in just this way.

For example, Fiat put a link on its Web site to evaluate users' needs for its next generation of the Fiat Punto model. Customers prioritized style, comfort, performance, price, and safety features. They were asked to share what they hated most about the car and to suggest ideas for new features. Then they could select from body styles, wheel designs, and front and rear designs, and they could see their design onscreen. Software captured the final results and also traced the sequence respondents used when selecting options. Fiat got back more than 3,000 surveys in a three-month period; ideas ranged from including an umbrella holder inside the car to building a model with a single bench front seat. The total cost to Fiat was $35,000; petty cash in the world of market research.[7]

Many firms are already using the Internet to get feedback from their own people, though a lot are reluctant to bring outsiders into the process. It's typical for software companies to put beta versions online for internal use only. For example, a company may put up a site internally and eventually post a "soft release" to its commercial Web site.

Deleting links to highly frequented parts of the site makes it more likely that only more technically aggressive users will stumble upon a beta release, rather than unsophisticated ones who might be frustrated by an error-ridden version.

Conversion to a Web-based format has several compelling advantages. Response time can be minimized because customers can provide feedback from the comfort of their own homes. It is easier to modify the research instrument or to create multiple experimental versions of it, and the feedback can be collected around the clock (and respondents can answer a survey in their pajamas). The researcher has the capability of reaching a larger and more diverse subject population, and it is possible that responses will be more truthful due to the anonymity afforded by the Web. Since data collection is automated and coding errors all but eliminated, data costs per respondent are considerably lower than with traditional research methods.[8]

Why isn't more design feedback collected online? There are several technical impediments to using a lot of visual materials in online consumer research. There may be variations in image resolution caused by the use of different computers, monitors, and browsers. The system architecture must be platform-independent so that Mac users aren't excluded. In addition, there is always the ubiquitous issue of download time due to bandwidth constraints for users accessing the site from a modem rather than a direct network connection. Finally, there's the problem of lack of Internet access by some segments of the population. This concern is diminishing as the rate of Internet penetration in private homes continues to escalate.

Still, some segments of consumers are likely to be especially comfortable with this kind of approach and to be willing to provide input on new product designs. For example, the Yankee Group, a high-tech consulting firm, has studied *TAFs—technologically advanced families*— that the company estimates constitute about 16 percent of American households. These households believe that faster, newer, more-advanced products will facilitate home and work life and make leisure time more fun. TAFs see themselves as more technologically and financially sophisticated than other consumers. They are usually the first on the block to own the newest digital gadget. Some TAFs admit they are big kids and simply must have the latest shiny toy, but they also believe in the power of technology to help them manage their busy lives.

TAFs are more than just an interesting phenomenon to high-tech companies. They also serve as guinea pigs, testing new products and offering clues about what will and won't work for the mass public. IBM uses TAFs to test new products at home before marketing them. As the marketing and sales program director at IBM's Home Networking Solutions observed, "[using TAFs] You can fine-tune the ease of setup, installation, and use of a product that you don't capture in a lab or storyboard."[9]

Although research firms were rather slow to take advantage of the Web because of some of the problems listed above, these initial drawbacks are rapidly being solved, and online consumer research is slowly but surely becoming much more accepted by major corporations. For example, General Motors is now conducting about 60 percent of its research in an Internet format, and Procter & Gamble divides its research expenditures equally between online and offline methods.

THE BOTTOM LINE

Conducting consumer research on the Internet has several advantages over mail or phone surveys or personal interviews. These include timeliness, access to large samples, and cost-efficiencies compared with traditional research methods. Statistically valid observations can be collected, including respondents' reactions to rich visual stimuli that heretofore were possible only in small-scale qualitative formats like focus groups.

The beauty of the Internet is that it opens the door to many innovative technologies that help to engage consumers in the research process. Our firm (Mind/Share, Inc.) employs online consumer research methodologies that 1) are visually-based; 2) allow the responses of large numbers of respondents to be aggregated for analysis; and 3) permit a nearly instantaneous and continuous flow of data to researchers. Our approach also tackles such technical impediments as download time and platform-dependence.

How do we do it? We use a Web-based interactive data collection technique that allows respondents to manipulate visual images of products as a means of expressing their tastes and preferences. This tool is composed of a browser-based software interface with an extensive database layer, which handles storage and retrieval of visual images.

A Web-based approach like this is very valuable for a range of merchandising and marketing decisions. Consider the apparel and home furnishings industries, for example. Typically, a fairly large number of styles—whether jeans or carpet samples—are manufactured and sent to retailers. Nobody really knows which will be stars and which will be dogs until market data are available. Letting customers vote with their dollars after the fact is a very expensive way to get market feedback! If customers can pick out the likely dogs before full-scale production, firms can trim their initial set of offerings and the savings can be enormous.

UNIFORMS ONLINE: A CASE STUDY

To illustrate this process, let's walk through a design study we conducted for Burns Security, a division of Wells Fargo Corporation. Burns decided to revamp its corporate image and as part of that effort the company wanted to redesign the uniforms worn by its security personnel. Uniforms play a crucial role in communicating corporate image, so choosing the right design is not a trivial issue in this competitive industry.

But what image should the uniforms communicate? Burns Security and its uniform supplier, Lion Apparel, needed answers—and fast. To provide this feedback we built a password-protected Web site exclusively for Burns employees we called Uniforms Online. We designed an online survey that gave respondents different design options from which to choose. Their choices were immediately transmitted back to our server, where they were combined with everyone else's for analysis. Soon afterwards, managers who were given access by Burns could log on to a secure Web site to see a visual summary of the options chosen. Quick responses, quick decisions!

The survey was designed and put on a Web site within a few days. In this case all respondents were employees of Burns, so they were notified by the company's president to visit the Web site, and each person was given a unique password identifier. Within three days, all completed surveys were received and analyzed.

First, participants were asked to select animals representing the image Burns has now, the image it wants to have, and the image it doesn't want to have (representing a company's image in terms of metaphors like animals is a common technique in marketing research). After the respondent "sorted" the animals into these categories, he saw his choices onscreen like the sample shown in Figure 5.1.

In the next step, the respondent is taken to a page that displays a set of uniform styles. Some were actual styles currently being worn by the firm's security personnel and others were new styles the company wanted to test. Once again, the employee "sorted" the options onscreen and rated each one on a series of attributes such as sophisticated or sloppy. An example is shown in Figure 5.2.

At this point the users of these products also can provide their own,

Figure 5.1: Studying corporate image online.

Courtesy of Mind/Share, Inc. (www.mind-share.net).

open-ended feedback. For example, what aspects of the design you selected would you change to make it even better? What problems are you encountering with your current uniform?

Now, things get really interesting. Instead of waiting weeks or months to receive a boring report that few will read, interested managers can log on to a restricted site and receive current updates on the respondents' uniform choices. Feedback can be accessed from anywhere. This information can be made available to as few or as many

Figure 5.2: Style-testing online.

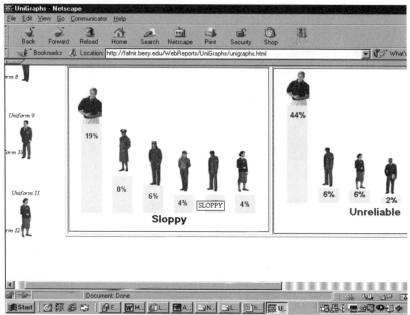

Courtesy of Mind/Share, Inc. (www.mind-share.net).

employees, clients, or consumers as desired. A sample report page is shown in Figure 5.3.

Turning consumers into codesigners is all about having conversations with customers. Companies need to understand that sometimes you need to be cruel to be kind; let people spout off about what they like and don't like—when there's still time to change. Early feedback increases the likelihood that what eventually gets offered is what people want. Turning pawns into partners is a win-win strategy for marketers and consumers alike. The online environment offers us a way to create a dialogue with customers almost effortlessly. That ability is crucial to compete in consumerspace—as we'll see in Chapter 6, consumers are going to be surfing through these virtual worlds whether we're there or not.

Figure 5.3: An online research report.

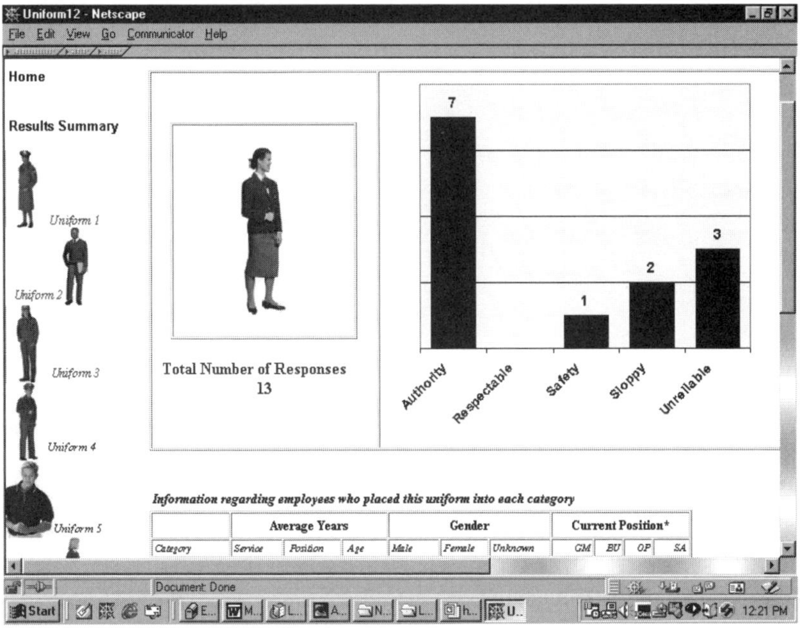

Courtesy of Mind/Share, Inc. (www.mind-share.net).

CHAPTER 6

Virtual Voices
Building Consumerspace Online

The band Widespread Panic has never had a music video on MTV nor cracked the Billboard Top 200. But, it's one of the top forty touring bands in the United States. How did it get to be so successful? Simple—the group built a virtual community of fans and laid itself bare to them. Hard-core followers can even log on to the band's Web site to find out what band members ate for lunch. Perhaps that's just a bunch of bologna to the rest of us, but Panic's fans need to know.

There's little doubt that consumerspace is thriving in its online forms. People around the world are projecting their identities (some real, some made up) into virtual communities where they work, play, court—and buy. Cyberspace is the place where many of us go to learn about what's happening out there. Whether checking in on the world via the *New York Times Online*, checking up on our stock portfolio, or checking out the latest music clips from our favorite bands, it's certainly a cliché to state that the Web is revolutionizing the way we relate to one another.

In the past few years many marketers have become discouraged by the dot-com bust and are now retrenching their efforts in the offline world. However, reports of the Web's demise are premature. The Web is not dead, it's just not taking on the forms that some people thought it would in the early days of the Internet gold rush.

There's still plenty of gold out there to be mined if you know where

135

to look for it. For example, singles continue to embrace sites like Match.com, Yahoo! Personals, Date.com, and LavaLife as an efficient way to find a mate. Jupiter Research estimates that the fifteen million Americans who posted personal ads online in 2002 will mushroom to twenty-four million in five years. In this chapter we'll explore how people are connecting with each other and with the companies they value in cyberspace.

Brand Communities

Matchmaking Web sites like LavaLife provide a form of community (think virtual singles bar) that has dramatically changed how we relate to one another. Surprisingly, many of these virtual communities are devoted not to people, not to politics or religion, but to specific brands. A *brand community* is a specialized, non–geographically bound group, based on a structured set of social relations among admirers of a brand.

Some of these communities are nurtured by companies that sponsor real-world, offline events to encourage enthusiasm about their products. For example, Saturn jumped on the brand community idea early on by staging its now famous owner reunions and barbecues. Another vehicle company, Harley-Davidson, attributes its return from near bankruptcy in the 1980s at least in part to the introduction of Harley Owner Groups that help HOGs everywhere pursue their common fervor for its bikes.

However, it's in the online world that brand communities often flourish. In these environments fellow travelers around the globe can find each other easily and create digital networks to nurture their shared passions. In some cases individuals create their own community Web pages on sites like geocities.com or sixdegrees.com. Companies also sponsor sites with the aim of giving devotees of a product or a lifestyle a congenial place to "meet." There are community sites for specific consumer profiles such as teenage girls (gurl.com) or college students (collegeclub.com), for themes such as relationships (swoon. com), or for people who are fans of a specific product (niketalk.com).

Needless to say, many of these communities focus on topics of great relevance to business, and in some cases the discussions sway the judgments of decision-makers. For example, participants in www. iii.co.uk, a British community devoted to financial issues, share buy/ sell recommendations with each other—and purportedly also influence the decisions of fund managers who monitor these discussions. These communities can be quite powerful insofar as knowledgeable opinion leaders who are crucial to a brand's acceptance populate them. In 1994 CEO Andrew Grove of Intel found out just how powerful, when he was forced to issue an apology on the Internet after chat groups discussing a possible flaw in the Pentium chip produced hordes of irate customers.

Virtual communities are a huge global phenomenon. Forrester Research estimates that as of 2000, 400,000 communities existed on the Internet and 27 percent of the online audience was community users. Another study conducted by Pew Internet and the American Life foundation found that 84 percent of all Internet users have been in contact with an online group, 79 percent have kept in contact with a particular group, and twenty-three million Internet users exchange e-mails with other group members several times a week.

THE BOTTOM LINE

The brand community is an emerging phenomenon that holds enormous potential as a marketing tool. Consumers who have a common allegiance to a brand can now bond with each other online, and these networks often exist independently of the brand's creators. Although community members are often leery about corporate involvement, the naturally occurring conversations about one's product are a powerful (and free) form of market feedback that is hard to ignore.

Types of Communities

Virtual communities come in many forms and perform a wide variety of functions. One typology describes them in terms of the social needs they provide to users and lays out four basic types of communities:[1]

1.   Communities of relationships: The WELL or match.com

2.   Communities of fantasy: Doom, EverQuest

3.   Communities of interest: Epinions, bolt.com

4.   Communities of transaction: eBay, Amazon

These descriptions are helpful but in some cases misleading. As the online regions of consumerspace continue to develop, we are witnessing a fusion of community types. Indeed, perhaps we are moving toward the goal of creating a utopian community that meets all of our needs. Ideally this virtual space will allow us to learn about topics that interest us, locate others who share those interests, engage in fantasies related to those interests, and then buy goods and services that enable us to take part of the experience back to the offline world.

We're not quite there yet, but as we'll see, some hybrid communities do bridge some of these functions. For example, Landsend.com (a community of transaction) lets you shop with a friend (to choose a gift for a third person perhaps) so that the consumer is also engaging in a relationship. Game sites are bursting with characters that use real brands, and transactional messages merge into the flow of the game. Matchmaking sites like match.com or HotJobs have a business model that depends upon the willingness of people to pay for the prospect of a new relationship in the form of a lover or an employer (just don't mix these up!).

Community Structures

Depending on the purpose of the community, there are different ways to enter and navigate these virtual meeting spaces. These are the three most prevalent forms:

1. *Multi-User Dungeons (MUD):* Originally, these were environments where players of fantasy games met. Now they refer to any computer-generated environment that lets people interact socially through a structured format of role- and game-playing.

2. *Rooms, Rings, and Lists:* These include Internet relay chat (IRC), otherwise known as *chat rooms. Rings* are organizations of related home pages, and *lists* are groups of people on a single mailing list who share information.

3. *Boards:* Online communities organized around interest-specific electronic bulletin boards. Active members read and post messages sorted by date and subject. There are boards devoted to musical groups, movies, wind, cigars, cars, comic strips, even fast-food restaurants.

"I Like to Watch": Types of Netizens

How do people get drawn into consumption communities? Internet users, or *netizens*, tend to progress from task-oriented information gathering to increasingly social involvement. *Lurkers* are surfers who like to watch but who don't participate. At first they will merely browse the site, but later they may well be drawn into active participation.

The intensity of identification with a virtual community depends upon two factors. The first is that the more central the activity to a person's self-concept, the more likely she will be to pursue an active membership in a community. The second is that the intensity of the social relationships the person forms with other members of the virtual community helps to determine her extent of involvement. As Figure 6.1 shows, combining these two factors creates four distinct member types:

1. *Tourists* lack strong social ties to the group and maintain only a passing interest in the activity.

2. *Minglers* maintain strong social ties but are not very interested in the central consumption activity.

Figure 6.1: Ways to participate in virtual communities.

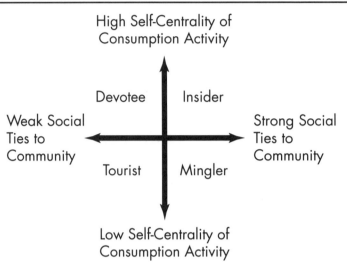

SOURCE: Michael R. Solomon, *Consumer Behavior: Buying, Having, and Being*, 5th ed., © 2002, p. 324. Reprinted by permission of Pearson Education, Inc., Upper Saddle River, N.J.

3. *Devotees* express strong interest in the activity but have few social attachments to the group.

4. *Insiders* exhibit both strong social ties and strong interest in the activity.

Devotees and insiders are the most important targets for marketers who wish to leverage communities for promotional purposes. They are the heavy users of virtual communities. And, by reinforcing usage, the community may upgrade tourists and minglers to insiders and devotees.[2]

Virtual Models: Beauty Is Only Skin Deep, but Ugly Is to the Bone

Corporate speakers lecturing about e-commerce often trot out a classic cartoon to illustrate the anonymity of the Web. It shows a dog sitting in front of a computer screen with the caption, ''On the Internet no one knows you're a dog." It's true that it's easier to pretend to be someone you're not when you're online, but the reality is that no one wants to look like a dog, either online or off. One of the intriguing aspects of the Web is its ability to let individuals and companies doctor their appearance to suit their moods, fantasies, or corporate image.

The virtual presence a company projects into consumerspace is, of course, a key branding component, and many firms have thrown many dollars into the pursuit of the slickest home page. But the projection of identity doesn't stop there. When we as consumers enter these spaces, we are relying upon the site's designers to help us navigate the space and easily make choices. One vital yet largely overlooked component is the visual forms we encounter as we make our way through online communities. Who do we want to be (virtually)? Who else do we want to encounter? What should they look like? How can we strangle whoever invented that incredibly annoying paper clip figure that keeps popping up in our word processing program?

Consumerspace is a place to try on identities and to interact with others—surfers who in many cases also are wearing a disguise to the virtual costume ball we call cyberspace. These figures can be related to our fantasies (many people seem to enjoy gender-switching when they enter communities), but this issue is also relevant for the transactional elements of communities. That's why at least a few companies are thinking more carefully about how they populate their Web sites with onscreen guides called avatars.

An *avatar* is the manifestation of a Hindu deity in superhuman or animal form. In the computing world it has come to mean a cyberspace presence represented by a character that you can move around inside a visual, graphical world. These entities originated in computer games and have over time spread into virtual communities. Avatars are now beginning to appear in online advertising and on e-commerce sites as a mechanism for enhancing the online experience. For example, Brown & Williamson Tobacco Corporation developed a high-tech vending machine featuring a cast of virtual characters on a video screen that "speak" to customers as they are choosing a brand. When a smoker tries to buy a pack of Marlboros made by rival Philip Morris, a virtual vixen with a sultry voice and lurid red lipstick entices him or her to switch to Lucky Strikes instead: "Toasted and delicious, and I'll give you a pack for 75 cents off."

Avatars can take many forms, ranging from that annoying paper clip in Microsoft Word to a lifelike (verging on anatomically correct) woman. Some dimensions we use to characterize avatars are shown in Figure 6.2.

An avatar may simply be a passive visible enhancement to the site, or it can be an active item with a physical form that collects and stores information on the user and facilitates the online experience. Miss Boo (www.boo.com), a caricature of a young hip female, is a decorative avatar used to sell clothes. BonziBuddy (www.bonzi.com) is an active avatar, a purple gorilla that collects information on the consumer's preferences. The avatar can appear motionless on the site, much like a still image (www.mySimon.com), or it can be animated like BonziBuddy, who moves around the Web page, reads books, and, when not being used, takes a nap.

Finally, the avatar can take the form of the actual site user, a "typical" consumer, a fashion model, or a celebrity, representing a continuum from the depiction of a realistic person to an idealized image.

Figure 6.2: Types of avatars.

Function	Action	Classification	Representation
Decorative	Motionless	User	Real Image
Active	Animated	Typical Consumer	Caricature
			Character
		Fashion Model	
		Celebrity	

SOURCE: Natalie T. Quilty, Michael R. Solomon, and Basil G. Englis (2003), "Icons and Avatars: Cyber-Models and Hyper-Mediated Visual Persuasion," *Advertising and Visual Persuasion*, edited by Linda Scott and Rajeev Batra (Mahwah, N.J.: Lawrence Erlbaum, in press).

Lands' End (www.landsend.com) and JC Penney (www.jcpenney.com) permit the user to create an avatar in the user's own image so that it may assist the user in selecting clothing to fit his or her body type. Users create their own avatar by selecting from predetermined descriptions (narrow, broad, etc.) for their shoulders, hips, waist, and bust. They can also select from a number of facial shapes, hairstyles, and hair and skin colors.

The creation of avatars for commercial formats is evolving into a cottage industry as demand for compelling figures begins to grow. For example, the German firm noDNA GmbH (www.nodna.com) offers a variety of "virtualstars." These are computer-generated figures that appear as caricatures, "vuppets" (cartoon-type mascots and animals), and "replicants" that are doubles of real people. According to Olaf Schirm, president of noDNA GmbH, models like Tyra (shown in Figure 6.3) receive hundreds of love letters and even a few marriage proposals.

Each of these actors can be developed to meet the needs of specific target markets. The physical appearance, personality, and communication message can be calibrated to a particular group of consumers. Some of the sites currently using these virtual models are time2bcool.com, virtopera.de and time4team.com. The French company W Interactive SARL provides synthetic talking faces that can deliver messages and product information in a number of languages. They can be created as cartoonlike people, real people, or famous personalities.

Elite Model Management, the agency that represents many of the supermodels that grace the catwalks of Paris and the pages of magazines worldwide, has created a virtual supermodel. Webbie Tookay is a digitally composed model. Armed with a personality profile produced specifically for the client's needs, Webbie is available for a licensing fee for all kinds of media-related work including virtual fashion shows and Internet advertising. Elite formed a brand-new division for the sole purpose of marketing virtual models.

The advantages of virtual avatars compared to flesh and blood models include the ability to change the avatar in real time to suit the

Figure 6.3: Tyra, a virtual model.

needs of the target audience or individual consumer. From an advertising perspective, they are likely to be more cost-effective than hiring a real person. From a personal selling and customer service perspective, they have the ability to handle multiple customers at any one time, they are not geographically limited, and they are operational 24/7, thus freeing up company employees and sales personnel to perform other activities.

THE BOTTOM LINE

Despite decades of research attesting to the impact of physical appearance on persuasion and attitude change, few companies think much about just how their virtual representatives should look. Depending upon the situation and the product being sold, this can be a crucial decision deserving of more attention. For example, in some cases consumers prefer to see a model that is a realistic depiction of an everyday person while in others they gravitate toward an idealized version much like a supermodel in the offline world.

My Life as a Sim . . . ulation

Get a life! Many consumers enter the online world to do just that. They experiment with new identities that often include a healthy dose of product-oriented fantasy. Nowhere is this more apparent than the incredibly popular interactive game called The Sims that allows players to create an entire family online. These "skins" are personalized to the user's wishes, including gender, body type, age, and personality. Players can set the stage and watch the actors they've created live out their virtual lives for their voyeuristic pleasure. As one promo for the game claims, "Are you interested in playing God? If You're Game, the Sims Are Ready." A striking aspect of the game is its materialistic emphasis. The Sims is all about creating little virtual consumers—it's the player's job to keep his or her characters happy by providing them with food, shelter, creature comforts, even partners.

Playing God can be a full-time job. The player can build or expand a house, including such details as wall coverings, landscaping, doors, and windows. He or she can choose from a huge array of objects to fill the house, including such "essentials" as a hot tub and a Vibromatic Heart Bed. Players literally direct their characters' lives, deciding if they will make friends, joke, flirt, dance, eat, shower, relieve their bladders, or throw parties. But overseeing a Sims character isn't all fun and games, because they are prey to the same problems that dog us in the offline world. For example, a Sims character can get depressed, urinate on itself, or otherwise have a bad hair day.

Figure 6.4: Populating a virtual dining room.

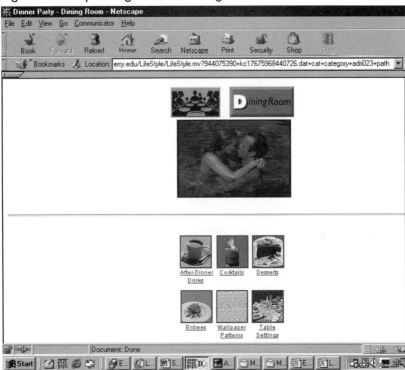

Courtesy of Mind/Share, Inc. (www.mind-share.net).

Machiavellian players can kill off others for their money, bulldoze their house and start again, or even create large adult "slave" families to make more money by employing them all in menial jobs.

The Sims is much more than a solitary game—it's a part of consumerspace. Players can take pictures of the houses and "skins" they've created and upload these to a Web site where they are shared with thousands of other players around the world. Any player can go to this Web site and download other Sims families and houses into their own neighborhood—modular housing in a virtual development.

The marketing potential of an online game like The Sims is enormous, yet until recently largely uncharted. Since most of the game is about acquiring stuff, it makes sense that actual brands have now been included in the sets of choices. Why not build in links to brand-sponsored Web sites when these are chosen? Why not use the platform as a marketing research tool to monitor the choices people make and to understand how these relate to other selections already taken to outfit "skins" and their habitats in this virtual world? The Sims has been the tip of the virtual iceberg when it comes to exploiting the potential of consumerspace.

We've created a similar environment in some of our online lifestyle research. Respondents navigate through "rooms" in a house, and in each they choose from among images of products in a variety of categories as they populate the room. For example, say a food manufacturer wanted to understand how consumers link its products to others or whether its offerings are associated with certain types of social occasions. As shown in Figure 6.4 on page 146, respondents might be asked to create a dining room, choosing everything from a table setting to the specific types of food and beverages that would appear on the table for a dinner party, family supper, etc.

THE BOTTOM LINE

Online consumer simulations like The Sims hold great promise as a research tool to help us understand how people use brands to populate the worlds they design in cyberspace. Marketers should

> pay more attention to the potential ability of data collection interfaces that take the form of games and other diversions to capture actual customer preferences.

The Corporate Paradox

Obviously, many marketers have spent many dollars to create online spaces to which they hope to attract droves of consumers. There's the rub—in many cases it's the grassroots spaces that are more effective as instigators of brand awareness and preference. This is, of course, but another example of the *Corporate Paradox*—the more involved a company appears to be in the dissemination of news about its products, the less convincing it becomes.

David Lewis, a British marketing researcher, makes a similar point when he distinguishes between buzz and hype: *Buzz* is word of mouth that is viewed as authentic and generated by customers. *Hype* is dismissed as inauthentic—corporate propaganda planted by a company with an ax to grind. The challenge to marketers who want to reach residents of consumerspace without being run out of town on a rail (virtually at least) is to create a presence without having it turn into a ghost town, abandoned by Web surfers in search of the "real thing."

Figure 6.5 characterizes communities on a continuum in terms of

Figure 6.5: The community-sponsorship continuum.

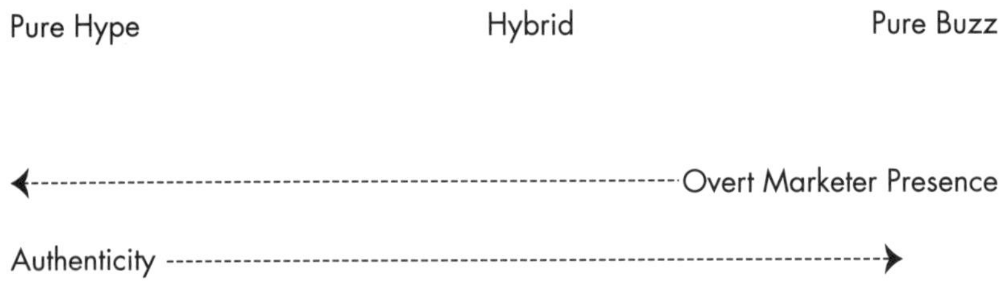

Pure Hype	Hybrid	Pure Buzz

←---Overt Marketer Presence

Authenticity ---→

the amount of input companies have in the site. The anchors are purely consumer-initiated communities and those blatantly sponsored by a commercial entity. As we'll see, both kinds can play an important role in consumerspace. Things get really interesting in the middle of this continuum where it's unclear where corporate hype ends and consumer buzz begins. Let's start with the blatantly commercial sites and then consider what other communities not overly linked to a sponsor might look like.

Pure Hype Communities

The most obvious and extreme form of a pure hype community is an e-commerce sales Web site. These communities of transaction are for many of us comparable to the "kiss-and-go" lane at the airport. They are task-oriented; we want to get on with our business and not linger there. That helps to explain why designing a "sticky" Web site that compels people to stay as long as possible is the holy grail for many designers. There's much to be said about pure e-commerce sites, but these are superficial communities at best (perhaps a contributing factor in the dot-com implosion we've seen in recent years).

Many firms are finding that, just as an offline mall needs a food court and other amenities to attract repeat shoppers, an e-commerce site needs to offer more than just a digitized catalog. Malls provide meeting places and social opportunities, and Web sites can do the same. Gartner G2 predicts that by 2005, 50 percent of all Fortune 1000 companies will launch virtual communities linked to their Web sites.[3]

Is a virtual community a good investment for a firm? The answer seems to be yes, at least in light of the recent finding that individuals who use community features have been found to make up two-thirds of online sales, while accounting for only a third of the visits. Furthermore, when community users post product reviews or messages, they are nine times more likely to visit again and twice as likely to buy and be brand loyal when compared with noncommunity users. Users who do not even post information but merely read the content are more apt to visit again and buy when compared with noncommunity users.

THE BOTTOM LINE ━━━━━━━━━━━━━━

> Adding features that encourage membership in a brand com-
> munity related to what is sold there can leverage the value of
> a company-sponsored e-commerce site. This strategy increases
> involvement with the product, encourages repeat visits, and
> builds loyalty over time.

Hybrid Communities

A virtual community devoted to motor oil—pretty slick! WD-40 began
its fan club Web site in early 2001. The company offered 1,000 ra-
dios in the shape of oilcans to individuals who signed up ten other
WD-40 fan club members. The campaign quadrupled the number of
people who registered at the site. A fan club site like this is one manifestation of what we can think of as a hybrid community—part buzz,
part hype.

   While consumption communities are largely a grassroots phenomenon founded by consumers for other consumers, this strategy holds
enormous potential for companies to connect with consumers—if they
are careful not to alienate members by being too aggressive or "commercial." At one point Warner Brothers noticed that many fans of
Bugs Bunny, Batman, and the Tasmanian Devil were downloading images and sound clips onto their personal Web pages and then selling
ad space on those pages. Instead of suing its fans, Warner created
an online community called ACME City that builds home pages for
registered members.

   Many corporate-sponsored sites build home pages for new members and ask for nothing in return except personal information on a
registration form. They can use this information to fine-tune the online
experience by making advertising, contests, and rewards programs
more relevant. Using newsgroup archives and search engines companies can create a detailed profile of any individual consumer who
has posted information. Already numerous firms including BellSouth,

Monsanto, and Motorola monitor bulletin boards and online chat rooms to glean product information and to better understand the current state of their brand image.

Hybrid communities are neither fish nor fowl because they are devoted to consumer activities yet retain a fair amount of corporate involvement (or interference, depending upon your perspective). A hybrid community is like a virtual petri dish—the marketer creates the growing area, sits back, and waits for something to happen.

Gaming and Advergaming

The most promising petri dish of them all may be the humble computer game. The Interactive Digital Software Association (IDSA) estimates that more than 219 million computer and video games were sold in 2000, almost two games for every household in America. In 2001, the video game industry raked in $10.8 billion, more than we spent in movie theaters.

Who is buying them? In the old days of computer gaming, scruffy teenage boys surrounded by old pizza boxes shot at TV screens in their basements. That stereotype is dated, however. Gamers are drawn from a surprisingly representative slice of the population, and a good number of them now include women and older people. According to Nielsen//NetRatings, 41 percent of people who frequent game sites like GamesSpot, Candystand, and Pogo are women, and 43 percent are aged 25 to 49.

This platform has come a very long way since the early days of Pong. It's hard to conceive of a piece of software that projects blood and guts on a screen as the gateway to a community, but that's what is happening in the online world. Increasingly, consumers are no longer satisfied to load a game on their computers and just play with themselves (so to speak). Now they want interactivity, they want to play with others, and they want it bad: Sony Online Entertainment's gaming Web site, the Station (www.station.com), has more than twelve million registered users, while Microsoft's Gaming Zone (www.zone.com) boasts a membership of twenty-nine million. This is an international phenomenon: In South Korea, gamers flock to Internet cafés called

"PC bangs" to play. In Japan, dance-by-numbers games like Dance Dance Revolution have turned arcades into nightclubs.

The emergence of gaming as an online, shared experience opens new vistas to marketers. Consider this: Toyota's digital racing game called Tundra Madness attracts 8,000 consumers who spend an average of eight minutes on the site daily. The company's research showed that the campaign raised brand awareness by 28 percent and intent to purchase by 5 percent. Heartened by the success of this experiment, Toyota launched games to promote other models. To target first-time car buyers, the company created the Matrix Video Mixer game, which it promoted through sites like RollingStone.com, GetMusic.com, and Launch.com. The effort was tied to a Gravity Games sponsorship and an in-theater commercial campaign. About three in ten registered users forwarded videos created through the game to their friends; 65 percent of those e-mails were opened.

The secret behind the appeal of this format is the huge chunks of time people spend immersed in these games. The average online player logs seventeen hours per week, and firms like Sony, Microsoft, and Sega are building their own virtual worlds to get a piece of the action. As one game company executive put it, "This is not a genre of game but a break-through new medium. It provides a completely new social, collaborative shared experience. We're basically in the Internet community business."[4]

Sony Online's EverQuest is among the most successful of the new breed of massively multiplayer online role-player games that allow people to live shadow lives. More than 430,000 registered players worldwide belong to "guilds" in a never-ending journey to slay monsters and earn points. EverQuest combines the stunning graphics of advanced gaming with the social scene of a chat room. As in The Sims, players create a character as a virtual alter ego, which may be a wise elf or a backstabbing rogue. Some players sell powerful characters on eBay for $1,000 or more.

The game is also the center of an active social scene. Players can travel around in groups of six. In many cases they settle into a regular group and spend two to three hours each night online with the same people. They may also mingle offline; Fan Faires attract several thousand people who often dress as their game characters. The average EverQuest subscriber spends about twenty hours a week living in this virtual world. Some view it as a possible addiction; EverCrack is a popular nickname for the game. One factor that makes it hard to kick the habit may be peer pressure because when a player logs off, this may hurt his guild's chances of advancing in the game.

These games are a key part of consumerspace because they are increasingly a new frontier for product placement strategies. As gaming goes mass market, the window is opening wide for a new form of hybrid community known as *advergaming*. This refers to the merging of interactive advertisements and product placement with online games that allow marketers to target specific demographic segments.

Companies are clamoring to have their products included in the action. Video games now feature real live brands such as Ford, Radio-Shack, General Motors, Toyota, Procter & Gamble, and Sony. Quiksilver, a clothing manufacturer for extreme-sport participants, puts its shirts and shorts into video games like Tony Hawk's Pro Skater 3. After its research showed that Hispanic kids are especially avid gamers, Procter & Gamble's 2001 Mission Refresh campaign for Head & Shoulders shampoo opened up a whole new market for the brand when it created an advergame specifically for Hispanic ports like Terra.com and YupiMSN.com. It's estimated that video game placements will generate $705 million a year by 2005.

Players spend an average of five to seven minutes on an advergame site, a clear advantage for advertisers over a thirty-second TV spot. Jupiter Media Metrix estimates that online advergaming revenue, including both traditional advertising and advertising within games (such as a Coke billboard displayed within a racing game), will reach $774 million by 2006, up from $134 million in 2002.[5]

Advergaming is a flexible, relatively inexpensive way to reach consumers where they live. Advergame developer Virtual Giveaway develops games of strategy to reach upscale educated users and action games for younger users. The firm places promotional messages for games depending upon the target. For example, about three-quarters of game players at the ESPN site are male, and 60 percent are under age 34, while the users at the Lycos Gamesville site are 60 percent female, and 65 percent are over the age of 35. Depending upon who is playing the game, even the way the game is won can be modified. Young males who are highly competitive and action-oriented are more likely to be exposed to games that allow a series of tiebreakers after a certain number of plays.

THE BOTTOM LINE

Advergaming, the use of product placement in computer games, is one of the new frontiers in online promotion. Games built around brands enhance realism and further reinforce the connection between brand images and social attributes.

Viral Marketing: Spread the Good Word

To promote its new Pocket Paks oral breath care strips, Listerine created a Germinator game on the brand's Web site. Players are encouraged to e-mail their scores to friends to goad them into playing also—presumably they learn about a new way to freshen their breath in the process. This is a typical form of *viral marketing*, a strategy that enlists consumers to promote a product or service by encouraging them to entice others to become involved in the promotion. For example, AllAdvantage.com pays you fifty cents an hour to surf the net, but you get a bonus of another ten cents an hour if you get friends to surf as well. And, if they in turn sign up still more friends, you get an extra five cents an hour. It's kind of like joining a virtual Amway.

Steven Jurvetson and his partners at the venture capital firm Draper Fisher Jurvetson coined the phrase *viral marketing* in 1997. They were describing how Hotmail's user base was growing exponentially because of a message it put at the bottom of every e-mail that let the receiver sign on to the free service. That strategy worked well for Hotmail; the company signed up five million subscribers in its first year.

According to the CEO of Gazooba, a viral marketing specialist, a viral marketing campaign can cost as little as $10,000. Since on average a person who likes the site recommends it to five or six friends, that's a pretty good investment. He noted that ". . . the return mail address of a friend is a brand that you trust."[6] According to a study by Jupiter Communications, only 24 percent of consumers say they learn about new Web sites in magazine or newspaper ads. Instead, they rely on friends and family for new site recommendations; so viral marketing is their main source of information about new sites.

Faux Buzz Communities

The now-famous *Blair Witch Project*, which led many viewers to believe the fictional treatment was in fact a real documentary, demonstrated the power of a brand that seems as if it's not one. Authenticity is key to the success of an online community. Pure buzz communities created by and for private consumers have this property, but some marketers are trying to borrow the veneer of buzz by going online with platforms that seem as if they are untouched by the corporate world. Buzz building has become the new mantra at many companies that recognize the power of underground word of mouth. Indeed, a bit of a cottage industry has sprung up as some firms begin to specialize in the corporate shill business by planting comments on Web sites made to look as if they originated from actual consumers.

Consider these recent forays into the shadowy world of faux buzz:

■ Building on the success of its resurrected Buddy Lee icon, Lee Apparel commissioned fifteen Web sites devoted to the diminutive doll that looked ". . . horrible, as if fans created them," according to an employee of the company that created the sites. The goal was to make it look as if people were spontaneously turning on to the Buddy Lee phenomenon.[7]

■ Dodge's Ram truck made a splash with a faux Web site and viral e-mail supposedly generated by fans to organize drag races in several cities. The e-mail featured amateurishly shot footage of a drag race and contained no reference to the Dodge connection, just a shot of the Ram's grille. Staged drag races were held where, of course, only Ram trucks emerged victorious. Videos of the wins were then posted to the Web site. Bogus letters were sent to editors of local newspapers protesting the rise in street racing and mentioning the Dodge Ram involvement. Supposedly the guerrilla campaign was so hush-hush even the top brass at the car company was kept in the dark.

■ When RCA records wanted to create a buzz around teen pop singer Christina Aguilera, they hired a team of young people to swarm the Web and chat about her on popular teen sites like alloy.com, bolt.com., and gurl.com. Posing as fans, they posted entries raving about her new material. Just before one of her albums debuted, RCA also hired a direct marketing company to e-mail electronic postcards filled with song snippets and biographical information to 50,000 Web addresses. The album quickly went to number one on the charts.

As powerful as these tactics are, they have the potential to poison the well in a big way. Web surfers, already skeptical about what they see and hear, may get to the point where they assume every "authentic" site they find is really a corporate front. Until then, however, buzz building online is going strong.

Just how effective is buzz building? Jupiter Media Metrix reports that 45 percent of online shoppers selected e-commerce Web sites based on word of mouth recommendations. However, only 7 percent of companies are able to identify individuals who share information via e-mail "passalongs." While this is still an inexact science, progress is being made toward measuring Internet buzz. One company called Opion (now a part of PlanetFeedback/Intelliseek), for example, identifies online opinion leaders and ranks the person's influence in a given subject area. Opion's system can rate the relative influence of celebrity Wall Street pundits, as well as those using pseudonyms on electronic bulletin boards devoted to stocks. The firm is already building buzz trackers for executives at three major studios to help them better understand the relationship among advertising, buzz, and box-office receipts.

Ratings and Rip-Offs

On the official *X-Files* homepage thex-files.com, fans debate the merits of each episode, but the show's groupies also critique and promote the most recent licensed *X-Files* merchandise. On newsgroup boards such as alt.tv.x-file they share pricing and quality hints and issue "rip-off alerts" about new products they deem offensive or inferior.

Anderson Consulting found that 62 percent of individuals who make purchases online stated that their purchase was attributable to customer reviews and recommendations. Reinforcing this finding, Forrester Research found that 30 percent of community users participate in this kind of forum because it facilitates their purchase decisions. Why are these peer-rating sites so popular?

Consumers don't trust "reliable sources" the way they used to. Professional reviewers are suspect—who knows which company may have bought them off? People are thirsting for input from "real" product users who don't have an ax to grind. Hybrid communities can also take the form of product ratings sites that let consumers chime in about their experiences with a myriad of products.

For example, a group of Silicon Valley venture capitalists started Epinions.com to provide a platform for product reviews. This service both rewards and rates product reviewers, in hopes of giving them enough incentive to provide useful opinions. Anyone can sign up to give advice on products that fit into the site's twelve categories, and shoppers can rate the reviews on a scale from not useful to very useful. To build credibility and eliminate suspicions that they are merely company shills advisers can build a page on the site with photos and personal information. Reviewers earn royalties of one to three dollars for every ten times their review is accessed, and their picture can be featured on the FrontPage if their reviews are widely read. According to one of the founders, the site relies on a "web of trust" in which viewers and advisers tend to be matched up over time with people whose opinions they have come to trust: "It mimics the way word of mouth works in the real world."[8] When a recommendation results in a sale, the company earns a referral fee from merchants.

More generally, many e-commerce vendors know that consumers give more weight to the opinions of real people, so they are finding ways to let these opinions be included on their Web sites. Amazon.com pioneered the trend of posting customer reviews way back in 1995. A great idea, but Amazon's tactics illustrate why many Web surfers retain a bit of cynicism about the authenticity of company-sponsored reviews. A high-visibility lawsuit accused Amazon of charging publishers to post positive reviews on the site. The company had to offer refunds for all books it recommended, and now Amazon tells customers when a publisher has paid for a prominent display on its site.

Are all opinions created equal? Unlikely—clearly the evaluations of some of us carry more weight. A study by Roper Starch Worldwide and Burson-Marsteller identified a group called *e-fluentials*. These persuasive folks number approximately eleven million people but influence the purchasing decisions of another 155 million American consumers both offline and online.[9]

According to Burson-Marsteller, in a recent year e-fluentials shared an estimated eighty-eight million opinions about companies and seventy-three million on products. They are asked for their advice three times more often than that of the average online users. They also share their views without being prompted; on average they notify seventeen individuals about negative company experiences and eleven others about positive encounters. Ninety-three percent tell individuals in person or on the phone about their experiences, and 87 percent e-mail their friends with the news. Men typically offer and seek advice concerning technology-related products, whereas women focus on health, beauty, and food-related products. E-fluential advice is usually well researched in that 85 percent of these consumers visit company Web sites, 62 percent online magazines, and 55 percent opinion Web sites, and a large majority double-check their information.[10]

Pure Buzz Communities
A homemade Web site created by two self-confessed "nerds" named Louis and Ish documented their quest for coolness—which for some

bizarre reason they decided would be found at a Wendy's restaurant. Perhaps deceased founder Dave Thomas is more like Elvis than many of us believed. Their search took on mystical qualities: "As though from the voice of God Himself, we realized our purpose: to visit every Wendy's we had knowledge of, limited only by our $5.50–$6 an hour jobs."[11]

Aside from the obvious fact that these guys really need to get out more, their pains to document their pilgrimages to fast-food heaven illustrate what marketers have known for many years: Consumer-generated word of mouth is far more powerful than paid advertising. That's why there is still no beating the appeal of a message that really is independent of corporate sponsorship—especially if it happens to be positive (we'll deal with those other pesky situations in Chapter 9).

Virtual Kingdoms

Some consumers have staked out their own personal claims in consumerspace by literally establishing their own virtual countries or kingdoms. These are a few sovereign territories:

■ Talossa.com: The King of Talossa lives with his father and sister near the University of Wisconsin—Milwaukee campus. At age 14 he proclaimed his bedroom a sovereign nation. The name of the country comes from a Finnish word meaning "inside the house." The roughly sixty citizens of Talossa boast a body of law, four political parties, an online journal, local holidays, and even a flag. They also have their own language and maintain a dictionary with 28,000 entries. The government meets monthly on the Web, and once a year citizens who live near Milwaukee gather in person for Talossafest. Becoming a citizen requires an investment: you are required to read one online book about the country and purchase at least two of the sixteen others for sale on the Web site. Candidates must pass a test on Talossan history, compose an essay titled "What Talossa Means to Me," and be approved by both parliamentary houses. This is for real: Some citizens spend more than twenty hours a week on the Web site, engaging in political discussions or posting gossip to a bulletin board.[12]

■ Freedonia.org: This micronation is a collective of libertarians based in Boston. Its monarch is a Babson College student who goes by the name of Prince John I. Members have minted their own line of currency, but for now the capital of the country is Prince John's house.

■ New-utopia.com: This micronation proposes to build a chain of islands in international waters and sells citizenship bonds over the Web for $1,500. The country's founder goes by the name of Prince Lazarus Long. Buyer beware: The prince does not have the best of diplomatic relations with the Securities Exchange Commission due to these sales.

The Corporate Paradox Redux

One of the most exciting aspects of the new digital world is that consumers can interact directly with other people who live around the block or around the world. *Consumer-to-consumer (C2C) e-commerce* refers to communications and purchases that occur among individuals without directly involving the manufacturer or retailer. Picture a small group of local collectors who meet once a month at a local diner to discuss their shared interests over coffee. Now multiply that group by thousands, and include people from all over the world who are united by a shared passion for sports memorabilia, Barbie dolls, Harley-Davidson motorcycles, or refrigerator magnets—all are participating in C2C e-commerce.[13]

Participants in pure buzz communities can feel free to praise, criticize, and guide to their hearts' content because these sites are genuine and unfettered with corporate trappings. These spaces are the incubators where genuine consumer opinion is born. That's what makes them such fertile ground for companies that want to get inside the heads of their customers. That's also what leads to the corporate paradox mentioned earlier: A consumption community's effectiveness increases the more removed it is from the locus of that consumption.

The challenge to marketers, of course, is to stay on top of what is being said without betraying the company's presence—in essence the company needs to turn itself into a "lurker" to learn as much as possible about its customers without interfering. One solution is to develop passive measurement systems that monitor activities in communities without revealing that comments are being tracked. For example, BrandPulse, an online buzz measurement tool, scours USENET groups, discussion forums, and other online sources for consumer-to-consumer communications about companies, products, competitors, and relevant issues.

THE BOTTOM LINE

Pure buzz communities are a rich source of information because they are the least scripted of all communities. It's a valuable exercise to monitor these environments, but as soon as a corporate presence reveals itself, the value of this information plummets. Marketers who can figure out how to walk this fine line will be amply rewarded with genuine insights regarding how consumers are thinking about and using their brands.

CHAPTER 7

The Disneyfication of Reality
Building Consumerspace Offline

Pilgrimages to sacred sites like Mecca, Lourdes, Bom Jesus da Lapa in Brazil, and now Ground Zero in Manhattan are a common occurrence. But don't forget to include Disney World on this list. Visits to the park are de rigueur for most families (and of course for NFL quarterbacks who proclaim their destination immediately upon winning the Super Bowl). For some devotees these trips take on religious overtones, much like the feelings expressed by the thousands who journey to Graceland each year ("Elvis has risen and was spotted at a Wendy's in Minneapolis . . .").

A Pilgrimage to Orlando

Consider the dedication of one George Reiger Jr., who has visited Disney World well over 200 times. He is an ex-cop who boasts 1,327 Disney tattoos, including an image of Walt himself. He turned down an offer by some Japanese businessmen to stuff his body after he dies and put it on display because he has stipulated in his will that he wants his ashes scattered in the water flowing through the Pirates of the Caribbean ride. Asked by an interviewer if he believes in God, Mr. Reiger pointed to the sky and said, "Yes. Mickey."[1] End of story.

Although the cost of a top-of-the-line admission ticket is higher, Disney World exhibits similarities to more traditional sacred places. Like Mecca, it's divided into two distinct domains. There is an outer, secular area and an inner, sacred one known as the Magic Kingdom. You initiate the experience by entering a parking lot where a mythological figure (Pluto, Goofy, etc.) guards your car. You hop on a monorail where you undergo what anthropologists call a *liminal experience* as you symbolically transition from the secular to the sacred area. A visitor to the external areas can smoke and eat, drink alcohol, and go barefoot—but these heathen behaviors are taboo once you board the monorail.

Upon entering the Kingdom, themed areas like Frontierland, Main Street U.S.A., and Tomorrowland remind you of traditional American values and juxtapose Walt's visions of the past, present, and future.[2] A similar experience awaits visitors to Disney Village at Euro Disney, which abounds in stereotypical images of the United States circa 1955. This sanitized version of America appears to feed Europeans' appetites for a wholesome, innocent country that never really existed, a sacred refuge against the real world.

Walt Disney recognized almost a half century ago that entertainment spaces could be transformed into consumerspaces that allow us to experience fantasy worlds—and to procure the souvenirs that prove we'd been there. The Disney Corporation boasts many talents, not least of which is a keen sense of synergy that lets it simultaneously merchandise many parts of its empire, from motion pictures to mouse ears. In this chapter, we'll look at some of the ways companies like Disney are engineering our physical environment to ensure that the places where we work and play are saturated by brands.

Themed Environments: Build It and They Will Shop

We expect to encounter "magical" happenings in Orlando, but fairy dust on the gritty streets of Manhattan? In consumerspace, many public venues like Times Square are evolving into theme parks that rival Disney's creations. They are essentially controlled environments that provide multiple forms of gratification—bread *and* circuses. These urban fantasylands include ambitious gentrification projects developed by the Rouse Corporation that are designed to lure people back downtown, such as New York's South Street Seaport, Boston's Fanueil Hall, and Baltimore's Harborplace. We find them in stores as well, where we can immerse ourselves in the commercial fantasy of Niketown or Sony Style —without having to spring for a pricey admission ticket.

Slowly but surely, shopping is blending with entertainment to emerge as a new form of activity some have termed *retailtainment*. Of course, this trend is not really a new development at all but actually a reincarnation of a very old one. Anthropologists tell us that the origins of the commercial marketplace lie in *festival marketplaces*. These entertainment zones traditionally sprang up on the borders of cities, where celebrations, exotic peoples, mysteries, and tricksters comingled.

We've moved from marketplaces to marketspaces, themed environments designed to stimulate our senses while motivating us to empty our wallets. These corporate-created fantasy worlds are a hallmark of consumerspace.[3] They are commercial venues based upon shared cultural meanings where design elements are carefully coordinated to produce an integrated consumer experience. Like Disney World, these meticulously controlled spaces often depict idealized versions of reality; the rough edges are smoothed out to deliver a seamless entertainment experience. As one architectural expert states, "Theming . . . is the largest and most notable trend in architecture today."[4] It is a trend that encompasses not only amusement parks such as Disney or Busch Gardens, but also casinos (like the Venetian in Las Vegas), hotels (Opryland in Nashville), shopping malls, airports, and museums.

While many consumers are able to identify themed environments as knockoffs of the "real thing," other consumers have a harder time delineating fact from fiction. As we saw way back in Chapter 1, hyperreality is the transformation of a simulation or hype into something that is taken by an audience as real. Consumers' experiences within these themed environments have become highly orchestrated, stylized, and even exaggerated to the extent that daily life has evolved into one in which fantasy and spectacle are accepted as normal. These environments are a sanitized version of the authentic, a world cleansed of strife, problems, and prejudices. Given the choice between going to Paris, France, and visiting the Paris Casino in Las Vegas, many of us seem to prefer the sanitized version (at least they speak English there like civilized people!).

For many, themed environments offer access to exotic places they would otherwise be unable to experience. As one Disney executive stated, "What we did is look at the world map, and ask where are the places people like to go for their vacation? And instead of them going there, we bring the place to them. We're telling the people, 'Look, you don't have to go to Wyoming to stay in a national lodge, you can come to Disney World.'"[5] A comment by one visitor to Epcot (certainly one of the bastions of hyperreality) captures this idea: "I don't need to go the South Pacific any more. I've already seen Tahiti in the Polynesian Village."[6]

The Store as Theme Park

In the old days, you had to journey to Anaheim or Orlando to embark on a fantasy experience. Now you can do it at your local mall by visiting a *themed store*, a hyperreal retail environment built around the mythos of a brand or company. Shops such as Niketown, the Everything Coca-Cola Store, the Lego Imagination Center, and the Sony Gallery of Consumer Electronics are basically lavish corporate advertisements fashioned from bricks and mortar. Manufacturers own them, and while they do sell merchandise, they are largely intended to build or perpetuate a brand image rather than to move product. To use the terminology introduced in Chapter 4, these concept stores aim to elicit a second-order response. They are about building long-term loyalty to a brand image rather than turning over inventory.

Some theme stores sell branded services rather than products and tend to have no brand history outside of the outlet itself. Examples include Planet Hollywood, the Hard Rock Cafe, the Rainforest Cafe,

Steven Spielberg's Dive! restaurants, and the (now-defunct) Fashion Cafe opened by supermodels. Still others, like the World of Coca Cola Museums in Las Vegas and Atlanta, build on an established brand to create an entertainment destination. At the General Mills Cereal Adventure, which recently opened at the Mall of America, children of all ages can cavort in the Cheerios Play Park and the Lucky Charms Magical Forest.

Themed flagship brand stores are an invaluable presence in consumerspace. They provide synergies by giving marketers a platform to broaden the impact of other brand-building activities. They let consumers experience the brand rather than just purchase it.

THE BOTTOM LINE

Concept stores like Niketown are invaluable outposts in consumerspace. They showcase a company's innovations and aim to build and maintain a corporate identity rather than simply sell products. These operations provide a way for consumers to physically experience the brand's mythos as it "comes to life" in a retail environment.

John Sherry and Robert Kozinets at Northwestern University have developed a typology that helps us to understand the practice and potential of retail theming. They identify four basic theme dimensions and speculate about opportunities to leverage these strategies even further:[7]

■ *Landscape themes* rely upon associations with images of nature, Earth, animals, and the physical body. Bass Pro Shops, for example, creates a simulated outdoor environment including pools stocked with fish. These analysts predict the appeal of "natural" environments will continue to grow, especially for urban dwellers. In addition, we may see increased interest in going "to the source" of the manufacturing process, which means breaking down the barriers between back-room and frontroom operations. Already, factory tours of such sites as the Crayola Factory, Hershey's Chocolate World, and Kellogg's Cereal City U.S.A. are popular tourist destinations. In a twist on this theme, Hershey opened a make-believe factory smack in the middle of Times Square. It appears to tower more than fifteen stories over Broadway and feature 4,000 "chasing" lights, four steam machines, 380 feet of neon lighting—plus a moving message board that can be programmed for consumers who want to flash messages to surprise their loved ones.

■ *Marketscape themes* build upon associations with man-made places. An example is the Venetian Hotel in Las Vegas, which lavishly re-creates parts of the Italian city. As we continue to move toward a global consumer culture, we see increased interest in experiencing local cultures (even as interpreted and sanitized in venues such as Epcot). Sherry and Kozinets note that the ESPN Zone store in Chicago mimics the architecture developed for other locations but customizes the content to emphasize Chicago sports teams. This model allows the store's management to maintain the identity of the brand across multiple venues by providing a construction template that can be tailored to local tastes.

■ *Cyberspace themes* are built around images of information and communications technology. They are often based on a virtual community (see Chapter 6). The retail interface developed by eBay instills a sense of community among its vendors and traders.

■ *Mindscape themes* draw upon abstract ideas and concepts, introspection, and fantasy and often possess spiritual overtones. The Kiva day spa in downtown Chicago offers health treatments based on a theme of Native American healing ceremonies and religious practices. Like Disney World, mindscape stores allow consumers access to the extraordinary where they can step outside of their normal routines and consume a sacred experience. Brands that will benefit most from this kind of theming will have (or create) a connection to self-improvement and spirituality. At the Seibu store in Tokyo, shoppers enter as neophytes at the first level. As they progress through the physical levels of the store, each is themed to connote increasing levels of consciousness until they emerge at the summit as completed shoppers.

The Ethnic Restaurant: Chowing Down on Culture

Although themed environments can take on a myriad of forms including hotels, casinos, and amusement parks, a more recent development is the proliferation of the themed restaurant. In these kinds of eating establishments, food is almost an afterthought. The real draw is the venue's entertainment value. The concept of "eatertainment" appeals to consumers who wish to expand their vistas beyond "meat and potatoes" by experiencing the flavors of other cultures—or at least a "safe" version of these gastronomical alternatives. For many consumers, these artificial qua real environments may literally constitute their sole contact with a foreign culture. Entering such a place offers the diner a sanitized version of the authentic.

One team of sociologists who have studied the topic in depth outline what they consider the main features of themed restaurants: 1) A uniting concept is taken from popular culture; 2) The concept is made apparent through the restaurant's interior and possibly the exterior. Modes of communicating include sound, decor, logos, menu terminology, uniforms, and merchandise; and 3) The food is only one aspect of the environment, often secondary to the ambience (as anyone who has tasted a burger at the Hard Rock Cafe can readily understand). Other distinguishing features include a standardized menu (not necessarily related to the theme), informal dining, locations close to metropolitan areas or well-traveled routes, and a theme that is easily understood by a majority of the clientele.

Consuming Authenticity

The Mom and Pop ethnic restaurant is yielding to large chains like the Olive Garden that slickly reproduce stereotypical decors as they feed the masses. Often the cuisine has melded so much into the host culture that authenticity is no longer a consideration. There is nothing remotely "Italian" conveyed in the decor of a Pizza Hut franchise. Perhaps this complete de-ethnicization of a foreign dish is appropriate since the type of pizza we are used to eating (along with many other "foreign foods" like chow mein) is an American invention to begin with!

Yet some consumers desire a more "authentic" eating experience. The claim to "authenticity" with regard to both the restaurants' environment and the food served is not only socially desirable but is also potentially a source of differentiation in a competitive business environment. However, this begs the question of just what is "authentic." This is not an objective, verifiable construct. Authenticity is rather a "locally constructed folk idea," a process of negotiation between the ethnic culture and host culture.[8] In other words, authenticity is in the eye of the beholder.

Frequently, a balance is struck between authenticity and practicality. Adaptations of the food, setting, and representations of the culture are presented to ensure that the consumers are experiencing an exotic experience, but not so much so that what they encounter violates their stereotypical expectations of that culture. For example, when cooks and owners of Chinese restaurants in the United States were asked in one study if it was possible to serve truly authentic food, they all responded negatively. Instead, they developed modified versions of ethnic dishes to offer consumers an "illusion of authenticity."[9] Hence the popularity of *faux* dishes like chow mein and the scarcity of snake entrees on Chinese menus in the United States.

In other cases the environment is blatantly fabricated, though only those in the know may be aware of inaccuracies. The Boomerock restaurant in Pasadena, California, for example, claims to be based upon Australian Aboriginal food and culture. The use of authentic tribal totem poles and heated granite cooking rocks, imported from Zimbabwe, may offer a unique dining experience but bears very little, if any, resemblance to the dining experience of Outback residents.

Ethnic restaurants signify their environments through the use of cultural symbols such as Japanese cherry blossoms, Italian red-and-white checked tablecloths, Chinese red lanterns, and Mexican cacti. These stereotypes are often reinforced by the use of costumes, such as the Italian waiter's black apron, the French chef's white hat, or the Japanese waitress's kimono. This "cultural shorthand" is almost universally recognized, at least among Western diners. But, these depictions have become clichés. Ironically, it seems that in many cases these design elements are more elaborate and more prevalent the farther one travels from the host culture. One is probably more likely to encounter a design prop like Chinese red lanterns in Baltimore than in Beijing.

Authentic, but Not Too Authentic

My colleagues and I have conducted several studies on ethnic restaurants and pubs to explore just how people experience "authenticity" in cuisine and ambience. In one study we gathered reactions of Australian and American consumers to the symbols (menu items, decor, etc.) used to connote Australian culture by the very popular Outback Steakhouse chain. This chain's Down Under formula has helped it to expand within a decade to 535 outlets in forty-six American states and ten foreign countries. The restaurants feature such "authentic" Aussie items as Walkabout Soup, Jackeroo Chops, Crocodile Dundee Steaks, Shrimp on the Barbie, Kookaburra Wings, and Wallaby Darned drinks.

We gave our respondents the opportunity to design their own versions of a restaurant that they felt would be more authentic than the Australian dining experience as interpreted by the company. Not surprisingly, our Aussie respondents took exception to the Outback's menu offerings. These reactions were typical:

- "The Outback Steakhouse is not a name I like. It is a bit corny! It conjures up an image that is from the past. I think Australians are a little more sophisticated these days." (Australian mother, 34)

- "I would choose a decor that represents the way we live, not something stuffed with kangaroos and koalas and that sort of tacky stuff. We're multicultural now. We're more adventurous. We expect variety." (Australian female, 18)

However, our American respondents thought that Outback did a good job of meshing with their ideas of what a "real" Australian eating establishment would and should be like. Indeed, when they were presented with a list of more authentic Aussie delights, they felt these were the imposters. Here's what one Yank suggested to make a menu more authentically Australian:

"The snail snacks, reptile toasters, and oxtail soup are not exactly what I would have selected. I would think of having shrimp, cheese fries, and definitely a bloomin' onion. . . . Under the beers I would add Fosters, Heineken, Samuel Adams, Bud Light, Budweiser, and Coors Light." Yes, there's nothing like quaffing a Budweiser to capture the true essence of the Land Down Under. . . .

In another study we examined stereotypes about "typical" Irish pubs, cornerstones of Irish community culture. We showed photographs of Irish pubs located in Ireland, Australia, and the United States to people in each of these three countries. Among other things, we asked them to guess the location of each pub. We often found that pubs not located in Ireland are seen as more authentic, especially by our non-Irish respondents! People seem to be more comfortable with the sanitized version than the real thing. That helps to explain the popularity of *faux* Irish pubs, a merchandising idea developed by Guinness PLC when it launched its Irish Pub Concept in an effort to spur the growth of bars serving its signature brew worldwide. Guinness prefabricates the pubs in Ireland, throws in some Irish recipes, and then exports them to markets in Singapore, Hong Kong, and elsewhere. The strategy of re-creating a sanitized version of "authenticity" does not seem to differ terribly much from the country pavilions we encounter at Epcot. Consumerspace is a hyperreal space, a themed zone engineered by marketers.

THE BOTTOM LINE

Restaurants and retailers are portals to foreign cultures. In many cases themed environments present idealized versions of these locales that may bear little resemblance to the actual location. Consumers crave authenticity—though they often prefer a marketer's version of it that is more consistent with their idealized expectations derived from mass media depictions of foreign cultures. As a rule, the less familiar people are with a culture, the more comfortable they will be with an idealized version of it that incorporates stereotypes they are expecting to see. We want the "real thing" but not if it's too real!

Reality Engineering

The village of Riverside, Georgia, has a colorful history. You can look at the sepia photographs depicting the town in the nineteenth century, or read excerpts from period novels lauding the settlement's cosmopolitan flair. You'll also discover that the town was used as a Union garrison during the War Between the States. There's only one hitch: Riverside didn't exist until 1998. The village is a clever fabrication created to promote a new housing and commercial development. The developer acknowledges the story ". . . is a figment of our imagination."[10]

As in the case of themed environments and ethnic fabrications, much of consumerspace is a figment of marketers' imaginations. Like Riverside, many of the environments in which we find ourselves, whether housing developments, shopping malls, sports stadiums, or theme parks, are largely composed of images and characters spawned by marketing campaigns.

Reality engineering occurs as elements of popular culture are appropriated by marketers and converted to vehicles for promotional strategies. These elements include sensory and spatial aspects of everyday existence, whether in the form of products appearing in movies, scents pumped into offices and stores, billboards, theme parks, video monitors attached to shopping carts, even faked "documenta-ries" like the *Blair Witch Project*. Reality engineering strategies di-vorce the consumer from his or her everyday reference points and dictate what is real and what is not. If you don't believe that, try find-ing a clock in a casino. The operators deliberately make it difficult to realize that it's getting to be time to cash in your chips.

How do reality engineers pull it off? One answer is that we've learned to believe what we see on TV, even as we are skeptical about the motives of the people who bring these images into our homes. We truly live in a mass-media(ted) reality. Historical analyses of Broadway plays, best-selling novels, and the lyrics of hit songs clearly show large increases in the use of real brand names over time. A novel by Fay Weldon called *The Bulgari Connection* deliberately showcases the Bulgari jewelry store in the first scene of the book.

Media images, whether of an actor drinking a can of Coke or driving a BMW, appear to significantly influence consumers' percep-tions of reality. These depictions affect viewers' notions about what the "real world" is like, including beliefs about dating behavior, racial stereotypes, and occupational status. Studies of the *cultivation hypoth-esis* focus upon the media's ability to distort consumers' perceptions of reality. They show that, among other effects, heavy television view-ers tend to overestimate how wealthy people are and the likelihood they will be victims of a violent crime.[11]

Consumerspace is very much about the blurring of boundaries. We no longer know what is "real" and what is contrived. And, it's not clear that we care. Perhaps what we want is to be part of the contrived, to blend in with the action we see on the tube. Just seeing your favorite logo on your favorite star not enough? Wait for the ad-vent of what some advertisers are calling "T-commerce." Right now you can go to the Web and buy an outfit you saw being worn on HBO's *Sex and the City*, but with "T-commerce" it will take a mere interactive click to literally buy a duplicate garment right off of Sarah Jessica Parker's back.

Advertising is out there, everywhere, and you may begin to doubt where it begins and ends. Indeed, a new campaign for the U.S. arm of Sony Ericsson Mobile Communications Ltd. blurs the boundaries even more. The company is sending teams of trained actors and actresses to tourist attractions such as the Empire State Building in New York and the Space Needle in Seattle. Posing as actual tourists, they will ask unsuspecting passersby to take their pictures—and in the process just happen to tout the benefits of the camera they're using. Another execution deploys female models to hang out in trendy lounges and bars with the goal of engaging strangers in conversation. As they're talking, the actress's phone will ring and the caller's picture will appear on the screen.

THE BOTTOM LINE

Marketers who are able to control sensory aspects of commercial environments act as reality engineers by manipulating our perceptions. Much of this activity occurs on the visual channel in the form of design elements such as color, texture, logos, and so on. However, reality engineering strategies can also be implemented using our other sensory channels. For example, odors pumped into a retail environment can alter our moods, as can the music playing in the background.

Guerrilla Marketing

The new school of "guerrilla marketing" is dedicated to making the contrived a reality. In the good old days of marketerspace, it was pretty easy to talk to customers. Fork over the money to create a snazzy TV commercial, air it on one of the three national networks, and wait for sales figures to climb. No longer. Network TV is a dinosaur. Major print outlets are losing circulation as specialized magazines proliferate. People are skeptical about ads they do happen to notice.

It's no longer about advertising; it's all about buzz (what we used to call positive word of mouth). That means creating events and giving away products in the real world, not just on TV—as when Kodak asked over 70,000 Super Bowl fans to join them in experiencing a simultaneous Kodak moment. How could they do this? Simple—give away disposable cameras to the crowd so everyone could take their own photos of the halftime show.

According to a report from consulting firm McKinsey & Co., 67 percent of U.S. consumer goods sales are now influenced by word of mouth. Creating a buzz calls for a lot more creativity than in the past. Reaching out to jaded, media-saturated consumers isn't such an easy job. That's why marketers are being challenged to be more and more resourceful. Don't use conventional military tactics that attack them straight on. Think like a guerrilla and ambush them before they have a chance to retaliate. *Guerrilla marketing* is hot—but what is it?

Broadly speaking, guerrilla tactics use unconventional marketing methods to gain conventional results, allowing smaller companies to compete with entrenched industry giants. Sometimes this simply translates into novel publicity stunts that get attention with minimal investment. Jay Levinson, one of the gurus of guerrilla marketing, observes that this can be as simple as putting a large number of small-denomination stamps on a direct mail piece instead of a single stamp, because people find it hard to ignore a letter plastered with stamps.[12] Evans Industries (a materials-handling supply company) got a lot of bang for its buck by buying $300 worth of California lottery tickets and sending them to distributors with a letter from the COO stating that if the lottery didn't make them rich, perhaps selling his products could.[13] The Kirshenbaum & Bond ad agency took their small client, Bamboo Lingerie, to the New York streets with a campaign of eye-catching stenciled sidewalk messages such as "From here it looks like you could use some new underwear."

Guerrilla marketing can take many forms, but most executions fall into one of three categories:

Attention-Getting Outdoor Advertising

■ Altoids, the makers of those curiously strong mints, hoped to raise curiosity along with sales in a 1999 advertising stunt that converted a New York tugboat into the image of a giant Altoids tin. Turning to the skies, Altoids placed a 1,000-square-foot banner on a building within view of the flight path for O'Hare International Airport in Chicago to draw the attention of a captive audience.

- Submedia, a New York–based advertising firm, is currently exploring a new venue for ad displays in the subway tunnels of some major cities. Riders along the Philadelphia line to Camden, New Jersey, experienced an ad for Coca-Cola's Dasani water that works like a zoetrope (a technology developed about 170 years ago). Riders on the train view what they perceive as an eye-catching cascading waterfall. The moving pictures are actually made of a series of panels seen through narrow slits; the illusion of movement is created when the viewer passes each at the appropriate rate of speed.

Teasers and Buzz Builders
- Lee jeans created a "phantom campaign" based on the retro hero Buddy Lee. The company quietly put up posters of the Buddy Lee doll in cities like New York and Los Angeles and waited for momentum to build before launching TV commercials that were shown during shows like *Dawson's Creek*.

- To promote its new Crest Whitestrips teeth-whitening product, Procter & Gamble mounted a billboard in Times Square with the come-on line: "September 20 find out why it's OK to wear white after Labor Day."

Street Teams and Stunts
- Days before VH1 put on its annual fashion awards show, models dressed as police officers fanned out on the streets of Los Angeles, New York, and Chicago to write up fashion citations. The term "fashion police" became a reality if only for a few days.

- A man dressed as a giant mosquito delivered baskets of cookies to the offices of trade publications. The goal of the stunt by the Discovery Channel was to generate favorable editorials for its new dot-com venture, Discovery.com.

- Amaretto di Saronno, marketer of the sweet liqueur Blucaos (pronounced "blue chaos"), entered the competitive shot market hoping to bring order(s) out of chaos. Blucaos Strike Teams descended on bars, blowing whistles and screaming for "caos!" The goal was to teach patrons to echo the cry to "order caos."

THE BOTTOM LINE

As it becomes more difficult to reach jaded consumers through conventional advertising media, many marketers are devising alternative ploys to grab people's attention. Guerrilla marketing tactics aim to surprise the consumer by putting commercial messages in places we don't expect. The most common ways to do this are eye-catching outdoor ads, teasers that stimulate word of mouth, and public relations stunts.

Product Placement: Brands *Are* the Story

You invest megabucks in a great commercial, but when it comes on, everyone leaves the room to take a "bio-break." Don't you hate when that happens? The future of conventional television advertising is cloudy at best because of this problem as well as others—such as the growing popularity of devices like TiVo that let us avoid seeing ads altogether.

Advertisers are now looking toward the technique of directly embedding their messages into the shows to address this big problem. Media vehicles like *Survivor* offer many opportunities to build products right into the story line. Real-life "actors" wearing clothing articles emblazoned with their makers' logos create "zap-proof" advertising. In some cases companies are choosing to produce their own programming in order to exert control over what people see. For example, Nike funded *Road to Paris,* a documentary about the U.S. cycling team in its training for the Tour de France. In return, Nike ads are aired continuously.

Product placement refers to the insertion of specific products and/or the use of brand names in movies and TV scripts. According to marketing lore, this practice took off after sales of Reese's Pieces jumped by 65 percent when the brand was eaten in the film *E.T.* The producers initially wanted to include the more familiar M&M candy product, but they were rebuffed. Presumably, the executive who decided to decline this offer is now seeking employment elsewhere.

Product placement has become commonplace, whether it involves Rosie O'Donnell eating a Wendy's salad during an episode of her talk show as part of an ad deal or (as we saw in Chapter 6) when characters in a video game wear Vans sneakers. We are no longer surprised to see actual brands in shows, though many people may not realize how new this practice really is.

Traditionally, networks demanded that brand names be "greeked" or changed before they could appear in a show, as when a Nokia cell phone was changed to Nokio on *Melrose Place.* No more. Still, to bypass Federal Communications Commission regulations requiring the disclosure of promotional deals, marketers typically don't pay for placements. Instead they pay product placement firms that work with set decorators looking for free props and realism. Product placement is so successful that even old shows are getting the treatment courtesy of digital technology—TBS is inserting virtual products in *Law & Order* reruns.

Some researchers claim that product placement can aid in consumer decision-making because the familiarity of these props creates a sense of cultural belonging while generating feelings of emotional security. For example, director Steven Spielberg deliberately featured brands such as Nokia, Lexus, Pepsi, Guinness, Reebok, and American Express to lend veracity to his futuristic movie *Minority Report.*

In some cases these placements even have the potential to create demand for a product that doesn't yet exist: A candy-apple red Swingline stapler played a prominent role in the dark comedy *Office Space*, a cult hit centered on the frustrations of corporate cubicle-dwellers. After the movie went into video, Swingline fielded a torrent of requests for the stapler. But, there was a small problem—the company didn't actually make the product in that color. A prop designer created it just for the shoot. People wanted the item so badly that a market developed on eBay for staplers spray-painted bright red. Three years later, Swingline caught on and came out with its "Rio Red" stapler. "Staple and be heard!" proclaims the Swingline Web site (swingline.com). "WHAM-cubicles! WHAM-dress code! WHAMWHAMWHAM!"

In the "old days" we saw Archie Bunker drink out of a red-and-white beer can that looked vaguely like a Budweiser. If *All in the Family* were being shot today, Archie would probably find his favorite easy chair draped in a Bud logo. While we have gotten used to seeing actors use real goods, product placement is moving to a new level as entire story lines are being written (or rewritten) to accommodate a sponsor. The WB network even named a reality series *No Boundaries* after a slogan for vehicles sold by the Ford Motor Company. When the product becomes the story, programming will never be the same:

■ Lincoln and NBC's *The Tonight Show* struck a deal that gives NBC Ford advertising valued at about $9 million. In return, Lincoln will build a concert stage adjacent to the soundstage used by Jay Leno's show. Music groups will perform on the stage and segments of those performances, dubbed "The Lincoln Garage Concert Series," will air each Friday as the musical feature of *The Tonight Show*. The new stage will hold a variety of Lincoln models, including the luxury Navigator SUV. Lincoln also would like to have the musical performers be driven onto the stage in Lincoln vehicles, or have Jay Leno, an avid car buff, mention the brand on air.

■ The TV show *Lost* was funded by a group of four clients: Coca-Cola, Johnson & Johnson, Lowe's, and Marriott International. In exchange, the clients took most of the ad time and featured their products on the air. Participants in the show drink Dasani water (Coca-Cola) and open survival kits that come in crates conveniently supplied by Lowe's.

■ NBC's *The Other Half* talk show has had representatives from advertisers like Clorox, Hyundai Motor America, and even Tan Towel, a "self-tanning towelette," appear on the show as part of the regular programming. During the Clorox-sponsored segment, for example, the hosts faced off against members of the studio audience in a make-believe game show about housekeeping.

THE BOTTOM LINE

Product placement is one of the most potent mechanisms for branding reality. In contrast to the recent past, actual brands appear regularly in TV shows, movies, and books—and increasingly the brands are integrated directly into the plot. This strategy is very effective, partly because it sidesteps consumers' skepticism about traditional advertising messages.

The ubiquity of brands in our everyday lives is hard to ignore. As we've seen, they pop up in movies, on TV, in novels. Many of us use our precious vacation time to pay homage to corporate entities like Mickey Mouse or to acquire merchandise from "exotic" places like the Hard Rock Cafe. This incessant exposure only seems to whet our appetite for more, more, more. That craving helps to make shopping a recreational activity, a sport, and, for some, a raison d'être. But, more on that in Chapter 8.

CHAPTER 8

I Buy, Therefore I Am
Shopping in Consumerspace

A job or an adventure? Shopping can be both. Some of us like to "shop 'til we drop" while others consider time spent in a mall as a particularly gruesome form of torture. Grin and bear it: In order to deploy products in our personal arsenal to express our identities, we first have to acquire them one way or another. The process of accumulating all this stuff is itself part and parcel of the consumption experience. Whether we do so gleefully or with great trepidation, that involves surrendering oneself to a shopping space (either physical or virtual). This chapter will focus on ways that marketers can design these spaces to lure consumers to them and make them happy they came.

The Thrill of the Hunt

We can distinguish generally between two reasons to shop: enjoyment (hedonic value) and accomplishment of a task (utilitarian value). This dichotomy applies to both bricks-and-mortar and cyber-shopping. For example, one study of 4,000 adult Internet users identified customer segments such as shopping lovers, fearful browsers, and shopping avoiders.

The diversity of shopping motives is illustrated by scale items researchers use to assess people's underlying reasons for shopping.

One item that measures hedonic value is "During the trip, I felt the excitement of the hunt." When that type of sentiment is compared with a more down-to-earth statement like "I accomplished just what I wanted to on this shopping trip," the contrast between these two dimensions is clear.[1]

Hedonic shopping motives can include the following:[2]

- *Social Experiences:* The shopping center or department store has replaced the traditional town square or county fair as a community gathering place. Many people (especially in suburban or rural areas) literally may have no place else to go to spend their leisure time.

- *Sharing of Common Interests:* Stores frequently offer specialized goods that allow people with mutual interests to communicate.

- *Interpersonal Attraction:* Shopping centers are prime places to people-watch. The shopping mall has become "hangout central" for teenagers. It also represents a controlled, secure environment for the elderly, and many malls now feature "mall walkers' clubs" for early-morning workouts.

- *Instant Status:* As every salesperson knows, some people savor the experience of being waited on, even though they may not necessarily buy anything. One men's clothing salesman offered this advice: "Remember their size, remember what you sold them last time. Make them feel important! If you can make people feel important, they are going to come back. Everybody likes to feel important!"[3]

- *The Thrill of the Hunt:* Some people pride themselves on their knowledge of the marketplace. They may relish the process of haggling and bargaining, viewing it as a sport with points measured in dollars shaved off the retail price.

Which way is it? Do people hate to shop or love it? It depends. Consumers can be segmented in terms of their *shopping orientation,* or general attitudes about shopping. These orientations may vary depending on the particular product categories and store types considered. A person may hate to shop for a car, but he may love to browse in clothing stores. And of course there are often strong gender differences. Industry experts claim what the rest of us know intuitively: Men and women tend to differ in their shopping styles. At least stereotypically, women are more likely to be recreational shoppers ("when the going gets tough, the tough go shopping"), and men tend to be task-oriented. All those resigned-looking men you see at the mall lounging on benches while their spouses do their thing certainly support that assertion.

For those who hate to shop, technological advances offer some hope in the form of automating many of our purchasing activities. Consider the prototype Barbie doll devised by Accenture. It is being billed as an *autonomous purchasing object*—a toy that shops for itself. Instead of silicon implants, this version has wireless chips embedded within it that let the doll communicate with other jacked-up dolls and accessories within range. This wired Barbie can scan the doll's clothing in a friend's closet and compare it with her wardrobe to see what's missing. She can send a purchase order to a home PC or buy straight from the manufacturer. The owner can limit Barbie's expense account, but otherwise she's on her own. In fact, the doll can be constantly shopping even though the owner might not know it. Accenture refers to the prototype as part of its "brave new world of silent commerce."

Welcome to the next step in the quest to simplify shoppers' lives: smart products that make decisions for us. In Singapore, cars "talk" to the streets they drive on. Now under development are frozen dinners that will automatically give cooking instructions to microwave ovens. Smart refrigerators monitor inventory and automatically submit replenish commands to the grocery store, which delivers the replacements on a regular schedule. In the future, we'll see cars and appliances that order their own replacement parts and schedule repairs and packaged foods that monitor their own inventory levels. Even our houses will be "smart." When roof tiles fall, they will send a message to a PC or PDA to e-mail the roofer ASAP.

Shop . . . and Bond

A futuristic vision of a world where all purchasing decisions are made automatically may be attractive to some cantankerous consumers, but it's hardly realistic. Like it or not, most of us spend a good portion of our waking lives shopping (and some of us dream about it as well). For many, this is about more than just acquiring things; it's a social experience. The reality is that if we really wanted to hibernate at home and not shop at all, that would be just about feasible—catalogs, delivery services, and the Web provide alternative means to obtain almost anything these days.

While many people obviously are taking advantage of these solutions to the "shop 'til you drop" syndrome, the malls aren't exactly empty yet. Shopping malls have tried to gain the loyalty of shoppers by appealing to their social motives as well as providing access to desired goods. The mall is often a focal point in a community. In the United States, 94 percent of adults visit a mall at least once a month. More than half of all retail purchases (excluding autos and gasoline) are made in a mall. In many cases these malls are evolving as entertainment centers that provide a (reasonably) pleasurable backdrop to permit shoppers to experience exotic new products, experiment with new identities, or just hang out with their friends in the food court.

For many, shopping truly is a social experience. It is a collaborative effort, an opportunity to get a "reality check" from significant others to validate one's taste in clothes, music, and home furnishings. It's also a way to share experiences and bond. Lands' End understands this aspect of shopping. As shown in Figure 8.1, its Web site provides a "Shop with a Friend" feature that lets two people browse together. Each can add items to a common shopping bag even though they may be physically separated by thousands of miles. This co-shopping ability is not prominently featured on Lands' End's site, but it should be. In some ways it's a revolutionary development, insofar as it brings us a step closer to simulating the actual shopping experience in an online environment.

It is in retailers' interests to encourage these joint shopping expeditions, offline or on. Some evidence suggests that people who shop

Figure 8.1: Lands' End "Shop with a Friend."

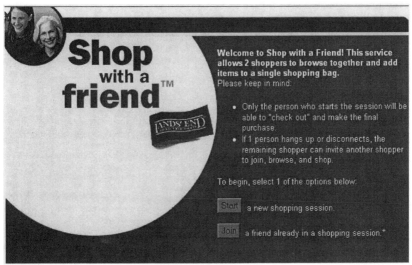

Welcome to Shop with a Friend! This service allows 2 shoppers to browse together and add items to a single shopping bag.
Please keep in mind:

- Only the person who starts the session will be able to "check out" and make the final purchase.
- If 1 person hangs up or disconnects, the remaining shopper can invite another shopper to join, browse, and shop.

To begin, select 1 of the options below:

Start a new shopping session.

Join a friend already in a shopping session.*

© 2002 Lands' End, Inc. Used with Permission.

with at least one other person tend to make more unplanned purchases, buy more, and cover more areas of a store than those who go it alone. Group members may be convinced to buy something to gain the approval of the others, or they may simply be exposed to more products and stores by pooling information with their associates. They say that shoppers often display a herd mentality, and it behooves the retailer to exert some control over where that herd chooses to graze.

THE BOTTOM LINE

We shop for many reasons, most of which are not task-related. Shopping often is a highly social process, and retailers that understand this have a competitive advantage. In particular, activities that facilitate group shopping (even online) should be encouraged.

Gift unto Others . . .

We know that we use many of the things we buy to make a statement about ourselves. However, the reality is that we also bestow material objects upon others that make important statements about our relationships and social connections. Indeed a healthy proportion of our shopping time is devoted to procuring goods for people other than ourselves.

Gifting is a richly symbolic act in just about every culture, and therefore not a buying decision to be taken lightly. In the typical gift-giving ritual, the giver procures the perfect object, meticulously removes the price tag, and carefully wraps it (symbolically changing the item from a commodity to a unique good), and delivers it to the recipient. Every culture prescribes certain occasions and ceremonies for giving gifts, whether for personal or professional reasons. The giving of birthday presents alone is a major undertaking. Each American on average buys about six birthday gifts a year—about one billion gifts in total. Business gifts are used strategically to define and nurture professional relationships, to the tune of more than $1.5 billion per year. These exchanges can be so crucial that a cottage industry of corporate gifting consultants now dispenses advice on just what kind of largesse one needs to make that perfect impression.

The importance of gifting rituals is especially clear during designated occasions in every culture like Christmas and weddings that mandate some transfer of assets among group members. Gifting is a potent medium of social communication, a way to measure one's worth against others. Often there are significant ramifications if the gift is inappropriate in some way (either too cheap or too lavish). Thorstein Veblen documented a classic example of strategic gifting when he was doing his seminal work on conspicuous consumption about a century ago. He was inspired by anthropological studies of the Kwakiutl Indians, who lived in the Pacific Northwest. At a ceremony called a *potlatch*, the host showed off his wealth by giving extravagant presents to his guests. The more he gave away, the better he looked to his tribesmen. Sometimes, the host would publicly destroy some of his property just to demonstrate how much he had.

And, because guests were expected to reciprocate, a poorer rival could be humiliated by inviting him to a lavish potlatch. The need to give away as much as the host, even though he could not afford it, would essentially force the hapless guest into bankruptcy. If the potlach sounds "primitive," think for a moment about many modern weddings. Parents commonly invest huge sums of money to throw a lavish party and compete with others for the distinction of giving their daughter the "best" or most extravagant wedding, even if they practically have to bankrupt themselves to do it.

One hundred years later, wedding gifts are as vexing a decision as ever. Gift registries help invitees navigate this ambiguous terrain by spelling out explicitly what will be considered an appropriate form of homage. Although registries have been around since the early 1930s, they used to be much more subtle. In the old days, for example, Macy's published a guide called "Hints on Hinting" to help brides plant gentle suggestions about what they would like to receive.

That kind of reticence is history, as the Web is transforming the age-old ritual of buying wedding gifts. Online registries encourage the new couple to be quite explicit about the resources they expect as they embark on their new life's journey. At weddingchannel.com, the lucky couple creates a personal wedding page where they post directions and pictures, plan toasts and seating arrangements, and tell stories about how they met. Guests pull up updated versions of a gift registry and purchase from retailers directly through the Web site.

The proliferation of these registries is understandable, since this business now takes in $19 billion a year. Revenues for Williams-Sonoma's registry alone were an estimated $120 million in 2001; the chain has registered more brides online than in all of its 200-plus physical stores combined. Think about the business potential: The average wedding party includes twelve people (including six who get stuck with those awful dresses) plus 150 guests. On average, the bride and groom register for more than fifty products and they receive an average of 171 wedding gifts. About half of the couples register at a place they have never shopped before, giving retailers a new customer base. According to the publisher of Bride's magazine, "If you can hook this consumer when she is in this life stage, you will fundamentally brand her for life."[4]

Wedding registries continue to evolve as our wish lists grow. Some couples have become so brazen that they request specific shares of stock (at Stockgift.com), contributions to fund an around-the-world trip, or even mortgage payments on that new dream house (available on a special registry maintained by the U.S. Department of Housing and Urban Development at hud.gov). At theknot.com the couple can even get their guests to subsidize their honeymoon airfare: They earn a frequent-flier mile for every dollar spent on them.

Of course, there are downsides to this new efficiency: Because the wedding couple specifies exactly what they want in advance, the giver doesn't really have to know very much about the recipients. Traditionally, part of the gifting ritual involves developing or reinforcing a symbolic relationship, but now the process is much more automated. As one etiquette expert disdainfully points out, in the old days (pre-Net) people were supposed to be "zealous with creativity" when selecting a gift. "Now, it's just gimme, gimme, gimme with a dollar amount attached." And in many cases the registry is listed on the invitation itself—a social no-no.[5]

The idea of sharing your specific material needs with friends and loved ones is expanding well beyond nuptials. Now a cottage industry of registries is springing up to enable consumers of all stripes to specify their desires online and sit back to wait for the products to roll in. These registries include:

- Twodaydreamers.com for doll collectors

- All Nations Stamp and Coin for philatelists and numismatists

- The Wishing Well for motorboat parts and supplies

- Clinique, Prescriptives, and Bobbi Brown for lipstick and cosmetics

- Restoration Hardware and Goodwood for furniture and home supplies

- SecretWish.com for teens who want to let their families know what they really want

- OfficeMax.com for back-to-school shoppers who need to know what teachers are requiring their students to have on the first day of class

THE BOTTOM LINE

Gifting is a pervasive activity, rich both in symbolism and economic potential. Consumers are becoming more brazen about specifying their wish lists. What once was an opportunity to affirm a special connection between two people is evolving into an online order fulfillment process. As this ritual changes, it brings many opportunities to develop other kinds of registries that will automate a wide range of gifting decisions.

The Dark Side of Shopping

Like those cargo cults discussed in Chapter 1 or the fanatic Disney fan mentioned in Chapter 7, we do in some sense worship products. If so, it's not that big a leap to proclaim that the shopping mall is the modern cathedral of consumption. For many of us, stores serve some of the same functions as churches: They let us get in touch with our inner selves, they provide sanctuary from the demons that bedevil us at home and at work, and they let us commune with others who share similar sensibilities. The more enthusiastic shoppers among us may even experience enlightenment and transcendence.

Sometimes, though, we can have too much of a good thing. The acquisition of objects is evolving into an obsession for many, where the need to purchase becomes pathological. *Consumer addiction* is a physiological and/or psychological dependency on products or services. While most people equate addiction with drugs, alcohol, or excessive overeating, virtually any product or service can be consumed to the point where reliance on it becomes extreme. There is even a Chap Stick Addicts support group with about 250 active members! Regardless of the object of the fixation, this form of addiction parallels the more familiar kinds. Generally, the gratification derived from the behavior is short-lived and the person experiences strong feelings of regret or guilt afterwards.

In some cases the expression "born to shop" is taken quite literally. People shop because they are compelled to do so, rather than because shopping is a pleasurable or functional task. *Compulsive consumption* refers to repetitive shopping, often excessive, as an antidote to tension, anxiety, depression, or boredom. *Shopaholics* turn to shopping much the way other addicts turn to drugs or alcohol. This compulsion is distinctly different from *impulse buying*. The sudden, spontaneous desire to buy a specific item is temporary, and it centers on a specific product at a particular moment. In contrast, compulsive buying is an enduring behavior where gratification is delivered by the process of buying, not by the items that happen to be bought. As one woman who spent $20,000 per year on clothing confessed, "I was possessed when I went into a store. I bought clothes that didn't fit, that I didn't like, and that I certainly didn't need."[6]

Fortunately, most of us like to fan the flames of capitalism, but we are not consumed by the fire. We are looking for stimulation, and the shopping mall often provides it. This reminds us why it's strategically crucial for retailers to create environments that enable us to act on these needs. As we'll see, that's why the physical elements of consumerspace are so crucial.

Retail Atmospherics: Build It and They Will Come

At Sony's Metreon entertainment center in San Francisco, a bank of movie theaters shows Sony films, while gleaming shops display cutting-edge cameras, computers, and video equipment that are hard to find elsewhere. Shoppers can take a break from browsing through this technology fantasyland by playing state-of-the-art computer games to their hearts' content on massive floor-to-ceiling screens. Sony gets it.

The physical layout and design of a retail environment helps to create an emotional experience, whether good or bad. That's why store designers pay a lot of attention to *atmospherics*, or the "conscious designing of space and its various dimensions to evoke certain effects in buyers."[7] These dimensions include colors, scents, and sounds. A store's atmosphere in turn affects purchasing behavior. According to one study, the emotional state experienced by a shopper five minutes after entering a store predicted both the amount of time and money he or she spent there.[8]

Many design elements can be cleverly (and often quite subtly) controlled to manipulate shoppers' perceptions. Light colors impart a feeling of spaciousness and serenity, bright colors create excitement. Designer Norma Kamali replaced fluorescent lights with pink ones in department store dressing rooms. The light had the effect of flattering the face and banishing wrinkles, making female customers more willing to try on (and buy) the company's bathing suits.

Many fast-food restaurants emphasize the color orange, which supposedly is energizing. Stores done in red tend to make people tense, whereas a blue decor imparts a calmer feeling. In fact, American Express chose to name its new card "Blue" after research showed the color evokes positive feelings about the future. Its advertising agency named blue "the color of the new millennium" because people associate it with sky and water, "providing a sense of limitlessness and peace."[9] In contrast, the color black evokes hostile feelings. Teams in both the National Football League and the National Hockey League that wear black uniforms are among the most aggressive; they consistently rank near the top of their leagues in penalties during the season.

THE BOTTOM LINE

Design elements play a crucial role in creating "store personality." Colors, textures, lighting, and other components can be subtly manipulated to alter shoppers' perceptions. In some cases these environmental cues may actually influence energy levels and interest in purchasing.

The Do-It-Yourself Mall

How can mall developers be sure that they will build the kind of mall that will attract consumerspace cruisers? In addition to "retailtainment" strategies discussed in Chapter 7, an important attribute of an attractive mall is the variety of stores a shopper will encounter there. Research supports the assertion that consumers' decisions about where to shop are influenced by the mix of stores available at a mall. Indeed, one study found that tenant variety was the strongest predictor of excitement in the mall shopping experience.[10]

If the tenant mix is a significant determinant of mall patronage, consumers' preferences for specific retailer types and stores should be a paramount goal in mall design and promotion. In reality, however, shoppers themselves do not participate in designing shopping centers. Chapter 5 made the case for integrating the voice of the consumer in new product development. The same argument applies here. Shopper feedback can potentially play a significant role in guiding a host of strategic decisions, including specifying the ideal mix of stores in a mall, the recreational and culinary options available, and even the center's physical decor and atmospherics.

As we saw in Chapter 5, involving actual consumers in this way reflects a trend in other industries toward *user-centered design*. The idea is to incorporate your current knowledge of users in the early stages of design, confront users repeatedly with early prototypes, and redesign as often as necessary. This ensures that customer requirements actually do guide the development process—and that mistakes can be avoided before it's too late.

CASE STUDY

My colleagues and I conducted a pilot project funded by the International Council of Shopping Centers.[11] The goal was to provide a way for shoppers to tell us what stores they would want to see if they got to choose the layout. We developed an online methodology to let consumers configure their ideal mall. A schematic was presented of a basic cross-shaped mall configuration consisting of four axs, each bounded by an anchor store with a food court in the middle. This layout provides for four retail stores in each of the four quadrants of the virtual mall as shown in Figure 8.2.

Respondents were asked to designate the type of store they would like to see at each of these sixteen locations. When the respondent clicked on each of the squares, a pull-down menu appeared with a list of fifteen store categories such as accessories, housewares, toys, women's fashions, etc. At this point he or she selected the desired store

Figure 8.2: The empty virtual mall.

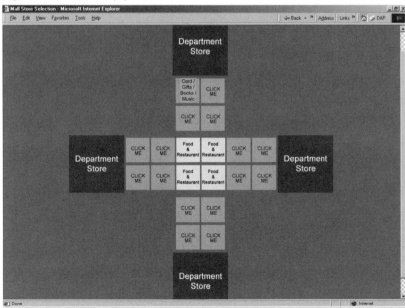

Courtesy of Mind/Share, Inc. (www.mind-share.net).

category with a click of the mouse. After choosing the type of store that should occupy a certain space, the respondent then selected a specific retailer within that category. Choices were made for all categories, including department stores (e.g., Sears, Nordstrom) and restaurants/ food outlets (e.g., Starbucks, Applebee's). A new screen then appeared that contained the actual logos of all the stores selected, so the "designer" could see his or her finished product.

This pilot project showed that respondents do indeed have strong preferences for certain types of stores and for specific retailers within each category. Furthermore, they expect certain types of stores to be placed in specific locations within the mall. For example, they told us that they would like to see stores selling accessories adjacent to anchor (department) stores, while entertainment-oriented stores (e.g., movie and tape retailers) are preferred closer to the food court and farther away from the anchor stores.

THE BOTTOM LINE

We talk about brand personality and sometimes even store personality. However, shopping malls also have personalities that are determined by their physical design and amenities as well as the particular variety of tenants they offer. Consumers should be enlisted as codesigners who provide input on the optimal mix of retailers and other services they would like to encounter when they visit a mall. This feedback is easily obtained by designing an online application that lets shoppers configure their ideal mall.

Scentual Marketing

Using colors strategically is intriguing, but atmospherics is about more than clever lighting. Indeed, many situational cues that we cannot even see influence our behavior in consumerspace, sometimes in subtle ways. Some retailers, for example, have figured out that they can create a desired effect by manipulating odors in the environment. That's why realtors advise us to bake a loaf of bread just prior to showing a house and also why some bakeries direct their exhaust fans out onto the sidewalk to lure passersby. One study even found that pumping stimulating odors into a Las Vegas casino increased the amount of money patrons fed into slot machines![12]

Aromachology is the field of olfactory research that investigates the psychological effects of fragrance. Japan is a leader in fragrance technology, and it is common there to find scents being pumped into office buildings, hospitals, and subways with the intent of either arousing or soothing people who pass through these areas.[13]

Some of our responses to scents result from early associations that call up good or bad feelings, and that explains why businesses are exploring connections among smell, memory, and mood. Researchers for Folgers found that for many people the smell of coffee summons up childhood memories of Mom cooking breakfast, so the aroma reminds them of home. The company turned this insight into a commercial where a young man in a military uniform arrives home early one morning. He goes to the kitchen, opens a Folgers package, and the aroma wafts upstairs. His mother opens her eyes, smiles, and exclaims, "He's home!"

Fragrance is processed by the *limbic system*, the most primitive part of the brain and the place where immediate emotions are experienced. This is where deep-seated connections are made, and some of these primordial linkages are both robust and surprising—one study even found that the scent of fresh cinnamon buns induced sexual arousal in a sample of male students![14] Many new scents are turning up in unexpected places to stimulate these feelings. Dirt cologne smells like potting soil and is one of sixty-two "single note" natural scents produced by Demeter Fragrances. Others include Carrot, Celery, and

Cucumber, and single note fragrances in development include Gasoline and Sweat. You can't get much more primordial than that.

Scented marketing (now a $90 million business) is taking interesting turns. One new wrinkle in the use of scents: fragrant clothes. The textile industry is developing new-age fabrics with "scentual" properties by embedding fragrances in microcapsules sewn into clothing. A French lingerie company is selling lingerie that emits scents when touched. Korean men are even buying lavender-scented suits to cover up liquor and cigarette odors. The capsules "pop" when jostled, so the more the man moves the better he smells—until the capsules wear out, at least.

The Sound of Muzak

Behavior in the shopping/consuming environment also is influenced by the sounds that surround us. Take background music, for example. Patrons of country-and-western bars drink more when the jukebox music is slower. According to a researcher, "Hard drinkers prefer listening to slower paced, wailing, lonesome, self-pitying music. . . ."[15] Similarly, music can affect eating habits. Another study found that diners who listened to loud, fast music ate more food. In contrast, those who listened to Mozart or Brahms ate less and ate more slowly. The researchers concluded that diners who choose soothing music at mealtimes can increase weight loss by at least five pounds a month![16]

The Muzak Corporation estimates that 80 million people hear its recordings every day. This so-called "functional music" is played in stores, shopping malls, and offices to either relax or stimulate consumers. Research shows that workers tend to slow down during midmorning and midafternoon, so Muzak uses a system it calls "stimulus progression" that increases the tempo during those slack times. Muzak has been linked to reductions in absenteeism among factory workers, and the company claims that even the milk and egg output of cows and chickens increases when the right soundtrack is pumped into the barn.

Shop the Store, Buy the Soundtrack

The recognition that a store, hotel, or restaurant's audio environment can be a key driver of its personality has created a new niche. Numerous companies including W Hotels, the Gap, Structure, Au Bon Pain, Starbucks, and Lane Bryant now are selling their own musical collections so that customers can re-create the store's vibes at home. While companies have long known that ambient music affects shoppers—from subliminally discouraging theft to putting people in the mood to buy—only recently did they think to package background music as a product itself. The soundtracks are a newly discovered source of free advertising that even provides a modest profit.

Victoria's Secret led the way when it released a disc of classical music in 1998. Sales managers had only to slip the disc into the store player, and soon women were snapping up bras, panties, and Beethoven. The first two volumes of the store's compilation discs, called *Classics by Request*, went double platinum, meaning they sold more than two million copies. To date, the store has sold fifteen million CDs. Similar releases include RCA Victor's *Classical Music for Home Improvements* and Sony's *Cyber Classics*, billed as music specifically for computer hackers to listen to while they program!

POP Goes the Shopper

Retailers' manipulations of sight, sound, and smell attest to the power of the immediate environment to shape our behaviors. A truly stimulating space can overpower us with the desire to be part of it, to buy into the dream. Scintillating displays of alluring clothing, chic home furnishings, and mouth-watering gourmet foods tempt us at every turn. There's a reason why many stores invest so heavily in fanciful window displays.

But even a more prosaic trip to pick up a gallon of milk can turn into a buying adventure. Researchers estimate that about two out of every three supermarket purchases are decided in the aisles. The proportion of unplanned purchases is even higher for some product categories. Roughly 85 percent of candy and gum, almost 70 percent of cosmetics, and 75 percent of oral hygiene purchases are un-planned.[17] For retailers, the moment of truth often is at the *point-of-purchase* (POP).

To cater to these urges, impulse items such as candy and gum are conveniently placed near the checkout. Similarly, many supermarkets have installed wider aisles to encourage browsing, and the widest tend to contain products with the highest profit margins. Low markup items that are purchased regularly tend to be stacked high in narrower aisles, to allow shopping carts to speed through. Some retailers have now added a high-tech tool to their arsenal in order to encourage impulse buying. The Portable Shopper is a personal scanning gun that allows customers to ring up their own purchases as they shop. The gun was initially developed for Albert Heijn, the Netherlands' largest grocery chain, to move customers through the store more quickly. It's now in use in over 150 groceries worldwide.

The prevalence of impulse purchases reminds us of the need to engineer the buying environment so that the appropriate drivers are operative at the time the shopper is actually deciding what to pur-chase. Each year, U.S. companies spend more than $13 billion on POP materials in the form of store displays ranging from simple shelf talkers to elaborate, interactive sideshows intended to entertain and arouse. These expenditures are increasing, often to the detriment of conventional advertising. Firms are slowly but steadily shifting their promotional allocations to reflect the reality that we often don't pro-cess brand information until we need it at the time of purchase.

How effective are these in-store communications? One study found that store displays boost purchases by a hefty 10 percent.[18] When Cotton Inc.'s *Lifestyle Monitor* asked women aged 16 to 70 where they get their clothing ideas, store displays were a leading influence, second only to clothing that they already owned and liked. Seventy-two percent of women cited the impact of displays on their decisions, which represents a 9.3 percentage point gain over the same period in 2000. Frito Lay, Procter & Gamble, and Anheuser-Busch sponsored an ambitious five-year study of 250 supermarkets in twenty-two cities that covered ninety-four brands in eight categories.

The results also demonstrated a dramatic increase in sales when POP (point-of-purchase) materials were used.

In an in-store promotion for Mountain Dew, a lifesize figure of a mountain biker who looks as if he had dropped through the ceiling was suspended above convenience store cash registers. That's bound to get your attention. A point-of-purchase stimulus can be an elaborate product display or demonstration, a coupon-dispensing machine, or even someone giving out free samples of a new cookie in the grocery aisle. An impactful display will entertain as it graphically demonstrates the product's capabilities. Some dramatic POP displays include:[19]

- *Timex:* A ticking watch sits in the bottom of a filled aquarium.

- *Kellogg's Corn Flakes:* A button with a picture of Cornelius the Rooster is placed within the reach of children near the cereal. When a child presses the button, he hears the rooster cock-a-doodle-doo.

- *Elizabeth Arden:* The company introduced "Elizabeth," a computer and video makeover system that allows customers to test out their images with different shades of makeup, without having to actually apply the products first.

- *Trifari:* This company offered paper punch-out versions of its jewelry so that customers could "try on" the pieces at home.

- *Charmin:* Building on the familiar "Please don't squeeze the Charmin" theme, the company deployed its Charmin Squeeze Squad. Employees hid behind stacks of the toilet tissue and jumped out and blew horns at any "squeezers" they caught in the aisles.

- *The Farnam Company:* As somber music plays in the background, a huge plastic rat draped in a black shroud lies next to a tombstone to promote the company's Just One Bite rat poison.

Participatory Shopping: The Mall as Amusement Park

For the shopper whose need for stimulation just isn't satisfied after
being accosted by obnoxious toilet paper snoopers, there are plenty
of other alternatives lurking out there. Shopping complexes are becoming giant entertainment centers, almost to the point where their
traditional retail occupants seem like an afterthought. As one retailing
executive put it, "Malls are becoming the new mini-amusement
parks."[20] Indeed, several large malls literally do incorporate amusement parks under their roofs. For example, the mammoth Mall of
America's seventy-eight acres of retail attractions include a theme
park named Camp Snoopy, complete with log flume. But you don't
have to build a roller coaster to provide shoppers with thrills and chills:

- Walk into REI, a Seattle-based store that sells gear for climbing,
  cycling, skiing, and camping. REI is more than an outdoor
  goods merchant, however. The store features a 65-foot-high,
  artificial climbing rock, a vented area for testing camp stoves,
  and an outdoor trail for checking out mountain bikes. Buying a
  water pump? Test it in an indoor river. Eyeing that new Gore-
  Tex jacket? See how it holds up in a simulated rainstorm.

- Vans Inc., a Los Angeles–based sporting goods retailer, opened
  a 60,000-square-foot skate park and off-road bicycle track at
  the Ontario Mills Mall.

- Bass Pro Shops, a chain of outdoor sports equipment stores,
  feature giant aquariums, waterfalls, trout ponds, archery and
  rifle ranges, putting greens, and free classes on topics from ice
  fishing to conservation.[21]

Retailers who are willing to explore innovative ways to build interactivity in to an otherwise humdrum purchasing environment can
achieve a participatory shopping experience. Creative merchants
have the ability to ramp up customer involvement in many ways,
whether they are working with bricks or clicks.

Participatory Shopping: Bricks

Customers at Ed Debevic's diners in Los Angeles and Chicago get more than a cheeseburger for their money. They enter an "authentic" 1950s-era diner and engage in spirited give-and-take with gum-popping, big-haired waitresses. Similarly, patrons of Jekyll and Hyde in Manhattan become involved in a theatrical performance. Creepy characters roam the building to entertain diners (really, audience members), and animated wall hangings pipe up without warning to deliver some dire prediction of death and dismemberment (in case the lunch entrees haven't already accomplished that objective).

We saw in Chapter 7 that the act of dining out is becoming a theatrical event. Restaurant operators like Lettuce Entertain You, the innovative parent company of Ed Debevic's, understand that diners want to participate in the experience rather than just eat a meal. Unfortunately, most conventional retailers have been slower to satisfy shoppers' desires for stimulating experiences. People want to interact with products, not just pull them off a shelf and have them wrapped to go. A few merchants have figured this out:

- MARS: The Musician's Planet, a giant music supplies shop, allows aspiring Eric Claptons to try out a guitar or even record a demo tape. Spontaneous jam sessions have been known to break out in the store without warning.

- At the Color Me Mine store in Santa Monica, California, customers sit at tables and paint their own pottery, which they have selected from dozens of different shapes.

- Cosmetics shoppers at Lush do more than buy a tube of lipstick. The retailer (which got started by supplying the Body Shop and is rapidly expanding in Europe) encourages consumer interaction. Women pick their poison from bins of self-serve skin-care and cosmetics products, most of which are sold by weight and with little packaging.

Participatory Shopping: Clicks

The desire to be part of the action extends to the online aspects of consumerspace as well. Despite the gloom-and-doom proclamations sounding the death knell for e-commerce, many of us are hanging in there. While total retail sales grew by only 2.8 percent in 2001, on-line retail sales spiked by 21 percent to $51.3. billion.[22]

Lingering fears about security and privacy notwithstanding, shop-ping on the Internet offers several compelling advantages. In addition to convenience and privacy, there is also the potential for instant grati-fication (even if you have to wait to have your purchases delivered). The immediacy of the Web (sit at 3:00 A.M. in your pajamas, point and click) has yet to be fully exploited. Down the road we can expect to see even greater connections between the "virtual social worlds" we discover with our browsers and the things we choose to buy for ourselves.

We can see hints of these linkages by looking at what a few inno-vative retailers, including F.A.O. Schwarz and the Canal Jean Com-pany, are doing to yoke their Web sites to their bricks-and-mortar operations. They are installing "voyeur-cams" to beam real-time im-ages from their stores over the Internet. Web surfers can virtually browse the actual inventory (and satisfy their voyeuristic urges by checking out the shoppers who are actually cruising the aisles). Lands' End customers can even check themselves out in cyberspace with "My Virtual Model," software that stores a scanned body image to create a 3-D model of the shopper. After having her body digitally mapped in a scanning booth, a customer can virtually "try on" clothing online.

THE BOTTOM LINE

Shoppers want to immerse themselves in participatory experi-ences, not just static collections of products stacked on shelves. In both bricks and clicks contexts, retailers need to build in oppor-tunities for greater involvement in the shopping experience.

Despite these scattered innovations, continued growth in the online space is hardly assured. Just as in the offline retailing world, e-commerce merchants need to find new ways to make the more mundane shopping experience enjoyable and easy. They have a way to go: One survey of 10,000 Internet customers of leading U.S. firms found that only 36 percent of the respondents were satisfied with their online interactions.[23]

It shouldn't have to be this way, but as with bricks-and-mortar stores, design is key. Many e-tailers continue to put up confusing Web sites that are a turnoff to frustrated Web surfers. By one estimate, 65 percent of online shoppers empty their carts before they complete their purchase due to confusion and the inaccessibility of customer service representatives to help with the process. That's serious—30 percent of Web visitors who have problems with a Web site while they're trying to shop say they won't shop there again, and another 10 percent say the experience was so aversive they won't continue to shop online at all.[24]

Talk about poisoning the well. On the other hand, this neglect of the online shopping experience opens the door to savvy e-merchants who understand that even people who are shopping from home often are looking for a little social stimulation and a lot of convenience. For now though, there's plenty of angst to go around in consumerspace. Will we just lie there and take it? As we'll see in Chapter 9, not necessarily.

CHAPTER 9

Trouble in Paradise
Culture Jamming in Consumerspace

A British musician who performs under the name Radio Boy pulverizes clothing, fast-food wrappers, and other residue from corporations to protest the evils of global consumerism. The first track on his album *The Mechanics of Destruction* is called "McDonald's." He created the song by electronically altering the noises made by thumping a hamburger bun, slurping a drink through a straw, and rustling a Golden Arches bag.

Vox Populi

This artist's anticorporate angst is hardly music to the ears of the business community. Online or off, many consumers are venting about the downside of materialism, corporate greed, the transgressions of specific companies, even about each other. These complaints can take the form of amateurish Web sites or graffiti scrawled on billboards. Unfortunately, they can also occur as highly sophisticated mass boycotts, cyberterrorism, or deadly product tampering.

Companies cannot ignore these protests, much as they might like to. The Disney Corporation discovered how effective these movements could be when the Southern Baptist Convention voted to persuade all its members to boycott its operations. This edict included all of the Disney Company theme parks, ABC Television, Disney Studios, ESPN,

Dimension Films, Miramax Films, and Disney's Go.com Web site. The anti-Mickey rebellion was instituted because of the "Gay Days" held at the theme parks and a view that Disney had a radical homosexual agenda that it promoted through its broadcasts. Soon other organizations joined the cause, including the American Family Association, the General Council of the Assemblies of God, Congregational Holiness Church, the Catholic League for Religious and Civil Rights, and the Free Will Baptists. The fallout from the boycott was significant, resulting in a layoff of 4,000 employees. One year after the boycott, Disney theme parks saw business drop by 8 percent from the previous year's corresponding quarter, and ABC Television and Disney Studios also announced cuts because releases failed to achieve expected profits. You can't please everybody all of the time, but mass actions like this can really make a dent in the bottom line.

America™: Culture Jamming and Brand Bashing

"Absolut Impotence." So reads a parody ad created by Adbusters, a nonprofit organization that advocates for ". . . the new social activist movement of the information age." The editor of the group's magazine argues that America is no longer a country, but rather a multitrillion-dollar brand subverted by corporate agendas. He claims that America™ is no different from McDonald's, Marlboro, or General Motors. Adbusters sponsors numerous initiatives, including Buy Nothing Day and TV Turnoff Week, intended to discourage rampant commercialism. These efforts, along with biting ads and commercials that lampoon advertising messages, are part and parcel of a strategy called *culture jamming* that aims to disrupt efforts by the corporate world to dominate our cultural landscape. The movement believes ". . . culture jamming . . . will change the way information flows, the way institutions wield power, the way TV stations are run, the way the food, fashion, automobile, sports, music, and culture industries set their agendas. Above all, it will change the way meaning is produced in our society."[1] The *Culture Jammers Manifesto* proclaims opposition to the "mind-polluters": "On the rubble of the old culture, we will build a new one with non-commercial heart and soul."[2]

While some in Corporate America may dismiss these extreme sentiments as the ravings of a lunatic fringe, they deserve to be taken seriously. Indeed, the recent peccadilloes by such corporate icons as Enron, Arthur Andersen, WorldCom, and Merrill Lynch have fueled a growing bonfire of mistrust and skepticism among the consuming public. Time will tell if this disillusionment will die down or continue to grow as new scandals continue to come to light. Clearly, dramatic steps are needed to restore public confidence as the business page of the newspaper starts to read like the crime blotter.

Negative WOM

Whether directed against customers, employers, or entire corporations, satirical messages created by activist organizations and even disapproving comments posted by customers can be quite damaging. Consumers weight negative word of mouth far more heavily than they do positive comments about a product or service. According to a study by the White House Office of Consumer Affairs, 90 percent of unhappy customers will not do business with a company again. Each of these people is likely to share their grievance with at least nine other people, and 13 percent of these disgruntled customers will go on to tell more than thirty people of their negative experience. That's how an avalanche begins.

Many dissatisfied customers and disgruntled former employees have been inspired to create their own Web sites just to share their tales of woe with others. For example, a Web site for people to complain about the Dunkin' Donuts chain got to be so popular the company bought it in order to control the bad press it was getting. A customer initially created the site to express his outrage over the fact that he was unable to get skim milk for his coffee. Indeed, the Web is bulging with sites set up by individuals for the sole purpose of expressing their displeasure with a company. A typical one is a hate site dedicated to the IKEA furniture store chain, complete with photos and commentary, that can be found at www.charlise.com/ikea.

THE BOTTOM LINE

A dissatisfied customer can inflict more damage on a company than a satisfied customer can help it. Negative word of mouth needs to be carefully addressed. A company can monitor customers' complaints at sites like Planetfeedback.com and ewatch.com that provide ongoing feedback to subscribers, or it can do this on its own. What it cannot do is ignore the problem. Complaints do not go away; they fester and multiply unless nipped in the bud.

Protest Sites

For a brief period a few years ago, visitors to Nike's home page found themselves taken instead to an alternative Web site put up by the S11 Alliance. This Australian group figured out how to divert browsers to its site in order to protest Nike's employment practices. As a media lawyer observed, "The person who, twenty years ago, was confined to walking up and down outside Chase Bank with a placard can now publish to millions of people with the click of a button."[3] Indeed, a single individual can do a lot of damage in cyberspace. One famous hacker who went by the nom de guerre of Pimpshiz hacked into more than 200 Web sites to insert a message supporting Napster before he was finally arrested.

The Web is a very efficient staging ground for mass demonstrations. Political activists protesting corporate policies are able to mobilize large numbers of consumers by touting their causes online. Some Web sites, like fightback.com, maintained by consumer activist David Horowitz, focus on a range of consumerism issues, while others, like mcspotlight.org, chronicle the ostensible misdeeds of a specific company like McDonald's. Indeed, while their life spans are often brief, at any point in time there are a surprising number of Web pages out there devoted to trashing specific companies, such as walmartsucks .com, chasebanksucks.com, and starbucked.com.

A portal site called protest.net serves as a clearinghouse for many of these movements. It offers access to an *Activists Handbook* and a calendar of upcoming protests organized by geographic region as well as by such issues as globalization and imperialism, animal rights, and the environment. While many of the focal points for citizens' anger are political in nature, a myriad of protests are directed against corporate policies ranging from child labor to unethical accounting practices. Although arguably the level of consumer involvement in antibusiness causes has diminished since the 1960s, clearly many of us are mad as hell and aren't going to take it anymore. A few examples of coordinated consumer protest movements are:

■ The Truth (sponsored by the American Legacy Foundation) was established in 1998 with significant funding from tobacco companies as part of settlements in lawsuits filed by numerous attorneys general around the country. The Truth's mission ". . . is to alert everyone to the lies and hidden practices of the cigarette companies, while giving people the tools to have a voice in changing that." This project develops marketing communications directed to adolescents and other at-risk populations to disseminate information about nicotine addiction, how tobacco products are advertised, and what these products do to the body.

■ Save the Redwoods/Boycott the Gap (SRBG) is an organization that specifically targets the Gap chain and its founders, the Fisher family. The group protests such policies as clear-cutting the redwood forests in Mendocino, California, and the alleged use of sweatshop labor on the island of Saipan, which produces some of the store's clothing. In one highly visible demonstration staged in several cities called "We'd Rather Wear Nothing Than Wear Gap!" activists stripped naked to call for the protection of redwood forests and workers' rights. Another organization called BehindTheLabel.org pushes the cause against the Gap by using a listserv to recruit protesters.

■ The Pittsburgh Coalition Against Pornography (PCAP) claims that the clothing company Abercrombie and Fitch produces pornographic advertising targeted to thirteen- to seventeen-year-olds. Many of the cited advertisements depict barely dressed youthful models promoting the latest adolescent styles. PCAP claims to have 12,000 people on its mailing list. The organization has designed its Web site to encourage a boycott of Abercrombie products. One section is entitled: "Take Action: Five Steps You Can Take to Ditch Fitch!"

The Rumor Mill

A clever online ad campaign for Lipton Tea at puppetsagainstbrisk. com features a mock "protest" by puppets that ostensibly were fired as product endorsers for the drink mix. Hopefully it's obvious that this ". . . pledge in the name of all good Puppets to solemnly kick Brisk butt!" is a fake (if not, we have a bridge to sell you).

There is a long and honored tradition of people inventing fake stories to see who will swallow them—like the one in 1824 where a man convinced 300 New Yorkers to sign up for a construction project. He claimed all the new building in the lower part of Manhattan (what is now the Wall Street area) was making the island bottom-heavy. As a result it needed to be sawed off and towed out to sea or all of New York City would tip over.[4] Since then, rumors have bedeviled companies like McDonald's (worms instead of beef in its burgers), Bazooka (spiders' eggs in bubble gum) and Procter & Gamble (its man-in-the-moon corporate logo is a sign of devil worship).

The Web compounds the problem because it is a perfect medium for spreading rumors and pranks. Many modern-day hoaxes surface in the form of e-mail chain letters promising instant riches if you pass the message on to ten friends. Here's a great one for professors: In a scam called "Win Tenure Fast," academics were told to add their names to a document and then cite it in their own research papers.

The idea is that everyone who gets the letter cites the professor's name and with so many citations you're guaranteed to get tenure! If only it were that easy. . . .

Other hoaxes involve major corporations. A popular scam promised that if you tried Microsoft products, you would win a free trip to Disneyland. Nike received several hundred pairs of old sneakers a day after the rumor spread that you would get a free pair of new shoes in exchange for your old, smelly ones (pity the delivery people who had to cart these packages to the company!).

Procter & Gamble got over 10,000 irate calls after a rumor began spreading in online newsgroups that its Febreze fabric softener kills dogs. In a preemptive strike, the company registered numerous Web site names like febrezekillspet.com, febrezesucks.com, and ihateprocterandgamble.com to be sure they weren't used by angry consumers. P&G now addresses questions about rumors on the FAQ section of its Web site. Other Web sites also are dedicated to tracking hoaxes and scams, including http://www.nonprofit.net/hoax/, http://scambusters.org, and http://www.hoaxkill.com. The moral: Don't believe everything you click on.

THE BOTTOM LINE

Rumors and hoaxes can be amusing, but they can cause real damage when taken seriously. The threat is compounded in the online space, where messages can be sent to thousands of people effortlessly and where it is difficult to assess their credibility. At the least, these stories need to be monitored. In some cases companies like P&G and Dunkin' Donuts have fought rumors more aggressively by buying out rumor-based Web sites or preemptively purchasing domain names that might be used to impugn them.

The Customer Is Never Right

Consumers are not the only ones who are angry. Many employees have an ax to grind as well. At a Web site put up by a disgruntled former employee of a certain fast-food franchise, we share the pain of this ex-burger flipper: "I have seen the creatures that live at the bottom of the dumpster. I have seen the rat by the soda machine. I have seen dead frogs in the fresh salad lettuce."[5] Fries with that?

A Web site called customerssuck.com gets 1,200 hits a day. This is a forum for restaurant and store workers who have to grin and bear it all day. Once off the clock, they can share their frustrations about the idiocy, slovenliness, and insensitivity of their customers. Some contributors to the Web site share stupid questions their customers ask, such as "How much is a 99-cent cheeseburger?" while others complain about working conditions and having to be nice to not-so-nice people. The slogan of the site is "the customer is never right."

In other cases employees are doing more than fantasizing about retaliation:

- A woman sued a car dealer in Iowa, claiming that a salesperson persuaded her to climb into the trunk of a Chrysler Concorde to check out its spaciousness. He then slammed the trunk shut and bounced the car several times, apparently to the delight of his coworkers. This bizarre act apparently came about because the manager offered a prize of $100 to the salesperson who could get a customer to climb in.[6]

- A Detroit couple filed a $100 million lawsuit against McDonald's, alleging three McDonald's employees beat them after they tried to return a watery milkshake.

- In Alabama a McDonald's employee was arrested on second-degree assault charges after stabbing a customer in the forehead with a ballpoint pen. The victim's attorney observed, "There was a great deal of profanity coming out of the employee prior to the stabbing." [7]

Anticonsumption: Power to the People

Some types of destructive consumer behavior can be thought of as *anticonsumption*, where products and services are deliberately defaced, mutilated, or used to embarrass others. Some of these actions are relatively harmless, as when a person goes online at dogdoo.com to send a bag of dog manure to a lucky recipient. This site even lets customers calibrate the size of the "gift" by choosing among three "Poo Poo Packages": Econo-Poop (20 lb. dog), Poo Poo Special (50 lb. dog) and the ultimate in payback, the Poo Poo Grande (110 lb. dog). The moral: Smell your packages before opening.

Anticonsumption includes practical jokes like poo poo grams and graffiti on buildings, subways, and roads, but it can also take the form of more organized efforts to make a political statement. The Institute for Applied Autonomy promotes "cultural insurrection" by providing detailed instructions on how to build a "contestational robot." This is an automated graffiti writer consisting of a rack of spray cans mounted on the rear of a remote-controlled vehicle. A human operator navigates the vehicle into the target area. At the flip of a switch, the vehicle rolls along the ground while the row of spray cans prints a protest message, much the way a dot-matrix printer operates.

In some cases these acts are a form of *cultural resistance*; consumers who are alienated from mainstream society single out objects that represent the values of the larger group and modify them as an act of rebellion or self-expression. In the hippie culture of the 1960s and 1970s, for example, many antiwar protesters began wearing cast-off military apparel, often replacing insignias of rank with peace signs and other symbols of "revolution." Other acts of anticonsumption include the creation of parody products to make a point. Mattel sued MCA Records over a song that labeled Barbie a "blond bimbo girl." The company also took an artist to court for creating a line of dolls including Exorcist Barbie, Tonya Harding Barbie, and Drag Queen Barbie.

Other forms of "expressive litigation" are more banal; some people have figured out that they can benefit from lawsuits against companies like McDonald's that have the temerity to serve hot coffee that can spill on sensitive places. Consumer chutzpah is rampant; a case in point is the woman who sued Celebrity Cruise Line for more than $2 million in damages because she got hit in the head with a Coco Loco drink that was dropped by a passenger on a deck above her. She claims the line should have known that passengers would try to balance their drinks on the ship's railings![8]

The Dark Side of Consumers

While people often have good reason to vent their anger at corporate practices, it seems there's ample blame to go around. A survey conducted by the McCann-Erickson advertising agency revealed the following tidbits:

- Ninety-one percent of people say they lie regularly. One in three fibs about their weight, one in four about their income, and 21 percent lie about their age. Nine percent even lie about their natural hair color.

- Four out of ten Americans have tried to pad an insurance bill to cover the deductible.

- Nineteen percent say they've snuck into a theater to avoid paying admission.

- More than three out of five people say they've taken credit for making something from scratch when they have done no such thing. According to one executive, this ". . . behavior is so prevalent that we've named a category after it—speed scratch."

A retail theft is committed every five seconds. *Shrinkage* is the industry term for inventory and cash losses from shoplifting and employee theft. This is a massive problem for businesses that is passed on to consumers in the form of higher prices (though in fairness, about 40 percent of the losses can be attributed to employees rather than shoppers). Shopping malls spend $6 million annually on security, and a family of four spends about $300 extra per year because of mark-ups to cover shrinkage. Indeed, shoplifting is America's fastest-growing crime. A comprehensive retail study found that shoplifting is a year-round problem that costs U.S. retailers $9 billion annually. The most frequently stolen items are tobacco products, athletic shoes, logo and brand-name apparel, designer jeans, and undergarments. The average theft amount per incident is $58.43, up from $20.36 in a 1995 survey.[9]

The large majority of shoplifting is not done by professional thieves or by people who genuinely need the stolen items. About two million Americans are charged with shoplifting each year, but it's esti-mated that for every arrest, eighteen unreported incidents occur. About three-quarters of those charged are middle- or high-income peo-ple (including celebrities like Bess Myerson and Winona Ryder) who shoplift for the thrill of it or as a substitute for affection.

Consumer Terrorism

The events of 2001 were a wake-up call to the free-enterprise system. They revealed the vulnerability of nonmilitary targets and reminded us that disruptions of our financial, electronic, and supply networks can potentially be more damaging to our way of life than the fallout from a conventional battlefield. These incursions may be deliberate or not—economic shockwaves of mad cow disease in Europe (and now spreading to Japan and elsewhere) are still reverberating in the beef industry. Assessments by the Rand Corporation and other analysts point to the susceptibility of the nation's food supply as a potential target of bioterrorism.

Consumer Terrorism Offline

Even prior to the anthrax scares of 2001, pernicious substances placed in products threatened to hold the marketplace hostage. This tactic first drew public attention in the United States in 1982, when seven people died after taking Tylenol pills laced with cyanide. A decade later Pepsi weathered its own crisis when more than fifty reports of syringes found in Diet Pepsi cans surfaced in twenty-three states. In that case Pepsi pulled off a PR coup de grâce by convincing the public that the syringes could not have been introduced during the manufacturing process. The company even showed an in-store surveillance video that caught a customer slipping a syringe into a Diet Pepsi can while the cashier's head was turned. Pepsi's aggressive actions underscore the importance of responding to such a crisis head-on and quickly.

Although these incidents abated in the 1990s, obviously current concerns about bioterrorism have revived the prospect of tampering as a political act. Indeed, in the spring of 2002 drug manufacturer Eli Lilly issued a warning that tampering had been discovered in a few bottles of the psychiatric drug Zyprexa.

THE BOTTOM LINE

Product tampering is a form of bioterrorism that can cause great harm and potentially cripple a company. Although every case is unique, the history of companies' varied responses to tampering indicates that a prompt, forthright admission of the problem is far superior to an attempt to cover it up or reduce its perceived severity.

Consumer Terrorism Online

Periodic outbreaks of computer viruses such as Nimda or Code Red are potent reminders of our vulnerability when we surf the Web. There is even a school for computer hackers in Paris called the Hackademy that (ostensibly) teaches computer enthusiasts how to protect themselves from being hacked.

The consulting firm Computer Economics reports that virus attacks worldwide cost businesses over $13 billion in 2001. Data collected on *cyberattacks* show that companies in the energy industry suffer attacks at twice the rate of other industries. And many of those attacks appear to be sponsored by governments or organizations in the Middle East.[10]

Online terrorists have other weapons in their arsenal as well. Sophisticated hackers can gain access to company databases and even manipulate transactional data. For example, hackers who engage in *e-shoplifting* change price information in online shopping carts. A perpetrator might, for example, put $100 worth of items into his cart and then save the Web page to a local hard drive. The hacker then modifies the price to $10 and resubmits the page.

As we continue to migrate more aspects of our lives onto the Web, these forms of consumer terrorism will not go away. One increasingly popular partial solution: If you can't beat 'em, join 'em. Though they may not broadcast it, many companies are hiring so-called ethical hackers to check their IT security. By putting a computer thief on its payroll, a business can identify weaknesses in its network and learn how its systems can be penetrated.

The Value of Me: Who Owns Our Minds, Our Bodies—and Our Data?

In the digital world of consumerspace, identity is an ephemeral concept. You can change who you are on a whim. The downside is that other people can pretend to be you—and spend your hard-earned money. *Identity theft* is a growing problem—even the former chairman of the Joint Chiefs of Staff had his identity stolen. It's estimated that 400,000 to 500,000 people a year lose control of their social security number and other personal information to criminals who use this information to secure credit in their names. The Federal Trade Commission's toll-free number for consumers who believe they have been a victim of identity fraud (877-idtheft) receives an average of 400 calls a week.

Sophisticated hackers are only part of the problem. The Information Age enhances the ability of large organizations to intervene in our daily lives. Indeed, one of the negative aspects of marketerspace is the potential (real or perceived) of commercial conglomerates to exert control over what we see—and to determine who else sees private details about who we are.

Concerns about privacy are growing, though in the wake of the September 11 attacks we are witnessing a willingness to sacrifice some anonymity. Polls taken since that time indicate that a large majority of Americans favor wider use of facial-recognition systems and want closer monitoring of banking and credit-card transactions. A majority even support the creation of a national ID card, which until 9/11 had been anathema to most Americans.

Many high-tech surveillance tools that were deemed too intrusive before September 11, including the FBI's "Carnivore" Internet eavesdropping system, are being unleashed. Cameras equipped with facial-recognition software can pick out known criminals in a crowd at airports, stadiums, and other public areas. Cars and cell phones equipped with location technology make it possible to track down people to within about ten feet. Meanwhile, sophisticated X-ray machines that can see through people's clothes may be more widely deployed at airports, government buildings, and even in corporate lobbies.

Subliminal Subversion

Concerns about brainwashing began to surface during the Cold War following reports of American POWs in North Korea being persuaded to switch sides. These fears spread to include the insidious actions of corporations wanting consumers to do their bidding. If the Commies could do it, why not Procter & Gamble? Social scientists like fabled "motivation researcher" Ernest Dichter adapted psychoanalytic techniques to plumb the inner recesses of consumers' minds—and libidos—in the service of corporations (resulting in many classic advertising appeals such as "Put a tiger in your tank"). Paranoia about mind control led many to believe that advertisers had figured out a way to influence us even when we didn't know they were trying.

Spurred on by "exposés" such as Wilson Bryan Key's *Subliminal Seduction*, we started to look carefully at advertising—even scrutinizing pictures of ice cubes to discern the airbrushed messages that might be lurking within. *Embeds* are tiny figures that are inserted into magazine advertising by using high-speed photography or airbrushing. These hidden figures, usually of a sexual nature, supposedly exert strong but unconscious influences on innocent readers.

The public has been captivated by the notion of *subliminal perception* for over forty years, despite the fact that there is virtually no proof that visual or verbal messages presented below the level of conscious awareness have any effect on consumer behavior. A survey of American consumers found that almost two-thirds believe in the existence of subliminal advertising, and over one-half are convinced that this technique can get them to buy things they do not really want!

The Disney Corporation is one of the most recent victims of concerns about subliminal messages. In 1999 the company recalled 3.4 million copies of its animated video *The Rescuers* because the film included a very brief image of a topless woman (she appeared in 2 frames of a 110,000-frame film, each for one-thirtieth of a second). This picture was embedded as a prank in the master negative way back in 1977, but "the naked truth" surfaced only recently.

Disney has been combating rumors of subliminal images in its films for years, and this issue was one of the reasons given for the aforementioned boycott of the company's products by the Southern Baptist Convention. CEO Michael Eisner had to rebut charges on the TV show *60 Minutes* that the clergyman in *The Little Mermaid* is shown with an erection. He argued, "Everybody knows it's his knee. It's just people spending too much time looking for things that aren't there."[11]

In fact, most examples of subliminal perception that have been "discovered" are not subliminal at all—to the contrary these images are quite visible. By definition, if you can see it or hear it, it is not subliminal, because the stimulus is above the level of conscious awareness! Nonetheless, the continuing controversy about subliminal persuasion has been important in shaping the public's beliefs about advertising and marketers' ability to manipulate consumers against their will.

Many consumers are also fascinated by the possible effects of messages hidden on sound recordings. An attempt to capitalize on subliminal auditory perception techniques is found in the growing market for self-help cassettes. These tapes, which typically feature the sound of waves crashing or some other natural sound, supposedly contain subliminal messages to help the listener stop smoking, lose weight, or gain confidence. Despite the rapid growth of this market, there is little evidence that subliminal stimuli transmitted on the auditory channel can bring about desired changes in behavior.

Along with the interest in hidden self-help messages on recordings, some consumers have become concerned about rumors of satanic messages recorded backward on rock music selections. The popular press has devoted much attention to such stories, and state legislatures have considered bills requiring warning labels about these messages. These backward messages do indeed appear on some albums, including Led Zeppelin's classic song "Stairway to Heaven," which contains the lyric ". . . there's still time to change." When played in reverse, this phrase sounds like "so here's to my sweet Satan."

The novelty of such reversals might help to sell records, but the "evil" messages within have no effect. Humans simply don't have a speech perception mechanism operating at an unconscious level that is capable of decoding a reversed signal. On the other hand, subtle acoustic messages such as "I am honest. I won't steal. Stealing is dishonest" are broadcast in more than 1,000 stores in the United States to prevent shoplifting, and these do appear to have some effect. Unlike subliminal perception, though, these messages are played at a (barely) audible level, using a technique known as *threshold messaging*. Some evidence indicates, however, that these messages are effective only on individuals who are predisposed to suggestion. For example, someone who might be thinking about taking something on a dare but who feels guilty about it might be deterred, but these soft words will not sway a professional thief.

Whose Hand Is in the "Cookie" Jar?
A Web site called disgruntledhousewife.com features a "Dick List." Women share with thousands of others no-holds-barred, detailed sto-

ries about the inadequate sexual performance of former lovers. In 1999 a Florida-based company named Applied Digital Solutions was awarded a patent for an identity-verification and remote-monitoring system it calls Digital Angel. The system consists of an implantable transceiver to track and recover humans. Power for the remote-activated receiver is generated electromechanically through the movement of body muscle. The device is small enough to be implanted in a child.

None of Your Business

So much for privacy in consumerspace. Scott McNealy, CEO of Sun Microsystems, said in 1999: "You already have zero privacy—get over it." However, many consumers don't agree with this sentiment: A study of 10,000 Web users found that 84 percent object to reselling of information about their online activity to other companies. One of the highest profile cases is that of DoubleClick Inc., a company that places "cookies" in your computer to let you receive targeted ads. The trouble began when Double Click bought Abacus Direct, a ninety-million-name database, and began compiling profiles linking the two sets of data so clients would know who was receiving what kind of ads.[12]

DoubleClick's ability to track what you choose to buy and where you choose to surf is just one isolated example, though. Many companies can trace choices you make online and link them to other information about you. For example, when you register online for a product, a *Globally Unique Identity* (*GUID*) is linked to your name and e-mail address. Every time you log on to a Web site with a banner ad, a "cookie" is placed on your hard drive that includes a unique identifying number. As you cruise to other sites, more cookies are stored with that number. This allows the advertiser to create a log of all the sites you've visited and the times you've done so. To get a glimpse into this tracking process, log on to the site www.privacy.net and run a simple analysis of your Web connection. You'll see a laundry list of information about your computer and the route you took to the Web.

Many are not happy at the prospect they are leaving an electronic trail behind. A poll conducted by the National Consumers League found that consumers are more worried about personal privacy than health care, education, crime, and taxes. People are particularly concerned that businesses or individuals will target their children. Nearly 70 percent of consumers worry about keeping their information private, but according to a Jupiter Media Metrix survey, only 40 percent read privacy policies posted on business Web sites. This may be because these statements are laden in legalese, however—only 30 percent of consumers who do take the time to read them say they are understandable. Businesses and legislators do appear to be responding to these concerns. The Online Personal Privacy Act of 2002 became the first such proposal to pass out of the Senate Commerce Committee and is slated for a full Senate vote. The Act requires that consumers be able to review their nonsensitive data that would be provided to other parties. It also offers legal remedies for consumers who could sue up to $500 per violation for the misuse of sensitive data.

Many commercial Web sites are already reducing the amount of personal data they collect. A survey conducted for the Progress and Freedom Foundation showed that while a very large majority of popular Web sites still collect data, 84 percent of the sites surveyed reported that they collect less of it than they did two years ago. The study found a much broader use of privacy policies that are more prominently displayed and determined that more detail is being provided about how companies collect and use consumer names, addresses, and other personal information. A larger proportion of policies also give individuals a chance to decide ahead of time whether to share their personal details.

Sorry, Not Interested . . .
This positive attitude is a good sign since it's getting much harder to win the trust and cooperation companies rely upon when they go to consumers to collect marketing intelligence. In the good old days of marketerspace, many of us would happily respond to market surveys gratis—even if it meant being interrupted at dinner. Today, the market-

ing research industry is struggling to boost anemic response rates. The teleservices industry (they don't like to be called telemarketers) has helped to erode consumers' willingness to participate in phone surveys—and some have poisoned the well for legitimate researchers by hiding their pitches behind an illusion of conducting a fact-finding study.

Mail surveys aren't faring much better. Especially since the anthrax scares of 2001, many people are reluctant to open mail from sources they don't recognize. On average, Americans receive 500 pieces of junk mail a year, but according to PlanetFeedback, an online consumer feedback site tracking post–September 11 trends, 25 percent of consumers said they no longer open junk mail because of the threat of anthrax. In an article on privacy issues in the *Atlantic Monthly*, Toby Lester notes that the quest for increased privacy is creating a myriad of business opportunities. Sales of personal paper shredders are up. Personal bodyguards are in demand. Anonymous Web-browsing and e-mailing services are available from companies with names like Anonymizer, Hushmail, IDcide, PrivacyX, and ZipLip. An outfit called Disappearing developed an e-mail system that allows users to send messages that permanently unwrite themselves after a previously specified amount of time.[13] Zero-Knowledge Systems of Montreal sells a software package called Freedom that includes five digital pseudonyms to assign to different identities.[14] Venture capitalists refer to this business domain as the *privacy space.*

In recounting the history of the privacy movement, Lester observes that in 1967 legal scholar Alan Westin began to argue for the establishment of a zone of privacy that would protect individuals, their words and deeds, and information about themselves. Westin has conducted public surveys about attitudes toward privacy, and based upon this work, he divides the population into three categories. About one-quarter of us, he claims, are "privacy fundamentalists" who are deeply concerned about privacy rights and reject any consumer benefits that require the release of data about ourselves. In contrast the "privacy unconcerned" (about 12 percent of the population) are people who don't worry at all about the issue.

Then there are the rest of us, the "privacy pragmatists." This segment is willing to give up its privacy when necessary, but it is concerned about the secondary use of information that was originally divulged for another purpose. Lester notes that this broad middle category represents a big business opportunity. These consumers will be receptive to new arrangements that allow them to selectively share their personal information with companies—for a price.

In a *Harvard Business Review* article, John Hagel and Jeffrey Rayport broached the idea of an *infomediary* who would broker consumer information to interested companies.[15] Their basic premise was that consumers would come to realize their personal information has market value, and they will try to take ownership of it by retaining companies that will bargain with vendors on their behalf. As a Novell executive observed, "Slowly but surely consumers are going to realize that their profile is valuable. For loaning out their identity, they're going to expect something in return."[16]

Start-up companies including Persona, Privada, and Lumeria have embraced this idea and are gearing up to enter a brand new market. The head of Lumeria explained in the *Atlantic Monthly* interview with Toby Lester that a customer would store personal data in a SuperProfile. The more specific the information stored (about such things as age, sex, family status, sexual orientation, income level, assets, consumer preferences, and current shopping interests), the more valuable that profile will become to advertisers, and (presumably) the more they will pay to access the profile. Ideally, everyone wins. The consumer agrees to make her data available to the advertiser, and the advertiser will be able to build a long-term relationship with customers who are receptive to their offers.

CHAPTER 10

Simply, Consumerspace

Nipple rings. Leopard-skin pants. Sushi. High-tech furniture. Postmodern architecture. Lexus. Chat rooms. Double decaf cappuccino with a hint of cinnamon. Eminem. We inhabit a world brimming with different styles and possibilities. Is it possible to have too much of a good thing?

Escape from Freedom: The Paradox of Consumerspace

Consumerspace is teeming with choices. The food we eat, the cars we drive, the clothes we wear, and the places we live and work—a multitude of options confront us at every turn. Just sorting through these intriguing possibilities can be a full-time job. Need a refill on red lipstick or a new bottle of cologne? Here are hundreds of varieties from which to choose (or so it seems). And that's not even counting the important stuff, like menu entrees, novels, new music, or sneakers.

This consumer cornucopia means we literally suffer from an embarrassment of riches. Our biggest problem (in terms of consumption issues anyway) is that we have too many choices. We suffer from information overload. Too many brands, not enough time. Many of us are overwhelmed by the freedom to choose from so many different options. We want less choice, not more. That's the paradox of consumerspace.

The need to reduce our options rather than increase them helps to explain why many of us identify with the *voluntary simplicity* movement. Voluntary simplifiers believe that once basic material needs are sated, additional income does not add to happiness. Instead of adding yet another SUV to the collection in the garage, simplifiers are into community building, public service, and spiritual pursuits.

The notion of simplicity as a cultural virtue has emerged several times in American history. In our early years, it was associated with religious groups like the Quakers who opposed excessive consumption. During the Civil War, it surfaced as a political issue. Simplicity was promoted by Franklin D. Roosevelt as a patriotic act before and during World War II. This theme subsided somewhat during the go-go Reagan years, but has now been resurrected in various forms such as the communitarian movement.

Voluntary simplifiers range from senior citizens who downsize their homes to young, mobile professionals who don't want to be tied down to their possessions. These sentiments snowballed after the tragedy of September 11, when many people became more reflective and less materialistic. In the months that followed, stories abounded of successful careerists who gave it all up to spend time with their families.

Clearly, most mainstream consumers are not about to give up their Prada bags any time soon. However, many of us are overwhelmed by the profusion of stuff out there. Even if we still want to be a "Material Girl" (or Boy), we may not have the time or the stamina to navigate a crowded marketplace.

The thesis of this final chapter is that a key role for marketers who want to succeed among this profusion is not necessarily to offer yet another car model or lipstick shade. Instead, there is tremendous potential value in acting as a "tour guide" in consumerspace—both offline and online. Rewards await those who help consumers to navigate through the confusion, sifting the possibilities and pointing out the products and services that really do meet our needs. In consumerspace, the mantra is clear: Simplify!

It's About Time

One of the root causes of the urge to simplify is that there are only so many hours in the day. With the snowballing messages exhorting us to buy and the accelerating number of things we can buy if we so choose, being a consumer can be a 24/7 commitment. Many of us believe we are more pressed for time than ever before, a feeling called *time poverty*.[1]

Ironically, that harried feeling may be more of an illusion than we think. It's possible that, compared with our parents, we just have more ways to spend our time, and we feel pressured by the weight of all these choices. Consider that the average working day at the turn of the twentieth century was ten hours (six days per week). Still, about a third of us report always feeling rushed—up from 25 percent of the population in 1964. The average American now sleeps seven hours a night, about ninety minutes less than people did a century ago.

Those of us who lament that there just aren't enough hours in the day are very responsive to marketing innovations that save time. With the increase in time poverty, researchers also are noting a rise in *polychronic activity*, where consumers do more than one thing simultaneously. This multitasking is especially noticeable in our eating habits. Consumers often do not allocate a specific time to dining, but instead eat on the run. In a recent poll, 64 percent of respondents said they usually do something else while eating. As one food industry executive commented, "We've moved beyond grazing and into gulping."[2]

The British researcher David Lewis notes that our subjective experience of time varies with our immediate priorities and needs. As a result we are more likely to be in a consumption mode (where, for example, we are more susceptible to product advertising) at some times than others. He distinguishes among these time categories:[3]

- *Flow Time:* We become so absorbed in an activity that we notice nothing else. Not a good time to be hitting people with ads.

- *Occasion Time:* Special moments when something monumental occurs, such as a birth or an important job interview. Ads clearly relevant to the situation will be given our undivided attention.

■ *Deadline Time:* When we're working against the clock. This is the worst time to catch someone's attention.

■ *Leisure Time:* During down time, we are more likely to notice ads and perhaps try new things.

■ *Time to Kill:* Waiting for something to happen such as catching a plane or sitting in a waiting room. This is bonus time, where we feel we have the luxury to focus on extraneous things. As a result, we are more receptive to commercial messages, even for products we don't normally use.

THE BOTTOM LINE

People feel more harried than ever before and often are willing to pay a premium for marketplace services that allow them to save time. Situational demands on our attention determine the extent to which we will be receptive to marketing messages or willing to try new products. A carefully crafted advertisement may fall on deaf ears if people are not open to processing it due to other distractions. In contrast, opportunities abound to reach captive audiences when they are between tasks, waiting, or traveling.

Waiting Is a No-No

How can marketers reduce their customers' stress levels by alleviating feelings of time poverty? Some have adopted a variety of "tricks" to minimize psychological waiting time. These techniques range from altering customers' perceptions of a line's length to providing distractions that divert attention away from waiting:

■ In response to complaints about the wait for elevators, a hotel installed mirrors near the elevator banks. People's natural tendency to check themselves out in the mirror reduced complaints, even though the actual waiting time was unchanged.

■ Airline passengers often complain about waiting to claim their baggage. In one airport, they would walk one minute from the plane to the baggage carousel and then wait seven minutes for their luggage. By changing the layout so that the walk to the carousel extended to six minutes and bags arrived two minutes after that, complaints were almost entirely eliminated.

■ Restaurant chains are scrambling to put the fast back into fast food, especially for drive-through lanes, which now account for 65 percent of revenues. In a study that ranked the speed of twenty-five fast-food chains, cars spent an average of 203.6 seconds from the menu board to departure (Wendy's came in first). To speed things up and eliminate spills, McDonald's created a salad served in a container sized to fit into a car cup holder. Arby's is working on a "high viscosity" version of its special sauce that's less likely to spill. Burger King is testing see-through bags so customers can quickly check their orders before speeding off.[4]

■ Grocery stores are trying to reduce the "register rage" experienced by customers who get irritated by long lines and slow clerks. And with good reason: In one survey, 83 percent of women and 91 percent of men said long lines made them stop going to a particular store. Retailers are testing technologies to reduce or eliminate lines. One approach is called *smart packaging;* a product has a tag that gives off a signal using a radio frequency. A computer at the store's exit picks up the signal, registers the price, and calculates the bill.[5]

New online business concepts based on improved delivery are popping up all over the Web. In Manhattan you can even get a pair of Gap blue jeans messengered to your door. Some manufacturers are trying to automate the process even more. In a British pilot project, the Safeway grocery chain is providing 200 consumers with personal organizers to create shopping lists. By using frequent shopper data, the device can suggest items to replenish based on past purchase patterns. A "smart refrigerator" developed by Frigidaire comes with a bar code scanner so consumers can reorder a fresh bottle of salad dressing, ketchup, or other frequently used items by scanning the used container across the door. The refrigerator picks up the UPC code and automatically reorders a fresh supply from the grocery store. Now if it can learn to do the dishes. . . .

THE BOTTOM LINE

The pervasiveness of time poverty creates numerous opportunities to provide products and services that save precious moments and help people simplify their lives. The physical environment can be structured to reduce the perception of waiting time even when the actual time remains the same. Convenience is a competitive advantage for mundane categories like fast food, but also for more complicated purchases and activities ranging from clothes shopping to airline tickets. A funeral parlor in Chicago even offers a drive-through service for those who want to pay their last respects and still be home for supper.

I, Robot?

Many social scientists who study consumer decision-making endorse the *economics-of-information* perspective. This assumes that consumers will gather as much data as they need to maximize the likelihood of making the best decision. We continue to explore our product options as long as the rewards of doing so (what economists call the *utility*) exceed the costs. In other words, people will put themselves out to collect as much information as possible as long as the process of gathering it is not too onerous or time consuming.

Of course, one way to provide this information is to design product labels that communicate quickly and clearly. Unfortunately sometimes they can be . . . less than clear. Here are some examples of labels that don't quite simplify things the way they should:[6]

- On a Conair Pro Style 1600 hair dryer: *WARNING: Do not use in shower. Never use while sleeping.*

- Instructions for folding up a portable baby carriage: *Step 1: Remove baby.*

- A rest stop on a Wisconsin highway: *Do not eat urinal cakes.*

- On a bag of Fritos: *You could be a winner! No purchase necessary. Details inside.*

- On some Swanson frozen dinners: *Serving suggestion: defrost.*

- On Tesco's Tiramisu dessert (printed on bottom of box): *Do not turn upside down.*

- On Marks & Spencer bread pudding: *Product will be hot after heating.*

- On packaging for a Rowenta iron: *Do not iron clothes on body.*

- On Nytol sleeping aid: *Warning: May cause drowsiness.*

Mental Accounting

Whether the labels make sense or not, this begs the question of whether we bother to read them. Contrary to the economics-of-information assumption, it turns out that in many cases we are not very conscientious about gathering all the information we need to make the smartest decision. Instead, we often fall back on simple rules or assumptions to simplify the process.[7] The Nobel Prize winner Herbert Simon refers to this as *satisficing.* In this view we often put out just as much effort as is necessary to make a satisfactory choice rather than killing ourselves to make the selection that is absolutely the best.

Consider the following scenario: You've been given a free ticket to a big football game. At the last minute, though, a sudden snowstorm makes getting to the stadium somewhat dangerous. Would you still go? Now, assume the same game and snowstorm, except this time you paid handsomely for the ticket. Would you head out in the storm in this case?

Analyses of people's responses to this situation and to other similar puzzles illustrate principles of *mental accounting*, in which decisions are influenced by the way a problem is posed (called *framing*) and by whether it is put in terms of gains or losses. In this case, researchers find that people are more likely to risk their personal safety in the storm if they paid for the football ticket. Only the most die-hard fan would fail to recognize that this is an irrational choice, as the risk to the person is the same regardless of whether he or she got a great deal on the ticket. This decision-making bias is called the *sunk-cost fallacy*—having paid for something makes us reluctant to waste it.

CASE STUDY ▬▬▬▬▬▬▬▬▬▬▬▬▬▬▬▬▬▬▬▬▬▬▬▬▬▬

Research in mental accounting also demonstrates that extraneous characteristics of the choice situation can influence our selections, even though they wouldn't if we were totally rational decision-makers. As one example, participants in a survey were provided with one of two versions of this scenario:

> You are lying on the beach on a hot day. All you have to drink is ice water. For the last hour you have been thinking about how much you would enjoy a nice cold bottle of your favorite brand of beer. A companion gets up to go make a phone call and offers to bring back a beer from the only nearby place where beer is sold (either a fancy resort hotel or a small, run-down grocery store, depending on the version you're given). He says that the beer might be expensive and so asks how much you are willing to pay for it. . . . What price do you tell him?[8]

In this study, the median price given by participants who read the fancy resort version was $2.65, but those given the grocery store version were willing to pay only $1.50! In both versions the consumption act is the same, the beer is the same, and no "atmosphere" is consumed because the beer is being brought back to the beach. So much for rational decision-making!

Especially when limited problem solving occurs prior to making a choice, consumers often fall back on *heuristics*, mental rules of thumb that lead to a speedy decision. These rules range from the very general (e.g., "Higher-priced products are higher-quality products" or "Buy the same brand I bought last time") to the very specific (e.g., "Buy Domino, the brand of sugar my mother always bought"). Sometimes these shortcuts may not be in our best interests. A consumer who personally knows one or two people who have had problems with a particular make of car, for example, might assume he or she would have similar trouble with it and thus overlook the model's overall excellent repair record as experienced by many thousands of satisfied drivers.

Still, we continue to look for cues that will reduce the amount of thought needed prior to making a purchase. One frequently used shortcut is the tendency to infer hidden dimensions of products from observable attributes, such as packaging, price, country of origin, and whether the product is being sold in a discount store versus a luxury boutique. Typically, visible aspects of the product are used to infer qualities we can't immediately see. This explains why someone trying to sell a used car takes great pains to be sure the vehicle's exterior is clean and shiny: Potential buyers often judge the vehicle's mechanical condition by its surface appearance even though this means they may drive away in a shiny, clean clunker.

To Search or Not to Search
The dogged persistence of some hard-core shoppers aside, most consumers typically visit only one or two stores and rarely seek out unbi-

ased information sources prior to making a purchase decision. Lower-income shoppers, who have more to lose by making a bad purchase, actually search less prior to buying than do more affluent people. All things being equal, younger, better-educated people (especially females) who enjoy the shopping/fact-finding process tend to work the hardest to scout out their options.

Instead of searching, we often choose to buy what we know. That explains why a well-known brand is probably the most widely used heuristic of all. People form preferences for a favorite brand, and then they literally may never change their minds in the course of a lifetime. A study by the Boston Consulting Group of the market leaders in thirty product categories found that twenty-seven of the brands that were number one in 1930 are still going strong. These include such perennial favorites as Ivory Soap, Campbell's Soup, and Gold Medal Flour.

A major study on brand loyalty commissioned by the WPP Group of advertising agencies surveyed 70,000 consumers in seven world markets and assigned "bonding scores" to brands based on the percentage of respondents who said they had formed an attachment to the brand. In the United States, Gerber led the pack with a 56 percent score, while British Telecom won the day for the United Kingdom, and Lufthansa prevailed in Germany. Brands that command fierce loyalty are treasured by marketers, and for good reason. A market leader is as much as 50 percent more profitable than its nearest competitor. Small wonder, then, that companies work very hard to cultivate loyalty.

THE BOTTOM LINE

People often look for shortcuts when deciding among brands. More is not necessarily better—providing reams of product information does not necessarily mean consumers will bother to absorb it. Rather than scrupulously considering all of our options, we often fall back upon mental rules of thumb to guide our choices and to determine product quality. For example, consumers often assume that a higher-priced alternative must be superior. In addition, when people form loyalty to a brand, they are more reluctant to try other options. This inertia underscores the importance of building strong bonds with customers early on to create a barrier-to-entry for competing brands.

Anyone (perhaps even a hard-headed economist) who has observed people buying an item on impulse or splurging on something they don't really need or can't really afford would probably agree that—contrary to the view of the consumer as a rational decision-maker—we tend not to be very robotic when we make choices in the marketplace. Indeed, unless we are devoting serious time to recreational shopping instead of hitting the golf course, we often seek out ways to short-circuit the process by "cutting to the chase" and making snap judgments based upon cues that we believe will simplify the onerous task of filtering through mountains of product alternatives. That's where enterprising marketers come in. In both offline and online formats, those who help consumers to simplify have a leg up on the competition.

Offline Filtering Agents: Legs and Brains

As we've seen, we often rely upon shortcuts to filter the mountains of information we receive about products down to a manageable level. One of the most common strategies is to rely upon other people to do our homework for us. Whether in the form of personal recommendations (or warnings) or simply observing the products others use, we often tune into feedback from those around us to considerably reduce the number of brands we will even consider.

What Would Tiger Woods Do?

Of course, we aren't just influenced by the choices of any Tom, Dick, or Harry we might happen to observe. Some people are far more influential than others. The term *reference group* describes significant others who guide our judgments about what is right or wrong, good or bad, cool or uncool. The referent may be a celebrity whose product endorsements impact on many people (e.g., Britney Spears plugging Pepsi) or a person or group with whom an individual has regular contact (e.g., members of the local gardening club who advocate using a certain plant food). Reference groups that affect consumption can include our parents, fellow sports enthusiasts, the Democratic Party, or even the Red Hot Chili Peppers, Spike Lee, and the Chicago Cubs (for masochists).

A reference group can take the form of a large, formal organization that has a recognized structure, complete with a charter, regular meeting times, and officers. Or it can be small and informal, such as a weekly bridge club or students living in a dormitory. Formal groups often are easier to reach with marketing communications because these are easier to identify. However, as a rule, small, informal groups such as family, friends, and work associates are more likely to influence our decisions.

THE BOTTOM LINE

Reference groups, whether formal or informal, exert tremendous influence on consumers' buying decisions. In particular, consumers rely heavily upon personal recommendations to sift among competing brands or service providers. Identifying the relevant referents for a target market can be key to impacting individual brand preferences. That's one reason stimulating positive word of mouth (or "buzz") is so central to many marketing strategies while the long-standing emphasis on impersonal mass communications is declining.

Surrogate Consumers

It's true that reference groups play a pivotal role in defining (and delimiting) the products we will consider. In addition to friends, lovers, and celebrities, however, there are other very important intermediaries we often overlook. These are people who sift through product choices for a living. Many people blindly follow the advice of their doctors, lawyers, or stockbrokers. Others rely upon their therapists, interior designers, or physical trainers to mold their inner and outer selves.

These are all examples of what I call a *surrogate consumer*, an agent retained by a consumer to guide, direct, and/or transact marketplace activities. I first coined this term to refer to the cottage industry of wardrobe consultants that reached its apex in the 1980s during the "dress for success" craze. Droves of professional women hired these fashion experts to fill their closets with power outfits that would convey the desired impression and help them to advance in business. I was fascinated by the idea that take-charge executives would willingly abdicate responsibility to a third party for these highly personal decisions.

After working with these clothing experts for a while, I realized that, in fact, many different types of services perform the same basic function as do wardrobe consultants. When viewed more broadly, after all, a surrogate consumer is someone who is paid to simplify a person's decision-making process in the marketplace. This means interior decorators, stockbrokers, radio programmers, restaurant reviewers, and many other professionals all qualify as surrogates.

Whether or not they actually make the purchase on behalf of the consumer, surrogates' recommendations can be enormously influential. The consumer in essence relinquishes control over several or all decision-making functions including identifying the set of product options available, evaluating the pros and cons of each, and sometimes even making the actual purchase. In some cases the client displays an astounding amount of trust in the surrogate's judgment, as when an interior designer is given a purse and free rein to completely redo a home in the owner's absence.

My research in this area indicates that there are two broad reasons to retain a surrogate consumer: Put plainly, we value them either for their legs or their brains.

■ *Legs:* As we've seen, time poverty is a chronic problem today. Increasingly, consumers are willing to "subcontract" tasks they used to perform themselves in order to save time. Surrogates who perform a descriptive function spell out alternatives for us and expedite our marketplace experiences. Opportunities abound to provide timesaving services, from line-sitting at motor vehicle and passport offices to the home delivery of prepared meals. We are often willing to hire "legs" that will relieve us from onerous tasks. As the Greyhound motto states, "Leave the driving to us."

■ *Brains:* Other situations are more complicated because even if time is not a problem, we lack the knowledge or self-confidence to make a satisfactory selection. Surrogates who perform a *prescriptive* function are similar to the cultural gatekeepers referred to in Chapter 2. They help us to sift through the mountains of aesthetic possibilities to define the "right" choices and point out the dogs.

My work with female executives, for example, revealed an interesting yet counter-intuitive finding. While it is commonly assumed that younger women are more likely to be highly involved with clothing and more knowledgeable about current styles (what the industry terms "fashion-forward"), these are precisely the types most likely to turn to a consultant to help them dress for work.

A similar pattern emerged when we looked at the types of investors most likely to retain a full-service financial adviser rather than a discount broker who provides relatively little in the way of guidance. Not surprisingly in this case, those who expressed little confidence in their own stock-picking abilities were more likely to be willing to pay a premium to receive professional advice. A reasonable generalization is that, regardless of the product domain, newcomers to a role are good candidates for surrogates who provide expertise rather than merely convenience. In those cases we want "brains" actively working for us rather than "legs" that just help to make transactions easier.

These two very disparate product domains of dress and securities highlight the fact that surrogates operate in a wide range of spheres, from the very practical to the very personal. Thus we can also categorize these intermediaries in terms of whether their input is functional and fact-based (e.g., doctors, accountants) or stylistic and subjective (e.g., astrologers, image consultants). When we combine these two dimensions as in Figure 10.1, we can quickly see that many of our

Figure 10.1: Types of consumer surrogates.

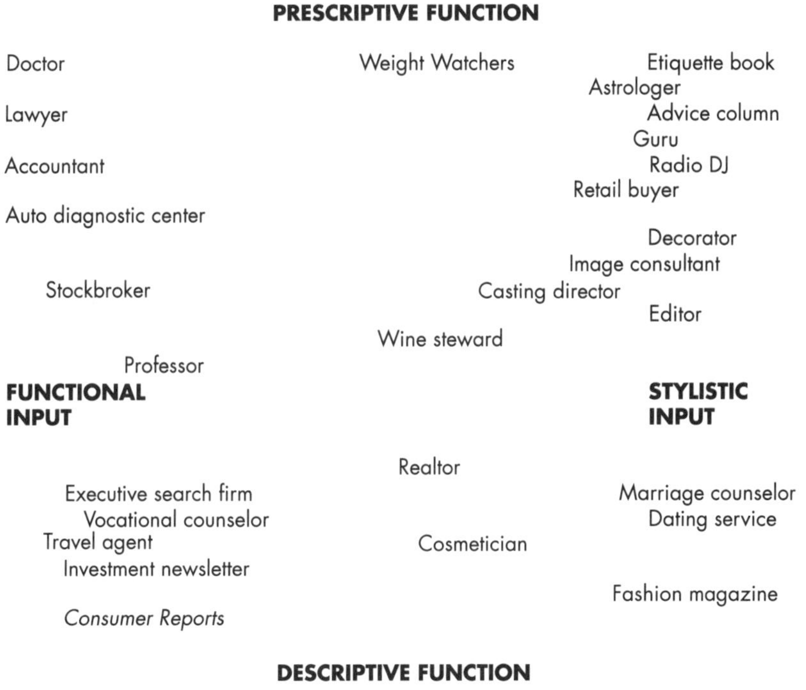

PRESCRIPTIVE FUNCTION

Doctor	Weight Watchers	Etiquette book
		Astrologer
Lawyer		Advice column
		Guru
Accountant		Radio DJ
		Retail buyer
Auto diagnostic center		
		Decorator
		Image consultant
Stockbroker	Casting director	
		Editor
	Wine steward	
Professor		

FUNCTIONAL INPUT ... **STYLISTIC INPUT**

	Realtor	
Executive search firm		Marriage counselor
Vocational counselor		Dating service
Travel agent	Cosmetician	
Investment newsletter		
		Fashion magazine
Consumer Reports		

DESCRIPTIVE FUNCTION

SOURCE: Michael R. Solomon, "Building Up and Breaking Down: The Impact of Cultural Sorting on Symbolic Consumption," in *Research in Consumer Behavior*, Vol. 3, edited by J. Sheth and E. C. Hirschman (Greenwich, Conn.: JAI Press, 1988).

marketplace interactions in fact require the assistance of surrogates of one kind or another.

It is hard to overestimate the potential impact of surrogate consumers in the marketplace. These service providers are key players in consumerspace, and marketers who recognize the need for simplification can carve out many unexploited niches. Ironically, the involvement of surrogates in a wide range of purchase decisions tends to be overlooked by many marketers. They may instead focus their efforts on persuading end consumers to buy their brands, when in fact there's a surrogate lurking in the background who is actually the key decision-maker.

THE BOTTOM LINE

Whether stockbrokers, interior designers, or restaurant reviewers, surrogate consumers make sense of a cluttered marketplace. Consumers delegate decision-making authority to a surrogate because they lack either the time or the confidence to make their own choices. It's important to understand whether, how, and why customers use surrogates so that the type of assistance one offers can be calibrated to the client's motivation for retaining help in the first place. And because consumers often delegate a surprisingly high amount of decision-making authority to surrogates, it may make more sense to promote products and services directly to these intermediaries.

Online Filtering Agents

A survey conducted by the Pew Internet & American Life Project in March 2000 found that Web surfers averaged ninety minutes per online session. When the same people were polled a year later, that number had dropped to eighty-three minutes. Respondents said they were using the Web more to conduct business than to explore new areas, aiming to get offline as quickly as possible.

Clearly the bloom is off the rose in the online domains of consumerspace. People are becoming more goal-oriented, and—as in the offline world—they want the experience streamlined and focused. For the most part, we simply don't want to be bothered sifting through massive amounts of information—many of us subscribe to the "ignorance is bliss" school of decision-making. That's where the Web offers an advantage—when used properly.

As anyone who's ever typed a phrase like "home theaters" into a search engine knows, the Web delivers enormous amounts of product and retailer information in seconds. That's why the biggest problem surfers face these days is narrowing down their choices, not beefing them up. Many of us solicit recommendations of movies, books, and restaurants at places like ifyoulike.com, alexlit.com and zagat.com. In one survey, twenty percent of online buyers stated that they would purchase more products via the Internet if these kinds of guides were more widely available.

Cybermediaries: Virtual Middlemen

With the tremendous number of Web sites available, and the huge number of people surfing the Web each day, how can people organize information and decide where to click? Search engines like Google prioritize the hits they report for a subject, but even so, it's not uncommon to get a mind-boggling list of hundreds of Web sites that may or may not be pertinent. Another problem is that these searches are not necessarily objective. Indeed, the Federal Trade Commission recently warned the operators of several major Internet search engines to make it clearer to their users when companies have paid to be included in Web search results. A Consumers Union survey revealed that 60 percent of Internet users who responded did not know that search engines accept fees for prominent positioning in their results. Clearly we need more help in efficiently narrowing down our choices.

One type of business that is growing to meet this demand is a *cybermediary*. This is an intermediary that helps to filter and organize online market information so that customers can identify and evaluate alternatives more efficiently. Cybermediaries take different forms:[9]

- *Directories and web portals* such as Yahoo!, WebMD, or fashionmall.com are general services that tie together a large variety of sites, often corresponding to an underlying theme.

- *Web-site evaluators* reduce the risk to consumers by reviewing sites and recommending the best ones. For example, Point Communications selects sites that it designates as Top 5 percent of the Web.

- *Forums, fan clubs*, and *user groups* offer product-related discussions to help customers sift through options. We discussed these earlier (see Chapter 6) in the context of the brand community phenomenon. Other sites like about.com help to narrow alternatives by providing human guides who make recommendations. This approach is especially prevalent in the travel industry, where several sites now connect surfers to travel experts (often volunteers who just like to share their expertise about travel). These sites include Allexperts.com, BootsnAll.com, and Exp.com.

Intelligent Agents: Do I Have a Book for You!

Some cybermediaries are smarter than others. The better ones have the ability to personalize feedback to our specific needs, an emerging priority identified in Chapter 4. In the future we can expect to see a plethora of online services that do more than organize information—they actually customize the results to conform to the user's individual profile.

Intelligent agents are sophisticated software programs that learn from past user behavior in order to recommend new purchases. For example, when you let Amazon.com suggest a new book, it's using a mathematical system called *collaborative filtering* to suggest novels based on what you and others like you have bought in the past. This approach was introduced in 1995 (the Stone Age in Web time!) by Firefly (which has since been bought by Microsoft) to make recommendations for taste-based products like music, books, and films.

Today a variety of agents called *shopping bots* act as online surrogates, including clickthebutton.com, mySimon.com, and DealTime.com. Lands' End's "My Personal Shopper" offers a glimpse of the future of cybermediaries. A consumer inputs her color and style preferences, and the software assigns her a score. Then the program matches this value against 80,000 items in Lands' End's inventory to recommend the best possible fit. As your fashion sense evolves, not to worry: This software learns and will adapt to the fluctuations in your choices over time.

The use of such systems reduces a consumer's search effort by narrowing the number of options he or she needs to consider. However, there is a "dark side" to the use of shopping bots and other intelligent agents: They virtually abolish the role of serendipity in our selections. The joy of discovering some unanticipated treasure in a bookstore, a clothing store, or even a hardware store is eliminated if recommendations are based strictly upon what we've done before. Very efficient, but very boring.

If and when intelligent agents proliferate, shopping will become far less recreational and more task-oriented. This would indeed be a shame—the appeal of these agents might be enhanced for many of us if a "randomizer" were included in the programming. For example, an agent could be programmed to include a recommendation extraneous to our normal preference pattern every nth time if the user chooses this option. If the enormous benefits in the way of simplification and efficiency could be tempered with just a little irrationality, intelligent agents have the potential to transform the way we make sense out of the maelstrom of data we call the Web.

THE BOTTOM LINE

Web-based technologies hold tremendous potential to simplify the way we search for product information. The value of a search engine is not its ability to generate a massive amount of options, but rather to condense and prioritize the data we need to make an informed decision. Portals and intelligent agents streamline and automate the process to a degree not possible in the offline world. However, there will always be a need for variety seeking and serendipity to complement the vast efficiencies of shopping in cyberspace.

Epilogue: Lessons Learned in Consumerspace

When all is said and done, the transition from marketerspace to consumerspace brings with it a number of insights. Those who wish to stay ahead of the curve and prosper in this environment need to adapt their marketing and communications strategies to compete in this brave new world. You're either on the train or under it!

Hopefully, this book has provided a modest start toward reframing this evolving producer-consumer relationship. It has emphasized that in our society, brands are part and parcel of our social identities. In addition, it has shown that consumers want to be partners rather than pawns as they access the marketplace to build these extended selves. Unlike the old days of marketerspace, consumers are actively looking for ways to be involved in product design, shopping, and evaluation. To recap, these are some of the major propositions we have discussed:

■ Consumers increasingly incorporate brand personalities as part of their social identities. Products are part of the extended self. Marketers who understand the role their brands play in creation of the self will have a competitive advantage over those who myopically think that people buy products for what they do, rather than for what they mean.

■ Self-definitions are not based upon the use of any one product. Consumers see relationships among products spanning many categories. They want to acquire product constellations that are consistent with who they are—and with who they aspire to be.

■ The self/product relationship is even stronger among young people. Gen Y is growing up in an MTV World, where youth tribes defined by common allegiance to musical genres, leisure activities, or other consumption subcultures rule. While skeptical of much traditional advertising, they take for granted that they are part of a larger, wired network of kids around the globe whose social identities transcend twentieth-century geographic boundaries.

■ As the world continues to shrink, nationalities recede in importance. The bedrock of our identities is formed by allegiance to common value systems, often expressed concretely through affiliation with common product sets. Branding provides security and clarity.

■ People will continue to search for product information both offline and online; young people in particular move seamlessly between these two domains. Companies must ensure that they are included in these dual contexts, and their corporate personas need to be consistent across bricks and clicks. Loyalty to a brand is often a shortcut to extended decision-making, so it's imperative to build bonds with a brand as early as possible to erect a barrier-to-entry against the competition.

■ Many spheres of consumption have become sacred, removed from the everyday, and imbued with mystical properties. These domains include celebrity worship, pilgrimages to tourist sites like Disney World, and the incorporation of products like coffee and bath oils into personal rituals.

■ Our reverence for products also enhances the potential for consumer terrorism as the marketplace becomes a forum for personal or organizational manipulation. The Web magnifies the power of individuals to voice displeasure with companies, organize boycotts, and generate negative word of mouth.

■ Customers value the opportunity to provide input to the creation of the products they buy. Companies need to transform their perceptions of consumers as passive couch potatoes by enlisting them as codesigners in the new product development process. Innovative product design that appeals to our senses is key to creating differential advantage.

■ Shopping is for many a recreational activity; we want to be immersed in the experience. Participatory marketing strategies, in both physical and virtual settings, amplify our personal connections with shopping, purchasing, and using. As consumers multitask to save time, they value retailtainment as a way to combine pleasure with provisioning. These experiences ramp up consumers' involvement with a product or service, giving it a vital edge over other options.

■ As traditional advertising messages lose their potency, marketers must constantly find new venues to reach consumers. The relentless need to identify new and unexpected formats causes a blurring of boundaries between traditional commercial spaces and those that used to be defined as off-limits. Increasingly, strategies such as guerrilla marketing and product placement make it more difficult to identify the agenda of those who make product recommendations. Word of mouth is categorized as either buzz (genuine) or hype (commercially manipulated). As a result, sources that can guarantee their objectivity will take on added value because buzz carries more weight than hype.

■ In many corners of consumerspace, consumers double as producers. They take on some of the traditional marketing functions that used to be the domain of companies operating in marketerspace. These roles include merchants (e.g., selling on eBay or engaging in multilevel marketing organizations such as Amway), product reviewers who recommend brands, and advertisers who create personal "shrines" to favored brands on personal Web pages.

■ Western consumer culture creates a paradox where we are faced with too many choices rather than too few. Customers will pledge their loyalty to companies that enable them to "escape from freedom" by simplifying and reducing options.

Welcome to consumerspace.

Notes

Chapter 1

1. Quoted in Benny Evangelista, "Advertisers Get into the Video Game," *San Francisco Chronicle*, 18 January 1999; available from www.sfgate.com/chronicle.
2. Quoted in "Video Game Company Tries Human Branding," *New York Times on the Web*, 12 August 2002; available from www.nytimes.com.
3. Packard (1957), quoted in William Leiss, Stephen Kline, and Sut Jhally, *Social Communication in Advertising: Persons, Products, and Images of Well-Being* (Toronto: Methuen, 1986), 11.
4. William Leiss, Stephen Kline, and Sut Jhally, *Social Communication in Advertising: Persons, Products, and Images of Well-Being* (Toronto: Methuen, 1986); Jerry Mander, *Four Arguments for the Elimination of Television* (New York: William Morrow, 1977), 11.
5. Danny Hakim, "Cadillac Too Shifting Focus to Trucks," *New York Times on the Web*, 21 December 2001; available from www.nytimes.com.
6. Quoted in Stephanie O'Donohoe, "Advertising Uses and Gratifications," *European Journal of Marketing* 28 (1994): 52–75.
7. Leslie Walker, "More Than the Sum of His Stuff," *Washington Post*, 11 August 2001, 1(E).
8. This section adapted from a discussion in Michael R. Solomon, *Consumer Behavior: Buying, Having, and Being*, 5th ed. (Upper Saddle River, N.J.: Prentice Hall, 2002).
9. Quoted in Dyan Machan, "Is the Hog Going Soft?" *Forbes*, 10 March 1997, 114–119.
10. Raymond Williams, *Problems in Materialism and Culture: Selected Essays* (London: Verso, 1980).
11. James B. Twitchell, *Living It Up: Our Love Affair with Luxury* (New York: Columbia University Press, 2002); Patricia Cohen, "In Defense of Our Wicked, Wicked Ways," *New York Times*, 7 July 2002, sec. 9, p. 1.
12. Marsha L. Richins, "Special Possessions and the Expression of Material Values," *Journal of Consumer Research* 21 (1994): 522–533.
13. Susan Fournier, "Consumers and Their Brands. Developing Relationship Theory in Consumer Research," *Journal of Consumer Research* 24 (March 1998): 343–373.
14. Erazim Kohák, "Ashes, Ashes . . . Central Europe After Forty Years," *Daedalus* 121 (Spring 1992): 197–215, quoted in Russell Belk, "Romanian Consumer Desires and Feelings of Deservingness," in *Romania in Transition*, ed. Lavinia Stan (Aldershot, U.K.: Dartmouth Press, 1997): 191–208.

15. Gerry Khermouch, "Whoa, Cool Shirt. 'Yeah, It's a Pepsi'," *Business Week*, 10 September 2001, 84.
16. Quoted in Bradley Johnson, "They All Have Half-Baked Ideas," *Advertising Age*, 12 May 1997, 8.
17. Quoted in Rebecca Piirto Heath, "The Once and Future King," *Marketing Tools* (March 1998): 38–43.
18. Quoted in Kathryn Kranhold, "Agencies Beef Up Brand Research to Identify Consumer Preferences," *Wall Street Journal Interactive Edition*, 9 March 2000; available from www.wsj.com.
19. Tim Triplett, "Brand Personality Must Be Managed or It Will Assume a Life of Its Own," *Marketing News* (9 May 1994): 9.
20. Teresa J. Domzal and Jerome B. Kernan, "Reading Advertising: The What and How of Product Meaning," *Journal of Consumer Marketing* 9 (Summer 1992): 48–64.
21. Charles Sanders Peirce, in *Collected Papers*, eds. Charles Hartshorne, Paul Weiss, and Arthur W. Burks (Cambridge, Mass.: Harvard University Press, 1931–1958).
22. Adapted from a discussion in Irving J. Rein, Philip Kotler, and Martin R. Stoller, *High Visibility* (New York: Dodd, Mead & Company, 1987).
23. Jean Baudrillard, *Simulations* (New York: Semiotext(e), 1983).
24. Eric Ransdell, "The Nike Story? Just Tell It!" *Fast Company*, January–February 2000, 44.
25. Quoted in Rafer Guzman, "Hotel Offers Kids a Room with a Logo," *Wall Street Journal Interactive Edition*, 6 October 1999; available from www.wsj.com.
26. Quoted in Wayne Friedman, "'Tomorrow' Heralds Brave New Ad World," *Advertising Age*, 24 June 2002, 3.
27. Quoted in Mary Kuntz and Joseph Weber, "The New Hucksterism," *Business Week*, 1 July 1996, 75.

Chapter 2

1. Quoted in Jonathan B. Weinbach, untitled article in *Wall Street Journal Interactive*, 7 December 1998; available from www.online.wsj.com.
2. William B. Hansen and Irwin Altman, "Decorating Personal Places: A Descriptive Analysis," *Environment and Behavior* 8 (December 1976): 491–504.
3. Quoted in Floyd Rudmin, "Property Crime Victimization Impact on Self, on Attachment, and on Territorial Dominance," *CPA Highlights, Victims of Crime Supplement* 9, no. 2 (1987): 4–7.
4. Emily Yoffe, "You Are What You Buy," *Newsweek*, 4 June 1990, 59.
5. "Man Wants to Marry His Car," *Montgomery Advertiser*, 7 March 1999, 11(A).
6. Russell W. Belk, "Possessions and the Extended Self," *Journal of Consumer Research* (September 1988): 139–168.
7. Ronald Alsop, "Lesbians Are Often Left Out When Firms Market to Gays," *Wall*

Street Journal Interactive Edition, 11 October 1999; available from www. online.wsj.com; Joseph Barstys, Subaru of America, personal communication.

8. Jean Halliday, "L. L. Bean, Subaru Pair for Co-Branding," *Advertising Age,* 21 February 2000, 21.

9. Michael J. Weiss, *The Clustering of America* (New York: Harper & Row, 1988).

10. Georg Simmel, "Fashion," *International Quarterly* 10 (1904): 130–155.

11. Malcolm Gladwell, *The Tipping Point* (New York: Little, Brown and Co., 2000).

12. Robert V. Kozinets, "Fandoms' Menace/Pop Flows: Exploring the Metaphor of Entertainment as Recombinant/Memetic Engineering," *Association for Consumer Research* (October 1999).

13. Janet Kornblum, "Everybody into the Memepool for Links to Some Very Odd Sites," *USA Today,* 4 May 2000, 3(D).

14. Quoted in Rachel Beck, "Power-Packing Mints Have Become Fashionable," *Montgomery Advertiser,* 10 June 1998, 1(D).

15. Richard A. Peterson, and D. G. Berger, "Entrepreneurship in Organizations: Evidence from the Popular Music Industry," *Administrative Science Quarterly* 16 (1971): 97–107.

16. Quoted in Herbert Blumer, *Symbolic Interactionism: Perspective and Method* (Englewood Cliffs, N.J.: Prentice Hall, 1969), 279.

17. Quoted in Julie Flaherty, "Ambient Music Has Moved to Record Store Shelves," *New York Times on the Web,* 4 July 2001; available from www.nytimes.com.

Chapter 3

1. "Teens Spent $172 Billion In 2001," in Teenage Research Unlimited (Northbrook, Ill., 2002 [cited 6 April 2002]); available from http://www.teenresearch. com.

2. Quoted in Ellen Goodman, "The Selling of Teenage Anxiety," *Washington Post,* 24 November 1979.

3. Quoted in "Teens Serious in Quest for Fun," in Teenage Research Unlimited (Northbrook, Ill., 2000 [cited 6 April 2002]); available from http://www. teenresearch.com.

4. Quoted in "Teens Serious in Quest for Fun," in Teenage Research Unlimited (Northbrook, Ill., 2000 [cited 6 April 2002]); available from http://www. teenresearch.com.

5. Quoted in Khanh T. L. Tran, "Plan to Roll Out Colored Tires Brings Politicians' Ire in California," *Wall Street Journal Interactive Edition,* 30 July 1999; available from www.wsj.com.

6. Howard W. French, "Vocation for Dropouts Is Painting Tokyo Red," *New York Times on the Web,* 5 March 2000, available from www.nytimes.com.

7. Mark Rechtin, "Surf's Up for Toyota's Co-Branded Roxy Echo," *Automotive News* 75, no. 5936, 25 June 2001, 17.

8. Chantal Liu, "Faces of the New Millennium," (Northwestern University, 1999

[cited 6 April 2002]); available from http://pubweb.acns.nwu.edu/~eyc345/final.html.

9. Hassan Fattah, "Hollywood, the Internet, and Kids," *American Demographics* 23, no. 5 (May 2001): 50–55.

10. Quoted in Julie Connelly, "A Ripe Target for Web Retailers, Teens Keep Heading to the Mall," *New York Times on the Web*, 22 September 1999; available from www.nytimes.com.

11. Mike Dano, "M-Commerce Will Outperform E-Commerce," *RCR Wireless News* 20, no. 2, April 2001, 4.

12. Quoted in Gabriel Kahn, "Virtual Rock Band Corresponds with Fans via Text Messaging," *Wall Street Journal Online*, 19 April 2002; available from www.wsj.com.

13. Michael Bociurkiw, "Text Messaging Thrives in the Philippines," *Forbes*, 10 September 2001, 28.

14. Patricia Riedman, "U.S. Patiently Awaits Wireless Texting That's Soaring Overseas," *Advertising Age*, 15 April 2002, S-6.

15. Mike Dano, "M-Commerce Will Outperform E-Commerce," *RCR Wireless News* 20, no. 2, April 2001, 4.

16. Marcel Danesi, *Cool: The Signs and Meanings of Adolescence* (Buffalo, N.Y.: University of Toronto Press, 1994).

17. Bruce Horovitz, "Gen Y: A Tough Crowd to Sell," USA Today.com, 21 April 2002.

18. Ibid.

19. Daniel McGinn, "Pour on the Pitch," *Newsweek*, 31 May 1999, 50–51.

20. Jack Neff, "P&G Targets Teens via Tremor, Toejam Site," *Advertising Age*, 5 March 2001, 12.

Chapter 4

1. Susan Fournier, "Consumers and Their Brands. Developing Relationship Theory in Consumer Research," *Journal of Consumer Research* 24 (March 1998): 343–373.

2. Quoted in Cara B. DiPasquale, "Navigate the Maze: Special Report on 1:1 Marketing," *Advertising Age*, 29 October 2001, S1 (2).

3. Bob Tedeschi, "Web Retailers Try to Get Personal," *New York Times on the Web*, 19 August 2002; available from www.nytimes.com.

4. Quoted in David Kushner, "From the Skin Artist, Always a Free Makeover," *New York Times on the Web*, 21 March 2002; available from www.nytimes.com.

5. Rebecca Gardyn, "Swap Meet," *American Demographics* 23, no. 7 (July 2001): 51–56.

6. Elisabeth Goodridge, "Portal Gives Workers Cruise Control," *InformationWeek*, no. 864 (19 November 2001): 73.

7. Quoted in Jennifer Lee, "In the U.S., Interactive TV Still Awaits an Audience," *New York Times*, 31 December 2001, 1(C).

8. This section adapted from a discussion in Michael R. Solomon and Elnora W. Stuart, *Marketing: Real People, Real Choices*, 3rd ed. (Upper Saddle River, N.J.: Prentice Hall, 2003).

9. Quoted in Robert V. Kozinets, "Utopian Enterprise: Articulating the Meanings of *Star Trek's* Culture of Consumption," *Journal of Consumer Research* 28 (June 2001): 74.

10. Quoted in Robert V. Kozinets, "Utopian Enterprise: Articulating the Meanings of *Star Trek's* Culture of Consumption," *Journal of Consumer Research* 28 (June 2001): 76.

11. Quoted in Ruth Ann Smith, "Collecting as Consumption: A Grounded Theory of Collecting Behavior" (unpublished manuscript, Virginia Polytechnic Institute and State University, 1994), 14.

12. Quoted in Philip Connors, "Like Fine Wine, a 'Collector' Visits McDonald's for Subtle Differences," *Wall Street Journal Interactive Edition*, 16 August 1999; available from www.wsj.com.

13. John F. Sherry Jr., "Dealers and Dealing in a Periodic Market: Informal Retailing in Ethnographic Perspective," *Journal of Retailing* 66, no. 2 (Summer 1990): 174.

14. H. J. Shrager, "Close Social Networks of Hasidic Women, Other Tight Groups, Boost Shaklee Sales," *Wall Street Journal Interactive Edition*, 19 November 2001; available from http://interactive.wsj.com/archive/retrieve.

15. This section adapted from Michael R. Solomon, *Consumer Behavior: Buying, Having, and Being*, 5th ed. (Upper Saddle River, N.J.: Prentice Hall, 2002).

16. Quoted in Amy Harmon, "Illegal Kidney Auction Pops Up on eBay's Site," *New York Times on the Web*, 3 September 1999; available from www.nytimes.com.

17. Quoted in G. Paschal Zachary, "A Most Unlikely Industry Finds It Can't Resist Globalization's Call," *Wall Street Journal Interactive Edition*, 6 January 2000; available from www.wsj.com.

Chapter 5

1. Dorothy Leonard and Jeffrey F. Rayport, "Spark Innovation Through Emphatic Design," *Harvard Business Review* 75, no. 6 (November–December 1997): 102–114.

2. James H. Gilmore II and B. Joseph Pine, "The Four Faces of Mass Customization," *Harvard Business Review* 75, no. 1 (January–February 1997): 91.

3. Jerry Wind and Arvind Rangaswamy, "Customerization: The Next Revolution in Mass Customization," *Journal of Interactive Marketing* 15, 1 (Winter 2001): 13–32.

4. Adapted from M. A. Kaulio, "Customer, Consumer, and User Involvement in Product Development: A Framework and a Review of Selected Methods," *Total Quality Management* 9, no. 1 (February 1998): 141.

5. Based upon a framework originally developed in K. D. Eason, "The Development of a User-Centered Design Process: A Case Study in Multidisciplinary Research" (Inaugural lecture, HUSAT Research Institute, Longhborough University of Technology, Loughborough, 14 October 1992; adapted by Kaulio, 1998).

6. Adapted from M. A. Kaulio, "Customer, Consumer, and User Involvement in Product Development: A Framework and a Review of Selected Methods," *Total Quality Management* 9, no. 1 (February 1998): 141.

7. Marco Iansiti and Alan MacCormack, "Developing Products on Internet Time," *Harvard Business Review* 75, no. 5 (September–October 1997): 108–118.

8. This section adapted from Basil G. Englis and Michael R. Solomon, "Life/Style OnLine: A Web-Based Methodology for Visually Oriented Consumer Research," *Journal of Interactive Marketing* 14, no. 1 (Winter 2000): 2–14.

9. Quoted in Ristina Ourosa, "Who Are the First Ones Out There, Buying the Latest Gadgets? Meet the TAFs," *Wall Street Journal Interactive Edition*, 16 June 1998; available from www.wsj.com.

Chapter 6

1. John Hagel III, Arthur G. Armstrong, *Net Gain: Expanding Markets Through Virtual Communities* (Boston: Harvard Business School Press, 1997).

2. Robert V. Kozinets, "E-Tribalized Marketing: The Strategic Implications of Virtual Communities of Consumption," *European Management Journal* 17, no. 3 (June 1999): 252–264.

3. M. Zetlin and B. Pfleging, "Creators of Online Community," *Computerworld*, 29 October 2001, 34.

4. Quoted in Marc Gunther, "The Newest Addiction," *Fortune*, 2 August 1999, 123.

5. Hassan Fattah and Pamela Paul, "Gaming Gets Serious," *American Demographics* 24, no. 5 (May 2002): 39–43.

6. Quoted in Karen J. Bannan, "Marketers Try Infecting the Internet," *New York Times on the Web*, 22 March 2000; available from www.nytimes.com.

7. Quoted in Eilene Zimmerman, "Catch the Bug," *Sales and Marketing Management*, February 2001, 78.

8. Bob Tedeschi, "Online Retailers Find That Customer Reviews Build Loyalty," *New York Times on the Web*, 6 September 1999; available from www.nytimes.com.

9. Seana Mulcahy, "Selling to E-Fluentials," *ClickZ Today*, 3 January 2002 (cited 27 April 2002); available from www.e-fluentials.com/news.

10. Burson Marsteller, "The e-fluentials: 2000" (cited 23 April 2002); available from http://bm.com; S. Khodarahmi, "Pass It On," *DotCEO* (cited 26 April 2002); available from www.dotceo.com; Seana Mulcahy, "Selling to E-Fluentials," *ClickZ Today*, 3 January 2002 (cited 27 April 2002); available from www. e-fluentials.com/news.

11. Quoted in Peter Romeo, "A Restaurateur's Guide to the Web," *Restaurant Business* 95, no. 14 (20 September 1996): 181.

12. Alex Blumberg, "It's Good to Be King," *Wired,* March 2000, 132–149.
13. This section adapted from Michael R. Solomon, *Consumer Behavior: Buying, Having, and Being,* 5th ed. (Upper Saddle River, N.J.: Prentice Hall, 2002).

Chapter 7

1. Quoted in Karon Haymon Long, "Tattooed Kingdom," *Opelika-Auburn News,* 16 June 2002, 6C.
2. Conrad Phillip Kottak, "Anthropological Analysis of Mass Enculturation," in *Researching American Culture,* ed. Conrad P. Kottak (Ann Arbor: University of Michigan Press, 1982): 40–74.
3. Material in this section was adapted from Caroline K. Lego, Natalie T. Wood, Stephanie L. McFee, and Michael R. Solomon, "A Thirst for the Real Thing in Themed Retail Environments: Consuming Authenticity in Irish Pubs," *Journal of Restaurant and Foodservice Marketing,* in press.
4. Quoted in William Booth, "Travel Trends—Will Fake Destinations Supplant the Real Ones?" *Seattle Times,* 28 July 1996, 7(K).
5. Quoted in "Fantasy Architecture," Broadcast transcript from the Best of the BBC. *Independent,* 19 September 1999, 52–53.
6. Quoted in Akiko Busch, "Get Real," *Interiors,* July 1999, 38.
7. Robert V. Kozinets, John F. Sherry, Benet DeBerry-Spence, Adam Duhachek, Krittinee Nuttavuthisit, and Diana Storm, "Themed Flagship Brand Stores in the New Millennium: Theory, Practice, Prospects," *Journal of Retailing* 78, no. 1 (2002): 17–31.
8. S. Lu and G. A. Fine, "The Presentation of Ethnic Authenticity: Chinese Food as a Social Accomplishment," *Sociological Quarterly* 36, no. 3 (Summer 1995): 535–554.
9. S. Lu and G. A. Fine, "The Presentation of Ethnic Authenticity: Chinese Food as a Social Accomplishment," *Sociological Quarterly* 36, no. 3 (Summer 1995): 535–554.
10. Quoted in "A Brand-New Development Creates a Colorful History," *Wall Street Journal Interactive Edition,* 18 February 1998; available from www.wsj.com.
11. Stephen Fox and William Philber, "Television Viewing and the Perception of Affluence," *Sociological Quarterly* 19 (1978): 103–112; W. James Potter, "Three Strategies for Elaborating the Cultivation Hypothesis," *Journalism Quarterly* 65 (Winter 1988): 930–939.
12. Susan Greco, "Thirty Seconds with Guerrilla Marketing's Guru," *Inc.* 17, no.11 (August 1995): 98.
13. Shari Caudron, "Guerrilla Tactics," *Industry Week,* 14 July 2001, 52–56.

Chapter 8

1. Barry J. Babin, William R. Darden, and Mitch Griffin, "Work and/or Fun: Measuring Hedonic and Utilitarian Shopping Values," *Journal of Consumer Research* 20 (March 1994): 644–656.

2. Edward M. Tauber, "Why Do People Shop?" *Journal of Marketing* 36 (October 1972): 47–48.

3. Quoted in Robert C. Prus, *Making Sales: Influence as Interpersonal Accomplishment* (Newbury Park, Calif.: Sage Library of Social Research, Sage Publications, Inc., 1989), 225.

4. Quoted in Cyndee Miller, "Nix the Knick-Knacks; Send Cash," *Marketing News* (26 May 1997): 13.

5. Quoted in "I Do . . . Take MasterCard," *Wall Street Journal,* 23 June 2000, W(1).

6. Quoted in Anastasia Toufexis, "365 Shopping Days Till Christmas," *Time,* 26 December 1988, 82.

7. Philip Kotler, "Atmospherics as a Marketing Tool," *Journal of Retailing* (Winter 1973–1974): 10.

8. Robert J. Donovan et al., "Store Atmosphere and Purchasing Behavior," *Journal of Retailing* 70, no. 3 (1994): 283–294.

9. Quoted in Adam Bryant, "Plastic Surgery at AmEx," *Newsweek,* 4 October 1999, 55.

10. Kirk L. Wakefield and Julie Baker, "Excitement at the Mall: Determinants and Effects on Shopping Response," *Journal of Retailing* 74, no. 4 (1998): 515–539.

11. Michael R. Solomon, Basil G. Englis, and John Cornett, "The Virtual Mall: Using the Internet to Configure the Ideal Shopping Environment," *Journal of Shopping Center Research* 9(1) (Spring/Summer 2002): 27–50.

12. Alan R. Hirsch, "Effects of Ambient Odors on Slot-Machine Usage in a Las Vegas Casino," *Psychology & Marketing* 12, no. 7 (October 1995): 585–594.

13. Annette Green, "The Fragrance Revolution," *Futurist* 27, no.2 (April 1993): 13–17.

14. Maxine Wilkie, "Scent of a Market," *American Demographics* 17, no. 8 (August 1995): 40–49.

15. Quoted in "Slow Music Makes Fast Drinkers," *Psychology Today,* March 1989, 18.

16. Brad Edmondson, "Pass the Meat Loaf," *American Demographics* 11, no. 1 (January 1989): 19.

17. Marianne Meyer, "Attention Shoppers!" *Marketing and Media Decisions* 23 (May 1988): 67.

18. Michael Janofsky, "Using Crowing Roosters and Ringing Business Cards to Tap a Boom in Point-of-Purchase Displays," *New York Times,* 21 March 1994, 9 (D).

19. Examples cited in Michael R. Solomon, *Consumer Behavior: Buying, Having, and Being,* 5th ed. (Upper Saddle River, N.J.: Prentice Hall, 2002).

20. Quoted in Jacquelyn Bivins, "Fun and Mall Games," *Stores,* August 1989, 35.

21. Janet Ginsburg, "Xtreme Retailing," *Business Week,* 20 December 1999, 120.

22. Nick Wingfield, "Online Retailing Is Still Growing Despite Some Losses Last Year," *Wall Street Journal Interactive Edition,* 12 June 2002; available from www.wsj.com.

23. De Wayne Lehman, "E-customers Not Satisfied," *Computer World,* 27 March 2000, 20.

24. Joan Raymond, "No More Shoppus Interruptus," *American Demographics* (May 2001): 39.

Chapter 9

1. Adbusters Media Foundation, "Adbusters," Vancouver, British Columbia [cited 27 June 2002]; available from http://adbusters.org/information/network/.
2. http://www.nikesweatshop.net; accessed 29 June 2002.
3. Quoted in Jan McCallum, "I Hate You, and Millions Know It," *BRW*, 7 July 2000, 84.
4. Tina Kelley, "Internet's Chain of Foolery," *New York Times*, 1 July 1999, 1(G).
5. www.protest.net; accessed June 17, 2000.
6. Calmetta Y. Coleman, "A Car Salesman's Bizarre Prank May End up Backfiring in Court," *Wall Street Journal*, 2 May 1995, 1(B).
7. Quoted in "Woman Stabbed Over McDonald's Meal Dispute," *Opelika/Auburn News*, 13 April 2002.
8. Frances A. McMorris, "Loaded Coconut Falls off Deck, Landing Cruise Line in Court," *Wall Street Journal Interactive Edition*, 13 September 1999; available from www.wsj.com.
9. "New Survey Shows Shoplifting Is a Year-Round Problem," *Business Wire*, 12 April 1998; Jennifer Lee, "Tracking Sales and the Cashiers" *New York Times on the Web*, 11 July 2001; available from www.nytimes.com.
10. Dan Verton, "Vulnerability Assessment Triggers Alarms," *Computerworld*, 21 January 2002, 14.
11. Quoted in Bruce Orwall, "Disney Recalls 'The Rescuers' Video Containing Images of Topless Woman," *Wall Street Journal Interactive Edition*, 11 January 1999; available from www.wsj.com.
12. The Associated Press, "Music Software Users Installed Tracking Program Unknowingly," *New York Times on the Web*, 5 January 2002; available from www.nytimes.com.
13. Toby Lester, "The Reinvention of Privacy," *Atlantic Monthly*, March 2001, 27–39.
14. Jennifer Lach, "The New Gatekeepers," *American Demographics* 21, no. 6 (June 1999): 41–42.
15. John Hagel III and Jeffrey F. Rayport, "The Coming Battle for Customer Information," *Harvard Business Review* (January–February 1997): 53.
16. Quoted in Jennifer Lach, "The New Gatekeepers," *American Demographics* 21, no. 6 (June 1999): 41–42.

Chapter 10

1. This section adapted from a discussion in Michael R. Solomon, *Consumer Behavior: Buying, Having, and Being*, 5th ed. (Upper Saddle River, N.J.: Prentice Hall, 2002).

2. Quoted in Dena Kleiman, "Fast Food? It Just Isn't Fast Enough Anymore," *New York Times,* 6 December 1989, 12 (C).
3. David Lewis and Darren Bridger, *The Soul of the New Consumer: Authenticity—What We Buy and Why in the New Economy* (London: Nicholas Brealey Publishing, 2000).
4. Jennifer Ordonez, "An Efficiency Drive: Fast-Food Lanes, Equipped with Timers, Get Even Faster," *Wall Street Journal Interactive Edition,* 18 May 2000; available from www.wsj.com.
5. Emily Nelson, "Mass-Market Retailers Look to Bring Checkout Lines into the 21st Century," *Wall Street Journal Interactive Edition,* 13 March 2000; available from www.wsj.com.
6. Examples provided by Dr. William Cohen, letter to author, October 1999.
7. Adapted from a discussion in Michael R. Solomon, *Consumer Behavior: Buying, Having, and Being,* 5th ed. (Upper Saddle River, N.J.: Prentice Hall, 2002).
8. Quoted in Richard Thaler, "Mental Accounting and Consumer Choice," *Marketing Science* 4 (Summer 1985): 206.
9. Material in this section adapted from Michael R. Solomon and Elnora W. Stuart, *Welcome to Marketing.com: The Brave New World of E-Commerce* (Englewood Cliffs, N.J.: Prentice Hall, 2001).

Recommended Reading

Ariely, Dan. "Controlling the Information Flow: Effects on Consumers' Decision Making and Preferences." *Journal of Consumer Research* 26 (2000): 233–248.

Arnould, Eric J., Linda L. Price, and Cele Otnes. "Making Consumption Magic: A Study of White-Water River Rafting." *Journal of Contemporary Ethnography* 28 (February 1999): 33–68.

Belk, Russell W. "Acquiring, Possessing, and Collecting: Fundamental Processes in Consumer Behavior." In *Marketing Theory: Philosophy of Science Perspectives*, edited by R. F. Bush and S. D. Hunt. Chicago: American Marketing Association, 1982.

———. "Hyperreality and Globalization: Culture in the Age of Ronald McDonald." *Journal of International Consumer Marketing* 8 (1996): 23–37.

———. "Possessions and the Extended Self." *Journal of Consumer Research* 15 (September 1988): 139–168.

———. "The Retro Sims." In *No Then There: Ecumenical Essays on the Rise of Retroscapes*, edited by Stephen Brown and John Sherry, forthcoming.

Belk, Russell W., Melanie Wallendorf, and John F. Sherry Jr. "The Sacred and the Profane in Consumer Behavior: Theodicy on the *Odyssey*." *Journal of Consumer Research* 16 (June 1989): 1–38.

Cova, Veronique, and Bernard Cova. "Tribal Aspects of Postmodern Consumption Research: The Case of French In-line Roller Skaters." *Journal of Consumer Behaviour* 1, no. 1 (June 2001): 67–76.

Danesi, Marcel. *Cool: The Signs and Meanings of Adolescence.* Toronto: University of Toronto Press, 1994.

Englis, Basil G., and Michael R. Solomon. "*Life/Style OnLine*©: A Web-Based Methodology for Visually Oriented Consumer Research." *Journal of Interactive Marketing*, 14 (2000): 1, 2–14.

Englis, Basil G., Michael R. Solomon, and Paula D. Harveston, "Web-Based, Visually Oriented Consumer Research Tools." In *Online Consumer Psy-*

261

chology: Understanding How to Interact with Consumers in the Virtual World, edited by Curt Haugtvedt, Karen Machleit, and Richard Yalch. Hillsdale, N.J.: Lawrence Erlbaum, 2002.

Etzioni, Amitai. "The Good Society: Goals Beyond Money." *Futurist* 35, no. 4 (July 2001).

Gatignon, Hubert, and Thomas S. Robertson. "A Propositional Inventory for New Diffusion Research." *Journal of Consumer Research* 11 (March 1985): 849–867.

Gladwell, Malcolm. *The Tipping Point*. New York: Little, Brown and Co., 2000.

Godin, Seth. *Permission Marketing: Turning Strangers into Friends, and Friends into Customers*. New York: Simon & Schuster, 1999.

Goffman, Erving. *The Presentation of Self in Everyday Life*. Garden City, N.Y.: Doubleday, 1959.

Gottdeiner, M. *The Theming of America Dreams, Visions and Commercial Spaces*. Boulder, Colo.: Westview Press, 1997.

Hagel III, John, and Arthur G. Armstrong. *Net Gain: Expanding Markets Through Virtual Communities*. Boston: Harvard Business School Press, 1997.

Hagel III, John, and Jeffrey F. Rayport. "The Coming Battle for Customer Information." *Harvard Business Review* (January–February 1997).

Hirsch, Paul M. "Processing Fads and Fashions: An Organizational Set Analysis of Cultural Industry Systems." *American Journal of Sociology* 77, no. 4 (1972): 639–659.

Hoffman, Donna L., and Thomas P. Novak. "Marketing in Hypermedia Computer-Mediated Environments: Conceptual Foundations." *Journal of Marketing* 60 (July 1996): 50–68.

Kozinets, Robert V. "E-Tribalized Marketing: The Strategic Implications of Virtual Communities of Consumption." *European Management Journal* 17, no. 3 (June 1999): 252–264.

Kozinets, Robert V., John F. Sherry, Benet DeBerry-Spence, Adam Duhachek, Krittinee Nuttavuthisit, and Diana Storm. "Themed Flagship Brand Stores in the New Millennium: Theory, Practice, Prospects." *Journal of Retailing* 78, no. 1 (2002): 17–31.

Lego, Caroline K., Natalie T. Wood, Stephanie L. McFee, and Michael R. Solomon. "A Thirst for the Real Thing in Themed Retail Environments: Consuming Authenticity in Irish Pubs." *Journal of Restaurant and Foodservice Marketing*, in press.

Leiss, William, Stephen Kline, and Sut Jhally. *Social Communication in Advertising: Persons, Products, and Images of Well-Being.* Toronto: Methuen, 1986.

Leonard, Dorothy, and Jeffrey F. Rayport. "Spark Innovation Through Emphatic Design." *Harvard Business Review 75*, no. 6 (November–December 1997): 102–114.

Lester, Toby. "The Reinvention of Privacy." *Atlantic Monthly*, March 2001, 27–39.

Lewis, David, and Darren Bridger. *The Soul of the New Consumer: Authenticity—What We Buy and Why in the New Economy.* London: Nicholas Brealey Publishing, 2000.

Lowery, Tina M., Basil G. Englis, Sharon Shavitt, and Michael R. Solomon. "Response Latency Verification of Consumption Constellations: Implications for Advertising Strategy." *Journal of Advertising 30* (2001): 1, 29–39.

Lynes, Russell. *The Tastemakers.* New York: Harper and Brothers, 1954.

Mander, Jerry. *Four Arguments for the Elimination of Television.* New York: William Morrow, 1977.

Mead, George H. *Mind, Self, and Society.* Chicago: University of Chicago Press, 1934.

O'Donnell, Kathleen A., and Daniel L. Wardlow. "A Theory on the Origin of Coolness." In *Advances in Consumer Research*, edited by Stephen J. Hoch and Robert J. Meyer (Provo, Utah: Association for Consumer Research, 2000).

Peterson, Richard A., and D. G. Berger. "Entrepreneurship in Organizations: Evidence from the Popular Music Industry." *Administrative Science Quarterly 16* (1971): 97–107.

Quilty, Natalie T., Michael R. Solomon, and Basil G. Englis. "Icons and Avatars: Cyber-Models and Hyper-Mediated Visual Persuasion." In *Advertising and Visual Persuasion*, edited by Linda Scott and Rajeev Batra. Hillsdale, N.J.: Lawrence Erlbaum, 2003 (in press).

Rein, Irving J., Philip Kotler, and Martin R. Stoller. *High Visibility.* New York: Dodd, Mead & Company, 1987.

Sherry Jr., John F. "A Sociocultural Analysis of a Midwestern American Flea Market." *Journal of Consumer Research* 17 (June 1990): 13–30.

Sherry Jr., John F., ed. *Servicescapes: The Concept of Place in Contemporary Markets.* Lincolnwood, Ill.: NTC Business Books, 1998.

Simmel, Georg. "Fashion." *International Quarterly* 10 (1904): 130–155.

Solomon, Michael R. "Building Up and Breaking Down: The Impact of Cultural Sorting on Symbolic Consumption." In *Research in Consumer Behavior,* Vol. 3, Edited by J. Sheth and E. C. Hirschman. Greenwich, Conn.: JAI Press, 1988.

———. *Consumer Behavior: Buying, Having, and Being,* 5th ed. Upper Saddle River, N.J.: Prentice Hall, 2002.

———. "The Missing Link: Surrogate Consumers in the Marketing Chain." *Journal of Marketing,* 50 (4) (October 1986): 208–219.

———. "The Role of Products as Social Stimuli: A Symbolic Interactionism Perspective." *Journal of Consumer Research* 10 (December 1983): 319–329.

———. "The Wardrobe Consultant: Exploring the Role of a New Retailing Partner" *Journal of Retailing* 63 (Summer 1987): 110–128.

Solomon, Michael R., and Susan P. Douglas. "Diversity in Product Symbolism: The Case of Female Executive Clothing." *Psychology & Marketing* 4 (Fall 1987): 189–212.

Solomon, Michael R., and Basil G. Englis. "Reality Engineering: Blurring the Boundaries Between Marketing and Popular Culture." *Journal of Current Issues and Research in Advertising* 16 (Fall 1994) 2: 1–18.

Solomon, Michael R., Basil G. Englis, and John Cornett. "The Virtual Mall: Using the Internet to Configure the Ideal Shopping Environment." *Journal of Shopping Center Research* 9(1) (Spring/Summer 2002): 27–50.

Solomon, Michael R., and Elnora W. Stuart. *Marketing: Real People, Real Choices* 3rd ed. Upper Saddle River, N.J.: Prentice Hall, 2003.

Stark, Myra. "Are You Ready for 'Naked Marketing'?" *Brandweek* 39, no.10 (9 March 1998): 26.

Stigler, George J. "The Economics of Information." *Journal of Political Economy* 69 (June 1961): 213–225.

Surprenant, Carol F. and Michael R. Solomon. "Predictability and Personalization in the Service Encounter." *Journal of Marketing* 51 (April 1987): 86–96.

Thaler, Richard. "Mental Accounting and Consumer Choice." *Marketing Science* 4 (Summer 1985): 199–214.

Thomke, Stefan, and Eric von Hippel. "Customers as Innovators: A New Way to Create Value." *Harvard Business Review* (April 2002): 74.

Twitchell, James B. *Living It Up: Our Love Affair with Luxury.* New York: Columbia University Press, 2002.

Veblen, Thorstein. *The Theory of the Leisure Class.* 1899. Reprint, New York: New American Library, 1953.

Wind, Jerry, and Arvind Rangaswamy. "Customerization: The Next Revolution in Mass Customization." *Journal of Interactive Marketing* 15, no. 1, (Winter 2001): 13–32.

Index